All the world's a stage,
And all the men and women merely players.

—William Shakespeare
As You Like It
ACT II SCENE 7

A Book of Plays

HOLT, RINEHART AND WINSTON

A Harcourt Classroom Education Company

Austin • New York • Orlando • Atlanta • San Francisco
Boston • Dallas • Toronto • London

Cover: (background, from *The Glass Menagerie*), © T. Charles Erickson;
(inset, top right, from *Our Town*), Martha Swope/TimePix; (inset, bottom right,
from *Twelve Angry Men*), Photofest.

HRW is a trademark licensed to Holt, Rinehart and Winston
registered in the United States of America and/or other jurisdictions.

Printed in the United States of America

ISBN 0-03-064428-3   5 6 043 03 02

Contents

Thornton Wilder
(1897–1975)

Thornton Wilder, who was born in Madison, Wisconsin, spent part of his youth in China, where his father was U.S. consul general to Hong Kong and Shanghai. Wilder later attended schools in America, spending two years at Oberlin College and earning his bachelor's degree at Yale.

His second novel was a best-seller. *The Bridge of San Luis Rey* (1927) is an ironic study of five travelers who happen to be crossing a rope bridge in Peru when it collapses and plunges them all to their deaths in the gorge below. The novel won a Pulitzer Prize for fiction and made Wilder famous.

Wilder won a Pulitzer Prize twice more—for drama, for *Our Town* (1938) and for *The Skin of Our Teeth* (1942). In 1954, he wrote a play called *The Matchmaker*, which became the basis for the enormously successful musical comedy *Hello, Dolly!*

Though Wilder was that rare literary creature, both a playwright and a novelist, and though he became one of the most distinguished literary figures of his time (he was often mentioned as a candidate for the Nobel Prize), he always liked to think of himself as a teacher. Indeed, he did spend a good deal of his life as a convivial teacher and lecturer of French, classical literature, and creative writing.

Unlike most other playwrights, Wilder liked to act; he frequently played the Stage Manager in regional summer-theater productions of *Our Town*.

Though anyone familiar with his life realizes that he was aware of the "dark side of the moon," he was, to the despair of some of his critics, essentially an optimist. Wilder emphasized the positive aspects of life: In *Our Town* it is the miracle of even the most ordinary day; in *The Skin of Our Teeth*, it is the human capacity through the ages to survive every conceivable calamity.

Wilder once wrote to a friend, "The positive still lives about us in sufficient fragments to live by."

Here is what Wilder said about his unorthodox staging of *Our Town:*

Those nineteenth-century audiences . . . loaded the stage with specific objects, because every concrete object on the stage fixes and narrows the action to one moment in time and place. (Have you ever noticed that in the plays of Shakespeare no one—except occasionally a ruler—ever sits down? There were not even chairs on the English or Spanish stages in the time of Elizabeth I.) So it was by a jugglery with time that the middle classes devitalized the theater. When you emphasize *place* in the theater, you drag down and limit and harness time to it. You thrust the action back into past time, whereas it is precisely the glory of the stage that it is always "now" there. Under such production methods the characters are all dead before the action starts. You don't have to pay deeply from your heart's participation. No great age in the theater ever attempted to capture the audience's belief through this kind of specification and localization. I became dissatisfied with the theater because I was unable to lend credence to such childish attempts to be "real." . . .

Our Town is not offered as a picture of life in a New Hampshire village; or as a speculation about the conditions of life after death. . . . It is an attempt to find a value above all price for the smallest events in our daily life. I have made the claim as preposterous as possible, for I have set the village against the largest dimensions of time and place. The recurrent words in this play (few have noticed it) are *hundreds, thousands,* and *millions.* Emily's joys and griefs, her algebra lessons, and her birthday presents—what are they when we consider all the billions of girls who have lived, who are living, and who will live? Each individual's assertion to an absolute reality can only be inner, very inner. And here the method of staging finds its justification—in the first two acts there are at least a few chairs and tables; but when she revisits the earth and the kitchen to which she descended on her twelfth birthday, the very chairs and table are gone. Our claim, our hope, our despair are in the mind—not in things, not in "scenery." Molière said that for the theater all he needed was a platform and a passion or two. The climax of this play needs only five square feet of boarding and the passion to know what life means to us.

The Happy Journey to Trenton and Camden

Thornton Wilder

Characters

The Stage Manager	**Pa (Elmer) Kirby**
Ma Kirby	**Beulah,** twenty-two
Arthur, thirteen	
Caroline, fifteen	

Setting: No scenery is required for this play. The idea is that no place is being represented. This may be achieved by a gray curtain backdrop with no sidepieces, a cyclorama, or the empty, bare stage.

[*As the curtain rises, the* STAGE MANAGER *is leaning lazily against the proscenium pillar at the left. He is smoking.* ARTHUR *is playing marbles down center in pantomime.* CAROLINE *is way up left talking to some girls who are invisible to us.* MA KIRBY *is anxiously putting on her hat (real) before an imaginary mirror up right.*]

Ma. Where's your pa? Why isn't he here? I declare we'll never get started.

Arthur. Ma, where's my hat? I guess I don't go if I can't find my hat. (*Still playing marbles*)

Ma. Go out into the hall and see if it isn't there. Where's Caroline gone to now, the plagued child?

Arthur. She's out waitin' in the street talkin' to the Jones girls—— I just looked in the hall a thousand times, Ma, and it isn't there. (*He spits for good luck before a difficult shot and mutters.*) Come on, baby.

Ma. Go and look again, I say. Look carefully.

4

[ARTHUR *rises, reluctantly, crosses right, turns around, returns swiftly to his game center, flinging himself on the floor with a terrible impact and starts shooting an aggie.*]

Arthur. No, Ma, it's not there.
Ma (*serenely*). Well, you don't leave Newark without that hat, make up your mind to that. I don't go no journeys with a hoodlum.
Arthur. Aw, Ma!

[MA *comes downstage, right to the footlights, pulls up an imaginary window and talks toward the audience.*]

Ma (*calling*). Oh, Mrs. Schwartz!
The Stage Manager (*down left, consulting his script*). Here I am, Mrs. Kirby. Are you going yet?
Ma. I guess we're going in just a minute. How's the baby?
The Stage Manager. She's all right now. We slapped her on the back and she spat it up.
Ma. Isn't that fine!—— Well, now, if you'll be good enough to give the cat a saucer of milk in the morning and the evening, Mrs. Schwartz, I'll be ever so grateful to you—— Oh, good afternoon, Mrs. Hobmeyer!
The Stage Manager. Good afternoon, Mrs. Kirby, I hear you're going away.
Ma (*modest*). Oh, just for three days, Mrs. Hobmeyer, to see my married daughter, Beulah, in Camden. Elmer's got his vacation week from the laundry early this year, and he's just the best driver in the world.

[CAROLINE *comes downstage right and stands by her mother.*]

The Stage Manager. Is the whole family going?
Ma. Yes, all four of us that's here. The change ought to be good for the children. My married daughter was downright sick a while ago——

The Stage Manager. Tchk—tchk—tchk! Yes. I remember you tellin' us.

Ma (*with feeling*). And I just want to go down and see the child. I ain't seen her since then. I just won't rest easy in my mind without I see her. (*To* CAROLINE) Can't you say good afternoon to Mrs. Hobmeyer?

Caroline (*lowers her eyes and says woodenly*). Good afternoon, Mrs. Hobmeyer.

The Stage Manager. Good afternoon, dear—— Well, I'll wait and beat these rugs until after you're gone, because I don't want to choke you. I hope you have a good time and find everything all right.

Ma. Thank you, Mrs. Hobmeyer, I hope I will—— Well, I guess that milk for the cat is all, Mrs. Schwartz, if you're sure you don't mind. If anything should come up, the key to the backdoor is hanging by the icebox.

Caroline. Ma! Not so loud.

Arthur. Everybody can hear yuh.

Ma. Stop pullin' my dress, children. (*In a loud whisper*) The key to the backdoor I'll leave hangin' by the icebox and I'll leave the screen door unhooked.

The Stage Manager. Now have a good trip, dear, and give my love to Beuhly.

Ma. I will, and thank you a thousand times.

[*She lowers the window, turns upstage and looks around.* CAROLINE *goes left and vigorously rubs her cheeks.* MA *occupies herself with the last touches of packing.*]

What can be keeping your pa?

Arthur (*who has not left his marbles*). I can't find my hat, Ma.

[*Enter* ELMER *holding a cap, up right.*]

Elmer. Here's Arthur's hat. He musta left it in the car Sunday.

Ma. That's a mercy. Now we can start—— Caroline Kirby, what you done to your cheeks?

Caroline (*defiant, abashed*). Nothin'.

Ma. If you've put anything on 'em, I'll slap you.

Caroline. No, Ma, of course I haven't. (*Hanging her head*) I just rubbed 'm to make 'm red. All the girls do that at high school when they're goin' places.

Ma. Such silliness I never saw. Elmer, what kep' you?

Elmer (*always even voiced and always looking out a little anxiously through his spectacles*). I just went to the garage and had Charlie give a last look at it, Kate.

Ma. I'm glad you did. (*Collecting two pieces of imaginary luggage and starting for the door*) I wouldn't like to have no breakdown miles from anywhere. Now we can start. Arthur, put those marbles away. Anybody'd think you didn't want to go on a journey to look at yuh.

[*They go out through the "hall."* MA *opens an imaginary door down right.* PA, CAROLINE *and* ARTHUR *go through it.* MA *follows, taking time to lock the door, hang the key by the "icebox." They turn up at an abrupt angle, going upstage. As they come to the steps from the back porch, each arriving at a given point, starts bending his knees lower and lower to denote going downstairs, and find themselves in the street. The* STAGE MANAGER *moves from the right to the automobile. It is right center of the stage, seen partially at an angle, its front pointing down center.*]

Elmer (*coming forward*). Here, you boys, you keep away from that car.

Ma. Those Sullivan boys put their heads into everything.

[*They get into the car.* ELMER's *hands hold an imaginary steering wheel and continually shift gears.* MA *sits beside him.* ARTHUR *is behind him and* CAROLINE *is behind* MA.]

Caroline (*standing up in the back seat, waving, self-consciously*). Goodbye, Mildred. Goodbye, Helen.

The Stage Manager (*having returned to his position by the left proscenium*). Goodbye, Caroline. Goodbye, Mrs. Kirby. I hope y' have a good time.

Ma. Goodbye, girls.
The Stage Manager. Goodbye, Kate. The car looks fine.
Ma (*looking upward toward a window right*). Oh, goodbye, Emma!
(*Modestly*) We think it's the best little Chevrolet in the
world—— (*Looking up toward the left*) Oh, goodbye, Mrs. Adler!
The Stage Manager. What, are you going away, Mrs. Kirby?
Ma. Just for three days, Mrs. Adler, to see my married daugh-
ter in Camden.
The Stage Manager. Have a good time.

[*Now* MA, CAROLINE, *and* THE STAGE MANAGER *break out into a
tremendous chorus of goodbyes. The whole street is saying goodbye.*
ARTHUR *takes out his peashooter and lets fly happily into the air.
There is a lurch or two and they are off.*]

Arthur (*leaning forward in sudden fright*). Pa! Pa! Don't go by
the school. Mr. Biedenbach might see us!
Ma. I don't care if he does see us. I guess I can take my children out of school for one day without having to hide down
back streets about it.

[ELMER *nods to a passerby.*]

(*Without sharpness*) Who was that you spoke to, Elmer?
Elmer. That was the fellow who arranges our banquets down
to the lodge, Kate.
Ma. Is he the one who had to buy four hundred steaks?

[PA *nods.*]

I declare, I'm glad I'm not him.
Elmer. The air's getting better already. Take deep breaths,
children.

[*They inhale noisily.*]

Arthur (*pointing to a sign and indicating that it gradually goes by*).
Gee, it's almost open fields already. "*Weber and Heilbroner Suits
for Well-Dressed Men.*" Ma, can I have one of them someday?

Ma. If you graduate with good marks perhaps your father'll let you have one for graduation.

[*Pause. General gazing about, then sudden lurch*]

Caroline (*whining*). Oh, Pa! Do we have to wait while that whole funeral goes by?

[ELMER *takes off his hat.* MA *cranes forward with absorbed curiosity.*]

Ma (*not sharp and bossy*). Take off your hat, Arthur. Look at your father—— Why, Elmer, I do believe that's a lodge brother of yours. See the banner? I suppose this is the Elizabeth branch.

[ELMER *nods.*]

(*sighs*) Tchk—tchk—tchk.

[*The children lean forward and all watch the funeral in silence, growing momentarily more solemnized. After a pause,* MA *continues almost dreamily but not sentimentally.*]

Well, we haven't forgotten the funeral that we went on, have we? We haven't forgotten our good Harold. He gave his life for his country, we mustn't forget that. (*There is another pause; with cheerful resignation*) Well, we'll all hold up the traffic for a few minutes someday.
The Children (*very uncomfortable*). Ma!
Ma (*without self-pity*). Well, I'm "ready," children. I hope everybody in this car is "ready." And I pray to go first, Elmer. Yes.

[ELMER *touches her hand.*]

Caroline. Ma, everybody's looking at you.
Arthur. Everybody's laughing at you.
Ma. Oh, hold your tongues! I don't care what a lot of silly people in Elizabeth, New Jersey, think of me—— Now we can go on. That's the last.

[*There is another lurch and the car goes on.*]

Caroline (*looking at a sign and turning as she passes it*). "Fit-Rite Suspenders. The Working Man's Choice." Pa, why do they spell "Rite" that way?
Elmer. So that it'll make you stop and ask about it, Missy.
Caroline. Papa, you're teasing me. —Ma, why do they say "Three Hundred Rooms Three Hundred Baths"?
Arthur. "Miller's Spaghetti: The Family's Favorite Dish." Ma, why don't you ever have spaghetti?
Ma. Go along, you'd never eat it.
Arthur. Ma, I like it now.
Caroline (*with gesture*). Yum-yum. It looked wonderful up there. Ma, make some when we get home?
Ma (*dryly*). "The management is always happy to receive suggestions. We aim to please."

[*The children scream with laughter. Even* ELMER *smiles.* MA *remains modest.*]

Elmer. Well, I guess no one's complaining, Kate. Everybody knows you're a good cook.
Ma. I don't know whether I'm a good cook or not, but I know I've had practice. At least I've cooked three meals a day for twenty-five years.
Arthur. Aw, Ma, you went out to eat once in a while.
Ma. Yes. That made it a leap year.

[*The children laugh again.*]

Caroline (*in an ecstasy of well-being, puts her arms around her mother*). Ma, I love going out in the country like this. Let's do it often, Ma.
Ma. Goodness, smell that air, will you! It's got the whole ocean in it—— Elmer, drive careful over that bridge. This must be New Brunswick we're coming to.
Arthur (*after a slight pause*). Ma, when is the next comfort station?

Ma (*unruffled*). You don't want one. You just said that to be awful.

Caroline (*shrilly*). Yes, he did, Ma. He's terrible. He says that kind of thing right out in school and I want to sink through the floor, Ma. He's terrible.

Ma. Oh, don't get so excited about nothing, Miss Proper! I guess we're all yewman beings in this car, at least as far as I know. And, Arthur, you try and be a gentleman—— Elmer, don't run over that collie dog. (*She follows the dog with her eyes.*) Looked kinda peaked to me. Needs a good honest bowl of leavings. Pretty dog, too. (*Her eyes fall on a billboard at the right*). That's a pretty advertisement for Chesterfield cigarettes, isn't it? Looks like Beulah, a little.

Arthur. Ma?

Ma. Yes.

Arthur. (*"route" rhymes with "out"*). Can't I take a paper route with the Newark *Daily Post*?

Ma. No, you cannot. No, sir. I hear they make the paper boys get up at four-thirty in the morning. No son of mine is going to get up at four-thirty every morning, not if it's to make a million dollars. Your *Saturday Evening Post* route on Thursday mornings is enough.

Arthur. Aw, Ma.

Ma. No, sir. No son of mine is going to get up at four-thirty and miss the sleep God meant him to have.

Arthur (*sullenly*). Hhm! Ma's always talking about God. I guess she got a letter from Him this morning.

Ma (*outraged*). Elmer, stop that automobile this minute. I don't go another step with anybody that says things like that. Arthur, you get out of this car.

[ELMER *stops the car.*]

Elmer, you give him a dollar bill. He can go back to Newark by himself. I don't want him.

Arthur. What did I say? There wasn't anything terrible about that.

Elmer. I didn't hear what he said, Kate.

Ma. God has done a lot of things for me and I won't have Him made fun of by anybody. Get out of this car this minute.

Caroline. Aw, Ma—don't spoil the ride.

Ma. No.

Elmer. We might as well go on, Kate, since we've got started. I'll talk to the boy tonight.

Ma (*slowly conceding*). All right, if you say so, Elmer.

[ELMER *starts the car.*]

Arthur (*frightened*). Aw, Ma, that wasn't so terrible.

Ma. I don't want to talk about it. I hope your father washes your mouth out with soap and water—— Where'd we all be if I started talking about God like that, I'd like to know! We'd be in the speak-easies and nightclubs and places like that, that's where we'd be.

Caroline (*after a very slight pause*). What did he say, Ma? I didn't hear what he said.

Ma. I don't want to talk about it.

[*They drive on in silence for a moment, the shocked silence after a scandal.*]

Elmer. I'm going to stop and give the car a little water, I guess.

Ma. All right, Elmer. You know best.

Elmer (*turns the wheel and stops; as to a garage hand*). Could I have a little water in the radiator—to make sure?

The Stage Manager (*in this scene alone he lays aside his script and enters into a role seriously*). You sure can. (*He punches the left front tire.*) Air all right? Do you need any oil or gas? (*Goes up around car*)

Elmer. No, I think not. I just got fixed up in Newark.

[THE STAGE MANAGER *carefully pours some water into the hood.*]

Ma. We're on the right road for Camden, are we?

The Stage Manager (*coming down on right side of car*). Yes, keep straight ahead. You can't miss it. You'll be in Trenton in a few minutes. Camden's a great town, lady, believe me.

Ma. My daughter likes it fine—my married daughter.

The Stage Manager. Ye'? It's a great burg all right. I guess I think so because I was born near there.

Ma. Well, well. Your folks still live there?

The Stage Manager (*standing with one foot on the rung of* MA's *chair. They have taken a great fancy to one another.*). No, my old man sold the farm and they built a factory on it. So the folks moved to Philadelphia.

Ma. My married daughter, Beulah, lives there because her husband works in the telephone company—— Stop pokin' me, Caroline!—— We're all going down to see her for a few days.

The Stage Manager. Ye'?

Ma. She's been sick, you see, and I just felt I had to go and see her. My husband and my boy are going to stay at the YMCA. I hear they've got a dormitory on the top floor that's real clean and comfortable. Have you ever been there?

The Stage Manager. No. I'm Knights of Columbus myself.

Ma. Oh.

The Stage Manager. I used to play basketball at the Y though. It looked all right to me. (*He reluctantly moves away and pretends to examine the car again.*) Well, I guess you're all set now, lady. I hope you have a good trip; you can't miss it.

Everybody. Thanks. Thanks a lot. Good luck to you.

[*Jolts and lurches*]

Ma (*with a sigh*). The world's full of nice people—that's what I call a nice young man.

Caroline (*earnestly*). Ma, you oughtn't to tell 'm all everything about yourself.

Ma. Well, Caroline, you do your way and I'll do mine—— He looked kinda pale to me. I'd like to feed him up for a few days. His mother lives in Philadelphia and I expect he eats at those dreadful Greek places.

Caroline. I'm hungry. Pa, there's a hot-dog stand. K'n I have one?
Elmer. We'll all have one, eh, Kate? We had such an early lunch.
Ma. Just as you think best, Elmer.

[ELMER *stops the car.*]

Elmer. Arthur, here's half a dollar——— Run over and see what they have. Not too much mustard either.

[ARTHUR *descends from the car and goes off stage right.* MA *and* CAR-OLINE *get out and walk a bit, upstage and to the left.* CAROLINE *keeps at her mother's right.*]

Ma. What's that flower over there? —I'll take some of those to Beulah.
Caroline. It's just a weed, Ma.
Ma. I like it——— My, look at the sky, wouldya! I'm glad I was born in New Jersey. I've always said it was the best state in the Union. Every state has something no other state has got.

[*Presently* ARTHUR *returns with his hands full of imaginary hot dogs which he distributes. First to his father, next to* CAROLINE, *who comes forward to meet him, and lastly to his mother. He is still very much cast down by the recent scandal and, as he approaches his mother, says falteringly*]

Arthur. Ma, I'm sorry. I'm sorry for what I said. (*He bursts into tears.*)
Ma. There. There. We all say wicked things at times. I know you didn't mean it like it sounded.

[*He weeps still more violently than before.*]

Why, now, now! I forgive you, Arthur, and tonight before you go to bed you . . . (*She whispers.*) You're a good boy at heart, Arthur, and we all know it.

[CAROLINE *starts to cry too.* MA *is suddenly joyously alive and happy.*]

Sakes alive, it's too nice a day for us all to be cryin'. Come now, get in. (*Crossing behind car to the right side, followed by the children*) Caroline, go up in front with your father. Ma wants to sit with her beau.

[CAROLINE *sits in front with her father.* MA *lets* ARTHUR *get in car ahead of her; then she closes door.*]

I never saw such children. Your hot dogs are all getting wet. Now chew them fine, everybody. —All right, Elmer, forward march.

[*Car starts.* CAROLINE *spits.*]

Caroline, whatever are you doing?
Caroline. I'm spitting out the leather, Ma.
Ma. Then say "excuse me."
Caroline. Excuse me, please. (*She spits again.*)
Ma. What's this place? Arthur, did you see the post office?
Arthur. It said "Lawrenceville."
Ma. Hhn. School kinda. Nice. I wonder what that big yellow house set back was—— Now it's beginning to be Trenton.
Caroline. Papa, it was near here that George Washington crossed the Delaware. It was near Trenton, Mama. He was first in war and first in peace, and first in the hearts of his countrymen.
Ma (*surveying the passing world, serene and didactic*). Well, the thing I like about him best was that he never told a lie.

[*The children are duly cast down. There is a pause.* ARTHUR *stands up and looks at the car ahead.*]

There's a sunset for you. There's nothing like a good sunset.
Arthur. There's an Ohio license in front of us. Ma, have you ever been to Ohio?

Ma. No.

[*A dreamy silence descends upon them.* CAROLINE *sits closer to her father, toward the left;* ARTHUR *closer to* MA *on the right, who puts her arm around him, unsentimentally.*]

Arthur. Ma, what a lotta people there are in the world, Ma. There must be thousands and thousands in the United States. Ma, how many are there?
Ma. I don't know. Ask your father.
Arthur. Pa, how many are there?
Elmer. There are a hundred and twenty-six million, Kate.
Ma (*giving a pressure about* ARTHUR's *shoulder*). And they all like to drive out in the evening with their children beside 'm. Why doesn't somebody sing something? Arthur, you're always singing something; what's the matter with you?
Arthur. All right. What'll we sing? (*He sketches.*)

"In the Blue Ridge Mountains of Virginia,
On the . . ."

No, I don't like that anymore. Let's do

"I been workin' on de railroad. . . ."

[CAROLINE *joins in.*]

"All de liblong day . . ."

[MA *sings.*]

"I been workin' on de railroad. . . ."

[ELMER *joins in.*]

"Just to pass de time away.
Don't you hear de whistle blowin'," [etc.]

[MA *suddenly jumps up with a wild cry and a large circular gesture.*]

Ma. Elmer, that signpost said "Camden." I saw it.
Elmer. All right, Kate, if you're sure.

[*Much shifting of gears, backing, and jolting.*]

Ma. Yes, there it is. "Camden—Five miles." Dear old Beulah.

[*The journey continues.*]

Now, children, you be good and quiet during dinner. She's just got out of bed after a big sorta operation, and we must all move around kinda quiet. First you drop me and Caroline at the door and just say hello, and then you menfolk go over to the YMCA and come back for dinner in about an hour.
Caroline (*shutting her eyes and pressing her fists passionately against her nose*). I see the first star. Everybody make a wish.

> "Star light, star bright,
> First star I seen tonight.
> I wish I may, I wish I might
> Have the wish I wish tonight."

(*Then solemnly*) Pins. Mama, you say "needles." (*She interlocks little fingers with her mother across back of seat.*)
Ma. Needles.
Caroline. Shakespeare. Ma, you say "Longfellow."
Ma. Longfellow.
Caroline. Now it's a secret and I can't tell it to anybody. Ma, you make a wish.
Ma (*with almost grim humor*). No, I can make wishes without waiting for no star. And I can tell my wishes right out loud too. Do you want to hear them?
Caroline (*resignedly*). No, Ma, we know 'm already. We've heard 'm. (*She hangs her head affectedly on her left shoulder and says with unmalicious mimicry.*) You want me to be a good girl and you want Arthur to be honest-in-word-and-deed.
Ma (*majestically*). Yes. So mind yourself.
Elmer. Caroline, take out that letter from Beulah in my coat pocket by you and read aloud the places I marked with red pencil.

Caroline (*laboriously making it out*). "*A few blocks after you pass the two big oil tanks on your left——*"
Everybody (*pointing backward*). There they are!
Caroline. *——you come to a corner where there's an A and P store on the left and a firehouse kitty-corner to it——*"

[*They all jubilantly identify these landmarks.*]

"*——Turn right, go two blocks, and our house is Weyerhauser Street, Number 471.*"
Ma. It's an even nicer street than they used to live in. And right handy to an A and P.
Caroline (*whispering*). Ma, it's better than our street. It's richer than our street. Ma, isn't Beulah richer than we are?
Ma (*looking at her with a firm and glassy eye*). Mind yourself, Missy. I don't want to hear anybody talking about rich or not rich when I'm around. If people aren't nice I don't care how rich they are. I live in the best street in the world because my husband and children live there. (*She glares impressively at* CAR-OLINE *a moment to let this lesson sink in, then looks up, sees* BEU-LAH *off left and waves*). There's Beulah standing on the steps looking for us.

[BEULAH *enters from left, also waving. They all call out, "Hello, Beulah—hello." Presently they are all getting out of the car, except* ELMER, *busy with brakes.*]

Beulah. Hello, Mama. Well, lookit how Arthur and Caroline are growing.
Ma. They're bursting all their clothes.
Beulah (*crossing in front of them and kissing her father long and affectionately*). Hello, Papa. Good old papa. You look tired, Pa.
Ma. Yes, your pa needs a rest. Thank heaven, his vacation has come just now. We'll feed him up and let him sleep late.

[ELMER *gets out of car and stands in front of it.*]

Pa has a present for you, Loolie. He would go and buy it.

Beulah. Why, Pa, you're terrible to go and buy anything for me. Isn't he terrible?

[STAGE MANAGER *removes automobile.*]

Ma. Well, it's a secret. You can open it at dinner.

Beulah (*puts her arm around his neck and rubs her nose against his temple*). Crazy old pa, goin' buyin' things! It's me that oughta be buyin' things for you, Pa.

Elmer. Oh, no! There's only one Loolie in the world.

Beulah (*whispering, as her eyes fill with tears*). Are you glad I'm still alive, Pa? (*She kisses him abruptly and goes back to the house steps.*)

Elmer. Where's Horace, Loolie?

Beulah. He was kep' over a little at the office. He'll be here any minute. He's crazy to see you all.

Ma. All right. You men go over to the Y and come back in about an hour.

Beulah. Go straight along, Pa, you can't miss it. It just stares at yuh.

[ELMER *and* ARTHUR *exit down right.*]

Well, come on upstairs, Ma, and take your things—— Caroline, there's a surprise for you in the back yard.

Caroline. Rabbits?

Beulah. No.

Caroline. Chickins?

Beulah. No. Go and see.

[CAROLINE *runs offstage, down left.*]

There are two new puppies. You be thinking over whether you can keep one in Newark.

Ma. I guess we can.

[MA *and* BEULAH *turn and walk way upstage right.* THE STAGE MAN-AGER *pushes out a cot from the left, and places it down left on a slant so that its foot is toward the left.* BEULAH *and* MA *come downstage center toward left.*]

It's a nice house, Beulah. You just got a *lovely* home.
Beulah. When I got back from the hospital, Horace had moved everything into it, and there wasn't anything for me to do.
Ma. It's lovely.

[BEULAH *sits on the cot, testing the springs.*]

Beulah. I think you'll find this comfortable, Ma. (BEULAH *sits on downstage end of it.*)
Ma (*taking off her hat*). Oh, I could sleep on a heapa shoes, Loolie! I don't have no trouble sleepin'. (*She sits down upstage of her.*) Now let me look at my girl. Well, well, when I last saw you, you didn't know me. You kep' saying, "When's Mama comin'? When's Mama comin'?" But the doctor sent me away.
Beulah (*puts her head on her mother's shoulder and weeps*). It was awful, Mama. It was awful. She didn't even live a few minutes, Mama. It was awful.
Ma (*in a quick, light, urgent undertone*). God thought best, dear. God thought best. We don't understand why. We just go on, honey, doin' our business. (*Then almost abruptly*) Well, now (*stands up*), what are we giving the men to eat tonight?
Beulah. There's a chicken in the oven.
Ma. What time didya put it in?
Beulah (*restraining her*). Aw, Ma, don't go yet. (*Taking her mother's hand and drawing her down beside her*) I like to sit here with you this way. You always get the fidgets when we try and pet yuh, Mama.
Ma (*ruefully, laughing*). Yes, it's kinda foolish. I'm just an old Newark bag-a-bones. (*She glances at the backs of her hands.*)
Beulah (*indignantly*). Why, Ma, you're good-lookin'! We always said you were good-lookin'—— And besides, you're the best ma we could ever have.
Ma (*uncomfortable*). Well, I hope you like me. There's nothin' like bein' liked by your family—— (*Rises*) Now I'm going downstairs to look at the chicken. You stretch out here for a minute and shut your eyes. (*She helps* BEULAH *to a lying position.*) Have you got everything laid in for breakfast before the shops close?

Beulah. Oh, you know! Ham and eggs.

[*They both laugh.* MA *puts an imaginary blanket over* BEULAH.]

Ma. I declare I never could understand what men see in ham and eggs. I think they're horrible—— What time did you put the chicken in?

Beulah. Five o'clock.

Ma. Well, now, you shut your eyes for ten minutes. (MA *turns, walks directly upstage, then along the back wall to the right as she absent-mindedly and indistinctly sings*)

"There were ninety and nine that safely lay
In the shelter of the fold. . . ."

AND THE CURTAIN FALLS

Our Town
Thornton Wilder

Characters
(in order of appearance)

Stage Manager	Mr. Webb
Dr. Gibbs	Woman in the Balcony
Joe Crowell	Man in the Auditorium
Howie Newsome	Lady in the Box
Mrs. Gibbs	Simon Stimson
Mrs. Webb	Mrs. Soames
George Gibbs	Constable Warren
Rebecca Gibbs	Si Crowell
Wally Webb	Three Baseball Players
Emily Webb	Sam Craig
Professor Willard	Joe Stoddard

Act One

The entire play takes place in Grover's Corners, New Hampshire.

No curtain.

   No scenery.

   The audience, arriving, sees an empty stage in half-light.

   Presently the STAGE MANAGER, *hat on and pipe in mouth, enters and begins placing a table and several chairs downstage left, and a table and chairs downstage right.*

   "Left" and "right" are from the point of view of the actor facing the audience. "Up" is toward the back wall.

   As the houselights go down he has finished setting the stage and leaning against the right proscenium pillar watches the late arrivals in the audience.

When the auditorium is in complete darkness he speaks:

Stage Manager. This play is called "Our Town." It was written by Thornton Wilder, produced and directed by A—— [or produced by A——, directed by B——]. In it you will see Miss C——, Miss D——, Miss E——, and Mr. F——, Mr. G——, Mr. H——, and many others. The name of the town is Grover's Corners, New Hampshire—just across the Massachusetts line: longitude 42 degrees 40 minutes, latitude 70 degrees 37 minutes. The first act shows a day in our town. The day is May 7, 1901. The time is just before dawn. (*A rooster crows.*) The sky is beginning to show some streaks of light over in the east there, behind our mount'in. The morning star always gets wonderful bright the minute before it has to go. (*He stares at it for a moment, then goes upstage.*) Well, I'd better show you how our town lies. Up here—(*That is, parallel with the back wall*)—is Main Street. Way back there is the railway station; tracks go that way. Polish Town's across the tracks and some Canuck families. (*Toward the left*) Over there is the Congregational Church; across the street's the Presbyterian. Methodist and Unitarian are over there. Baptist is down in the holla' by the river. Catholic Church is over beyond the tracks. Here's the town hall and post office combined; jail's in the basement. Bryan once made a speech from these steps here. Along here's a row of stores. Hitching posts and horse blocks in front of them. First automobile's going to come along in about five years—belonged to banker Cartwright, our richest citizen, . . . lives in the big white house up on the hill. Here's the grocery store and here's Mr. Morgan's drugstore. Most everybody in town manages to look into those two stores once a day. Public school's over yonder. High school's still farther over. Quarter of nine mornings, noontimes, and three o'clock afternoons, the hull town can hear the yelling and screaming from those schoolyards. (*He approaches the table and chairs downstage right.*) This is our doctor's house—Doc Gibbs. This is the back door. (*Two arched trellises are pushed out, one by each proscenium pillar.*) There's some scenery for those who think they have to have scenery. There's a garden here.

Corn . . . peas . . . beans . . . hollyhocks . . . heliotrope . . . and a lot of burdock. (*Crosses the stage*) In those days our newspaper come out twice a week—*The Grover's Corners Sentinel*—and this is editor Webb's house. And this is Mrs. Webb's garden. Just like Mrs. Gibbs's, only it's got a lot of sunflowers, too. Right here—big butternut tree. (*He returns to his place by the right proscenium pillar and looks at the audience for a minute.*) Nice town, y'know what I mean? Nobody very remarkable ever come out of it—s'far as we know. The earliest tombstones in the cemetery up there on the mountain say 1670–1680—they're Grovers and Cartwrights and Gibbses and Herseys—same names as are around here now. Well, as I said: It's about dawn. The only lights on in town are in a cottage over by the tracks where a Polish mother's just had twins. And in the Joe Crowell house, where Joe Junior's getting up so as to deliver the paper. And in the depot, where Shorty Hawkins is gettin' ready to flag the 5:45 for Boston. (*A train whistle is heard. The* STAGE MANAGER *takes out his watch and nods.*) Naturally, out in the country—all around—they've been lights on for some time, what with milkin's and so on. But town people sleep late. So—another day's begun. There's Doc Gibbs comin' down Main Street now, comin' back from that baby case. And here's his wife comin' downstairs to get breakfast. Doc Gibbs died in 1930. The new hospital's named after him. Mrs. Gibbs died first—long time ago in fact. She went out to visit her daughter, Rebecca, who married an insurance man in Canton, Ohio, and died there—pneumonia—but her body was brought back here. She's up in the cemetery there now—in with a whole mess of Gibbses and Herseys—she was Julia Hersey 'fore she married Doc Gibbs in the Congregational Church over there. In our town we like to know the facts about everybody—— That's Doc Gibbs. And there comes Joe Crowell, Jr., delivering Mr. Webb's *Sentinel.*

[DR. GIBBS *has been coming along Main Street from the left. At the point where he would turn to approach his house, he stops, sets down his— imaginary—black bag, takes off his hat, and rubs his face with fatigue, using an enormous handkerchief.* MRS. GIBBS *has entered her kitchen, gone through the motions of putting wood into a stove, lighting it, and preparing breakfast. Suddenly,* JOE CROWELL, JR., *starts down Main Street from the right, hurling imaginary newspapers into doorways.*]

Joe Crowell, Jr. Morning, Doc Gibbs.

Dr. Gibbs. Morning, Joe.

Joe Crowell, Jr. Somebody been sick, Doc?

Dr. Gibbs. No. Just some twins born over in Polish Town.

Joe Crowell, Jr. Do you want your paper now?

Dr. Gibbs. Yes, I'll take it—— Anything serious goin' on in the world since Wednesday?

Joe Crowell, Jr. Yessir. My school teacher, Miss Foster's getting married to a fella over in Concord.

Dr. Gibbs. I declare—— How do you boys feel about that?

Joe Crowell, Jr. Well, of course, it's none of my business—but I think if a person starts out to be a teacher, she ought to stay one.

Dr. Gibbs. How's your knee, Joe?

Joe Crowell, Jr. Fine, Doc, I never think about it at all. Only like you said, it always tells me when it's going to rain.

Dr. Gibbs. What's it telling you today? Goin' to rain?

Joe Crowell, Jr. No, sir.

Dr. Gibbs. Sure?

Joe Crowell, Jr. Yessir.

Dr. Gibbs. Knee ever make a mistake?

Joe Crowell, Jr. No, sir.

[JOE *goes off.* DR. GIBBS *stands reading his paper.*]

Stage Manager. Here comes Howie Newsome delivering the milk.

[HOWIE NEWSOME *comes along Main Street, passes* DOCTOR GIBBS, *comes down the center of the stage, leaves some bottles at* MRS. WEBB's *back door, and crosses the stage to* MRS. GIBBS's.]

Howie Newsome. Git-ap, Bessie. What's the matter with you?—— Morning, Doc.

Dr. Gibbs. Morning, Howie.

Howie Newsome. Somebody sick?

Dr. Gibbs. Pair of twins over to Mrs. Goruslawski's.

Howie Newsome. Twins, eh? This town's gettin' bigger every year.

Dr. Gibbs. Going to rain, Howie?

Howie Newsome. No, no. Fine day—that'll burn through. Come on, Bessie.

Dr. Gibbs. Hello, Bessie. (*He strokes her.*) How old is she, Howie?

Howie Newsome. Going on seventeen. Bessie's all mixed up about the route ever since the Lockharts stopped takin' their quart of milk every day. She wants to leave 'em a quart just the same—keeps scolding me the hull trip.

[*He reaches* MRS. GIBB's *back door. She is waiting for him.*]

Mrs. Gibbs. Good morning, Howie.

Howie Newsome. Morning, Mrs. Gibbs. Doc's just comin' down the street.

Mrs. Gibbs. Is he? Seems like you're late today?

Howie Newsome. Yes. Somep'n went wrong with the separator. Don't know what 'twas.

[*He goes back to Main Street, clucks for Bessie and goes off right.* DR. GIBBS *reaches his home and goes in.*]

Mrs. Gibbs. Everything all right?

Dr. Gibbs. Yes. I declare—easy as kittens.

Mrs. Gibbs. Bacon'll be ready in a minute. Set down and drink your coffee. Child-*run*! Child-*run*! Time to get up—— George! Rebecca!—you can catch a couple hours' sleep this morning, can't you?

Dr. Gibbs. Hm! . . . Mrs. Wentworth's coming at eleven. Guess I know what it's about, too. Her stummick ain't what it ought to be.

Mrs. Gibbs. All told, you won't get more'n three hours' sleep. Frank Gibbs, I don't know what's goin' to become of you. I do wish I could get you to go away someplace and take a rest. I think it would do you good.

Mrs. Webb. Emileeee! Time to get up! Wally! Seven o'clock!

Mrs. Gibbs. I declare, you got to speak to George. Seems like something's come over him lately. He's no help to me at all. I can't even get him to cut me some wood.

Dr. Gibbs. Is he sassy to you?

Mrs. Gibbs. No. He just whines! All he thinks about is that baseball—— George! Rebecca! You'll be late for school.

Dr. Gibbs. M-m-m . . .

Mrs. Gibbs. George!

Dr. Gibbs. George, look sharp!

George's Voice. Yes, Pa!

Dr. Gibbs (*as he goes off the stage*). Don't you hear your mother calling you?

Mrs. Webb. Walleee! Emileee! You'll be late for school! Walleee! You wash yourself good or I'll come up and do it myself.

Rebecca Gibb's Voice. Ma! What dress shall I wear?

Mrs. Gibbs. Don't make a noise. Your father's been out all night and needs his sleep. I washed and ironed the blue gingham for you special.

Rebecca. Ma, I hate that dress.

Mrs. Gibbs. Oh, hush up with you.

Rebecca. Every day I go to school dressed like a sick turkey.

Mrs. Gibbs. Now, Rebecca, don't be impossible. You always look *very* nice.

Rebecca. Mama, George's throwing soap at me.

Mrs. Gibbs. I'll come up and slap the both of you—that's what I'll do.

[*A factory whistle sounds. The children enter and take their places at the breakfast tables:* EMILY *and* WALLY WEBB, GEORGE *and* REBECCA GIBBS.]

Stage Manager. We've got a factory in our town too—hear it? Makes blankets. Cartwrights own it and it brung 'em a fortune.

Mrs. Webb. Children! Now I won't have it. Breakfast is just as good as any other meal and I won't have you gobbling like wolves. It'll stunt your growth—that's a fact. Put away your book, Wally.

Wally. Aw, Ma!

Mrs. Webb. You know the rule's well as I do—no books at table. As for me, I'd rather have my children healthy than bright.

Emily. I'm both, Mama; you know I am. I'm the brightest girl in school for my age. I have a wonderful memory.

Mrs. Webb. Eat your breakfast.

Wally. I'm bright, too, when I'm looking at my stamp collection.

Mrs. Gibbs. I'll speak to your father about it when he's rested. Seems to me twenty-five cents a week's enough for a boy your age. I declare I don't know how you spend it all.

George. Aw, Ma—I gotta lotta things to buy.

Mrs. Gibbs. Strawberry phosphates—that's what you spend it on.

George. I don't see how Rebecca comes to have so much money. She has more'n a dollar.

Rebecca (*spoon in mouth, dreamily*). I've been saving it up gradual.

Mrs. Gibbs. Well, dear, I think it's a good thing every now and then to spend some.

Rebecca. Mama, do you know what I love most in the world—do you?—money.

Mrs. Gibbs. Eat your breakfast.

[*The school bell is heard.*]

The Children. Mama, there's first bell—— I gotta hurry—— I don't want any more.

Mrs. Webb. Walk fast, but you don't have to run. Wally, pull up your pants at the knee. Stand up straight, Emily.

Mrs. Gibbs. Tell Miss Foster I send her my best congratulations—can you remember that?
Rebecca. Yes, Ma.
Mrs. Gibbs. You look real nice, Rebecca. Pick up your feet.
All. Goodbye.

[*The children from the two houses join at the center of the stage and go up to Main Street, then off left.* MRS. GIBBS *fills her apron with food for the chickens and comes down to the footlights.*]

Mrs. Gibbs. Here, chick, chick, chick. No, go away, you. Go away. Here, chick, chick, chick. What's the matter with *you*? Fight, fight, fight—that's all you do. Hm . . . *you* don't belong to me. Where'd you come from? (*She shakes her apron.*) Oh, don't be so scared. Nobody's going to hurt you.

[MRS. WEBB *is sitting by her trellis, stringing beans.*]

Good morning, Myrtle. How's your cold?
Mrs. Webb. Well, it's better, but I told Charles I didn't know as I'd go to choir practice tonight. Wouldn't be any use.
Mrs. Gibbs. Just the same, you come to choir practice, Myrtle, and try it.
Mrs. Webb. Well, if I don't feel any worse than I do now I probably will. While I'm resting myself, I thought I'd string some of these beans.
Mrs. Gibbs (*rolling up her sleeves as she crosses the stage for a chat*). Let me help you. Beans have been good this year.
Mrs. Webb. I've decided to put up forty quarts if it kills me. The children say they hate 'em but I notice they're able to get 'em down all winter.

[*Pause.*]

Mrs. Gibbs. Now, Myrtle. I've got to tell you something, because if I don't tell somebody I'll burst.
Mrs. Webb. Why, Julia Gibbs!

Mrs. Gibbs. Here, give me some more of those beans. Myrtle, did one of those secondhand furniture men from Boston come to see you last Friday?

Mrs. Webb. No—o.

Mrs. Gibbs. Well, he called on me. First I thought he was a patient wantin' to see Dr. Gibbs. 'N he wormed his way into my parlor, and, Myrtle Webb, he offered me three hundred and fifty dollars for Grandmother Wentworth's highboy, as I'm sitting here!

Mrs. Webb. Why, Julia Gibbs!

Mrs. Gibbs. He did! That old thing! Why, it was so big I didn't know where to put it and I almost give it to Cousin Hester Wilcox!

Mrs. Webb. Well, you're going to take it, aren't you?

Mrs. Gibbs. I don't know.

Mrs. Webb. You don't know—three hundred and fifty dollars. What's come over you?

Mrs. Gibbs. Well, if I could get the doctor to take the money and go away someplace on a real trip, I'd sell it like that—— Myrtle, ever since I was *that* high I've had the thought that I'd like to see Paris, France. I suppose I'm crazy.

Mrs. Webb. Oh, I know what you mean—— How does the doctor feel about it?

Mrs. Gibbs. Well, I did beat about the bush a little and said that if I got a legacy—that's the way I put it—I'd make him take me somewhere.

Mrs. Webb. M-m-m . . . What did he say?

Mrs. Gibbs. You know how he is. I haven't heard a serious word out of him ever since I've known him. No, he said, it might make him discontented with Grover's Corners to go traipsin' about Europe; better let well enough alone, he says. Every two years he makes a trip to the battlefields of the Civil War and that's enough treat for anybody, he says.

Mrs. Webb. Well, Mr. Webb just *admires* the way Dr. Gibbs knows everything about the Civil War. Mr. Webb's a good mind to give up Napoleon and move over to the Civil War, only Dr. Gibbs being one of the greatest experts in the country just makes him despair.

Mrs. Gibbs. It's a fact! Doctor Gibbs is never so happy as when he's at Antietam or Gettysburg. The times I've walked over those hills, Myrtle, stopping at every bush and pacing it all out, like we was going to buy it.

Mrs. Webb. Well, if that secondhand man's really serious about buyin' it, Julia, you sell it. And then you'll get to see Paris, all right.

Mrs. Gibbs. Oh, I'm sorry I mentioned it. Only it seems to me that once in your life before you die you ought to see a country where they don't talk and think in English and don't even want to.

[*The* STAGE MANAGER *returns to the center of the stage.*]

Stage Manager. That'll do. That'll do. Thank you very much, ladies.

[MRS. GIBBS *and* MRS. WEBB *gather up their things, return into their homes, and disappear.*]

Now we're going to skip a few hours in the day at Grover's Corners. But before we go on, I want you to know some more things about the town—all kinds of things. So I've asked Prof. Willard of our state university to come down here and sketch in a few details of our past history—kind of scientific account, you might say. Is Prof. Willard here?

[PROF. WILLARD, *a rural savant, pince-nez on a wide satin ribbon, enters from the right with some notes in his hand.*]

May I introduce Prof. Willard of our university. A few brief notes, thank you, Professor—unfortunately our time is limited.

Prof. Willard. Grover's Corners . . . let me see . . . Grover's Corners lies on the old Archeozoic granite of the Appalachian range. I may say it's some of the oldest land in the world. We're very proud of that. A shelf of Devonian basalt crosses it with vestiges of Mesozoic shale, and some sandstone outcroppings, but that's all more recent—two hundred, three hundred million years old. Some highly interesting fossils have been found. . . . I may say, unique fossils . . . two miles out of town, in Silas Peckham's cow pasture. They can be seen at the museum in our university at any time. Did you wish the meteorological conditions?

Stage Manager. Thank you. We would.

Prof. Willard. The mean precipitation is 40 inches. The mean annual temperature is 43 degrees, ranging between 102 degrees in the shade and 38 degrees below zero in winter. The . . . the . . . uh . . .

Stage Manager. Thank you, Professor. And have you Prof. Gruber's notes on the history of human life here?

Prof. Willard. Hm . . . yes . . . anthropological data: early Amerindian stock. Cotahatchee tribes . . . no evidence before the tenth century of this era . . . hm . . . now entirely disappeared . . . possible traces in three families. Migration toward the end of the seventeenth century of English brachycephalic blue-eyed stock . . . for the most part. Since then some influx of Slav and Mediterranean types . . .

Stage Manager. And the population, Prof. Willard?

Prof. Willard. Within the town limits, 2,640. The postal district brings in 507 more. Mortality and birthrates are constant; by MacPherson's gauge, 6.032.

Stage Manager. Thank you *very* much, Professor. We're all very much obliged to you, I'm sure.

Prof. Willard. Not at all, sir, not at all.

Stage Manager. This way, Professor, and thank you again.

[*Exit* PROF. WILLARD.]

Now the political and social report: Editor Webb—— Oh, Mr. Webb?

[MRS. WEBB *appears at her back door.*]

Mrs. Webb. He'll be here in a minute. . . . He just cut his hand while he was eatin' an apple.

Stage Manager. Thank you, Mrs. Webb.

Mrs. Webb. Charles! Everybody's waitin'. (*Exit* MRS. WEBB.)

Stage Manager. Mr. Webb is publisher and editor of *The Grover's Corners Sentinel*. That's our local paper, y'know.

[MR. WEBB *enters from his house, pulling on his coat. His finger is bound in a handkerchief.*]

Mr. Webb. Hmm ... I don't have to tell you that we're run here by a board of selectmen—— All males vote at the age of 21. Women vote indirect. We're lower middle class, sprinkling of professional men ... 10 percent illiterate laborers. Politically, we're 86 percent Republicans, 6 percent Democrats, 4 percent Socialists, rest indifferent. Religiously, we're 85 percent Protestants, 12 percent Catholics, rest indifferent. Do you want the poverty and insanity statistics?

Stage Manager. Thank you, no. Have you any comments, Mr. Webb?

Mr. Webb. Very ordinary town, if you ask me. Little better behaved than most. Probably a lot duller. But our young people here seem to like it well enough: 90 percent of 'em graduating from high school settle down right here to live—even when they've been away to college.

Stage Manager. Thank you, Mr. Webb. Now, is there anyone in the audience who would like to ask editor Webb anything about the town?

Woman in the Balcony. Is there much drinking in Grover's Corners?

Mr. Webb. Well, ma'am, I wouldn't know what you'd call *much*. Satiddy nights the farmhands meet down in Ellery Greenough's stable and holler some. Fourth of July I've been known to taste a drop myself—and Decoration Day, of course. We've got one or two town drunks, but they're always having remorses every time an evangelist comes to town. No, ma'am, I'd say likker ain't a regular thing in the home here, except in the medicine chest. Right good for snakebite, y'know—always was.

Tall Man at Back of Auditorium. Is there no one in town aware of——

Stage Manager. Come forward, will you, where we can all hear you—— What were you saying?

Tall Man. Is there no one in town aware of social injustice and industrial inequality?

Mr. Webb. Oh, yes, everybody is—somethin' terrible. Seems like they spend most of their time talking about who's rich and who's poor.

Tall Man. Then why don't they do something about it?

Mr. Webb. Well, we're ready to listen to everybody's suggestion as to how you can see that the diligent and sensible'll rise to the top and the lazy and quarrelsome sink to the bottom. We'll listen to anybody. Meantime until that's settled, we try to take care of those that can't help themselves, and those that can we leave alone—— Are there any more questions?

Lady in a Box. Oh, Mr. Webb? Mr. Webb, is there any culture or love of beauty in Grover's Corners?

Mr. Webb. Well, ma'am, there ain't much—not in the sense you mean. Come to think of it, there's some girls that play the piano at high school commencement, but they ain't happy about it. Yes, and I see where my daughter's been made to read *The Merchant of Venice* over to the school. Seems all pretty remote to 'em, y'know what I mean. No, ma'am, there isn't much culture, but maybe this is the place to tell you that we've got a lot of pleasures of a kind here: We like the sun comin' up over the mountain in the morning, and we all notice a good deal about the birds. We pay a lot of attention to them, and trees and plants. And we watch the change of the seasons: Yes, everybody knows about them. But those other things—you're right, ma'am—there ain't much—*Robinson Crusoe* and the Bible; and Handel's "Largo," we all know that; and Whistler's Mother—those are just about as far as we go.

Lady in a Box. So I thought. Thank you, Mr. Webb.

Stage Manager. All right! All right! Thank you, everybody.

[MR. WEBB *retires*.]

We'll go back to the town now. It's middle of the afternoon. All 2,640 have had their dinners and all the dishes have been washed. There's an early-afternoon calm in our town: a buzzin' and a hummin' from the school buildings; only a few buggies on Main Street—the horses dozing at the hitching posts; you all remember what it's like. Doc Gibbs is in his office, tapping people and making them say "ah." Mr. Webb's cuttin' his lawn over there; one man in ten thinks it's a privilege to push his own lawn mower. No, sir. It's later than I thought. There are the children coming home from school already.

[EMILY WEBB *comes sedately down Main Street carrying some schoolbooks. There are some signs that she is imagining herself to be a lady of striking elegance. Her father's movements to and fro with the lawn mower bring him into her vicinity.*]

Emily. I *can't*, Lois. I've got to go home and help my mother. I *promised*.
Mr. Webb. Emily, walk simply. Who do you think you are today?
Emily. Papa, you're terrible. One minute you tell me to stand up straight and the next minute you call me names. I just don't listen to you. (*She gives him an abrupt kiss.*)
Mr. Webb. Golly, I never got a kiss from such a great lady before.

[*He goes out of sight.* EMILY *leans over and picks some flowers by the gate of her house.* GEORGE GIBBS *comes careening down Main Street. He is throwing a ball up to dizzying heights and waiting to catch it again. This sometimes requires his taking six steps backward.*]

George. Excuse me, Mrs. Forrest.
Stage Manager (*as* MRS. FORREST). Go out and play in the fields, young man. You got no business playing baseball on Main Street.
George. Awfully sorry, Mrs. Forrest—— Hello, Emily.
Emily. H'lo.
George. You made a fine speech in class.
Emily. Well . . . I was really ready to make a speech about the Monroe Doctrine, but at the last minute Miss Corcoran made me talk about the Louisiana Purchase instead. I worked an awful long time on both of them.

George. Gee, it's funny, Emily. From my window up there I can just see your head nights when you're doing your homework over in your room.

Emily. Why, can you?

George. You certainly do stick to it, Emily. I don't see how you can sit still that long. I guess you like school.

Emily. Well, I always feel it's something you have to go through.

George. Yeah.

Emily. I don't mind it really. It passes the time.

George. Yeah—— Emily, what do you think? We might work out a kinda telegraph from there to there, and once in a while you could give me a kinda hint or two about one of those algebra problems. I don't mean the answers, Emily, of course not . . . just some little hint . . .

Emily. Oh, I think *hints* are allowed—— So-ah—if you get stuck, George, you whistle to me, and I'll give you some hints.

George. Emily, you're just naturally bright, I guess.

Emily. I figure that it's just the way a person's born.

George. Yeah. But, you see, I want to be a farmer, and my Uncle Luke says whenever I'm ready, I can come over and work on his farm, and if I'm any good, I can just gradually have it.

Emily. You mean the house and everything?

[*Enter* MRS. WEBB.]

George. Yeah. Well, thanks. . . . I better be getting out to the baseball field. Thanks for the talk, Emily—— Good afternoon, Mrs. Webb.

Mrs. Webb. Good afternoon, George.

George. So long, Emily.

Emily. So long, George.

Mrs. Webb. Emily, come and help me string these beans for the winter. George Gibbs let himself have a real conversation, didn't he? Why, he's growing up. How old would George be?

Emily. I don't know.

Mrs. Webb. Let's see. He must be almost sixteen.

Emily. Mama, I made a speech in class today and I was very good.

Mrs. Webb. You must recite it to your father at supper. What was it about?

Emily. The Louisiana Purchase. It was like silk off a spool. I'm going to make speeches all my life—— Mama, are these big enough?

Mrs. Webb. Try and get them a little bigger if you can.

Emily. Mama, will you answer me a question, serious?

Mrs. Webb. Seriously, dear—not serious.

Emily. Seriously—will you?

Mrs. Webb. Of course, I will.

Emily. Mama, am I good-looking?

Mrs. Webb. Yes, of course you are. All my children have got good features; I'd be ashamed if they hadn't.

Emily. Oh, Mama, that's not what I mean. What I mean is: Am I *pretty*?

Mrs. Webb. I've already told you, yes. Now that's enough of that. You have a nice young pretty face. I never heard of such foolishness.

Emily. Oh, Mama, you never tell us the truth about anything.

Mrs. Webb. I *am* telling you the truth.

Emily. Mama, were *you* pretty?

Mrs. Webb. Yes, I was, if I do say it. I was the prettiest girl in town next to Mamie Cartwright.

Emily. But, Mama, you've got to say *some*thing about me. Am I pretty enough . . . to get anybody . . . to get people interested in me?

Mrs. Webb. Emily, you make me tired. Now stop it. You're pretty enough for all normal purposes. Come along now and bring that bowl with you.

Emily. Oh, Mama, you're no help at all.

Stage Manager. Thank you. Thank you! That'll do. We'll have to interrupt again here. Thank you, Mrs. Webb; thank you, Emily.

[MRS. WEBB *and* EMILY *withdraw.*]

There are some more things we've got to explore about this town. This time we're going to go about it in another way:

We're going to look back on it from the future. I'm not going to tell you what became of these two families we're seeing most of, because the rest of the play will tell you about them. But take some of these others: Take Joe Crowell, Jr. Joe was a very bright fellow. He graduated with honors and got a scholarship to Boston Tech—MIT, that is. But the war broke out and Joe died in France. All that education for nothing. Howie Newsome's still delivering milk at Grover's Corners. He's an old man now, has a lot of help, but he still delivers it himself. Says he gets the feel of the town that way. Carries all the accounts in his head; never has to write down a word. Mr. Morgan's drugstore ain't the same—it's all citified. Mr. Morgan retired and went out to live in San Diego, California, where his daughter married a real estate man, name of Kerby. Mr. Morgan died there in 1935 and was buried in a lot of palm trees. Kinda lost his religion at the end and took up New Thought or something. They read some newfangled poetry over him and cremated him. The New Hampshire in him sort of broke down in him in that climate, seems like. The Cartwrights got richer and richer. The house is closed most of the year. They're off eating big dinners in hotels now—in Virginia Hot Springs and Miami Beach. They say the winters are cold here. I see where they've become 'Piscopalians. The Cartwright interests have just begun building a new bank in Grover's Corners—had to go to Vermont for the marble, sorry to say. And they've asked a friend of mine what they should put in the cornerstone for people to dig up a thousand years from now. Of course, they've put in a copy of *The New York Times* and a copy of Mr. Webb's *Sentinel*. We're kind of interested in this because some scientific fellas have found a way of painting all that reading matter with a kind of glue—silicate glue—that'll make it keep a thousand—two thousand years. We're putting in a Bible . . . and the Constitution of the United States and a copy of William Shakespeare's plays. What do you say, folks? What do you think? Y'know—Babylon once had two million people in it, and all we know about 'em is the names of the kings and some copies of wheat contracts and . . . the sales of slaves. Yet, every night all those families sat down to supper, and the father came home from his work, and the smoke went up the chimney—same as here. And even in Greece and Rome, all we know about the real life of the people is what we can piece together out of the joking poems and the comedies they wrote for the theater back then. So I'm going to have a copy of this play put in the cornerstone, and the people a thousand years from now'll know a few simple facts about us—more than the Treaty of Versailles and the Lindbergh flight. See what I mean? Well—you people a thousand years from now—in the provinces north of New York at the beginning of the twentieth century, people et three times a day: soon after sunrise, at noon, and at sunset. Every seventh day, by law and by religion, was a day of rest and all work come to a stop. The religion at that time was Christianity. I guess you have some other records about Christianity. The domestic setup was marriage: a binding relation between a male and one female that lasted for life. Christianity strictly forbade killing, but you were allowed to kill animals, and you were allowed to kill human beings in war and government punishings. I guess we don't have to tell you about the government and business forms, because that's the kind of thing people seem to hand down first of all. Let me see now if there's anything else. Oh, yes—at death people were buried in the ground just as they are. So, friends, this is the way we were in our growing up and in our marrying and in our doctoring and in our living and in our dying. Now we'll return to our day in Grover's Corners. A lot of time has gone by. It's evening. You can hear choir practice going on in the Congregational Church. All the children are at home doing their schoolwork. The day is running down like a tired clock.

[*A choir partially concealed in the orchestra pit has begun singing "Blessed Be the Tie That Binds."* SIMON STIMSON *stands directing them. Two ladders have been pushed on to the stage; they serve as indication of the second story in the Gibbs and Webb houses.* GEORGE *and* EMILY *mount them and apply themselves to their schoolwork.* DR. GIBBS *has entered and is seated in his kitchen, reading.*]

Simon Stimson. Now look here, everybody. Music come into the world to give pleasure—— Softer! Softer! Get it out of your heads that music's only good when it's loud. You leave loudness to the Methodists. You couldn't beat 'em, even if you wanted to. Now again. Tenors!

George. Hssst! Emily!

Emily. Hello.

George. Hello!

Emily. I can't work at all. The moonlight's so *terrible.*

George. Emily, did you get the third problem?

Emily. Which?

George. The *third*?

Emily. Why, yes, George—that's the easiest of them all.

George. I don't see it. Emily, can you give me a hint?

Emily. I'll tell you one thing: The answer's in yards.

George (*!!!*). In yards? How do you mean?

Emily. In *square* yards.

George. Oh . . . in square yards.

Emily. Yes, George, don't you see?

George. Yeah.

Emily. In square yards of *wallpaper.*

George. Wallpaper—oh, I see. Thanks a lot, Emily.

Emily. You're welcome. My, isn't the moonlight *terrible*? And choir practice going on—— I think if you hold your breath you can hear the train all the way to Contookuck. Hear it?

George. M-m-m—— What do you know!

Emily. Well, I guess I better go back and try to work.

George. Good night, Emily. And thanks.

Emily. Good night, George.

Simon Stimson. Before I forget it: How many of you will be able to come in Tuesday afternoon and sing at Fred Hersey's wedding?—show your hands. That'll be fine; that'll be right nice. We'll do the same music we did for Jane Trowbridge's last month—— Now we'll do "Art thou weary; art thou languid?" It's a question, ladies and gentlemen, make it talk. Ready.

Dr. Gibbs. Oh, George, can you come down a minute?

George. Yes, Pa. (*He descends the ladder.*)

Dr. Gibbs. Make yourself comfortable, George; I'll only keep you a minute. George, how old are you?

George. I? I'm sixteen, almost seventeen.

Dr. Gibbs. What do you want to do after school's over?

George. Why, you know, Pa, I want to be a farmer on Uncle Luke's farm.

Dr. Gibbs. You'll be willing, will you, to get up early and milk and feed the stock . . . and you'll be able to hoe and hay all day?

George. Sure, I will. What are you . . . what do you mean, Pa?

Dr. Gibbs. Well, George, while I was in my office today I heard a funny sound . . . and what do you think it was? It was your mother chopping wood. There you see your mother—getting up early, cooking meals all day long, washing and ironing—and still she has to go out in the back yard and chop wood. I suppose she just got tired of asking you. She just gave up and decided it was easier to do it herself. And you eat her meals, and put on the clothes she keeps nice for you, and you run off and play baseball—like she's some hired girl we keep around the house but that we don't like very much. Well, I knew all I had to do was call your attention to it. Here's a handkerchief, son. George, I've decided to raise your spending money twenty-five cents a week. Not, of course, for chopping wood for your mother, because that's a present you give her, but because you're getting older—and I imagine there are lots of things you must find to do with it.

George. Thanks, Pa.

Dr. Gibbs. Let's see—tomorrow's payday. You can count on it—hmm. Probably Rebecca'll feel she ought to have some more too. Wonder what could have happened to your mother. Choir practice never was as late as this before.

George. It's only half-past eight, Pa.

Dr. Gibbs. I don't know why she's in that old choir. She hasn't any more voice than an old crow. . . . Traipsin' around the streets at this hour of the night . . . Just about time you retired, don't you think?

George. Yes, Pa.

[GEORGE *mounts to his place on the ladder. Laughter and good-nights can be heard onstage left and presently* MRS. GIBBS, MRS. SOAMES, *and*

MRS. WEBB *come down Main Street. When they arrive at the center of the stage, they stop.*]

Mrs. Soames. Good night, Martha. Good night, Mr. Foster.
Mrs. Webb. I'll tell Mr. Webb; I *know* he'll want to put it in the paper.
Mrs. Gibbs. My, it's late!
Mrs. Soames. Good night, Irma.
Mrs. Gibbs. Real nice choir practice, wa'n't it? Myrtle Webb! Look at that moon, will you! Tsk-tsk-tsk. Potato weather, for sure.
Mrs. Soames. Naturally I didn't want to say a word about it in front of those others, but now we're alone—really, it's the worst scandal that ever was in this town!
Mrs. Gibbs. What?
Mrs. Soames. Simon Stimson!
Mrs. Gibbs. Now, Louella!
Mrs. Soames. But, Julia! To have the organist of a church drink and drink year after year. You know he was drunk tonight.
Mrs. Gibbs. Now, Louella! We all know about Mr. Stimson, and we all know about the troubles he's been through, and Dr. Ferguson knows too, and if Dr. Ferguson keeps him on there in his job, the only thing the rest of us can do is just not to notice it.
Mrs. Soames. Not to notice it! But it's getting worse.
Mrs. Webb. No, it isn't, Louella. It's getting better. I've been in that choir twice as long as you have. It doesn't happen any-where near so often. . . . My, I hate to go to bed on a night like this—— I better hurry. Those children'll be sitting up till all hours. Good night, Louella. (*She hurries downstage, enters her house, and disappears.*)
Mrs. Gibbs. Can you get home safe, Louella?
Mrs. Soames. It's as bright as day. I can see Mr. Soames scowl-ing at the window now. You'd think we'd been to a dance the way the menfolk carry on.

[*Repeated good-nights.* MRS. GIBBS *arrives at her home.*]

Mrs. Gibbs. Well, we had a real good time.

Dr. Gibbs. You're late enough.

Mrs. Gibbs. Why, Frank, it ain't any later 'n usual.

Dr. Gibbs. And you stopping at the corner to gossip with a lot of hens.

Mrs. Gibbs. Now, Frank, don't be grouchy. Come out and smell my heliotrope in the moonlight. (*They stroll out arm in arm along the footlights.*) Isn't that wonderful? What did you do all the time I was away?

Dr. Gibbs. Oh, I read—as usual. What were the girls gossiping about tonight?

Mrs. Gibbs. Well, believe me, Frank—there is something to gossip about.

Dr. Gibbs. Hmm! Simon Stimson far gone, was he?

Mrs. Gibbs. Worst I've ever seen him. How'll that end, Frank? Dr. Ferguson can't forgive him forever.

Dr. Gibbs. I guess I know more about Simon Stimson's affairs than anybody in this town. Some people ain't made for small-town life. I don't know how that'll end, but there's nothing we can do but just leave it alone. Come, get in.

Mrs. Gibbs. No, not yet. . . . Oh, Frank, I'm worried about you.

Dr. Gibbs. What are you worried about?

Mrs. Gibbs. I think it's my duty to make plans for you to get a real rest and change. And if I get that legacy, well, I'm going to insist on it.

Dr. Gibbs. Now, Julia, there's no sense in going over that again.

Mrs. Gibbs. Frank, you're just *unreasonable!*

Dr. Gibbs. Come on, Julia, it's getting late. First thing you know you'll catch cold. I gave George a piece of my mind tonight. I reckon you'll have your wood chopped for a while anyway. No, no, start getting upstairs.

Mrs. Gibbs. Oh, dear. There's always so many things to pick up, seems like. You know, Frank, Mrs. Fairchild always locks her front door every night. All those people up that part of town do.

Dr. Gibbs. They're all getting citified, that's the trouble with them. They haven't got nothing fit to burgle and everybody knows it. (*They disappear.* REBECCA *climbs up the ladder beside* GEORGE.)

George. Get out, Rebecca. There's only room for one at this window. You're always spoiling everything.

Rebecca. Well, let me look just a minute.

George. Use your own window.

Rebecca. I did, but there's no moon there. . . . George, do you know what I think, do you? I think maybe the moon's getting nearer and nearer and there'll be a big 'splosion.

George. Rebecca, you don't know anything. If the moon were getting nearer, the guys that sit up all night with telescopes would see it first and they'd tell about it, and it'd be in all the newspapers.

Rebecca. George, is the moon shining on South America, Canada, and half the whole world?

George. Well—prob'ly is.

[*The* STAGE MANAGER *strolls on.*]

Stage Manager. Nine-thirty. Most of the lights are out. No, there's Constable Warren trying a few doors on Main Street. And here comes editor Webb, after putting his newspaper to bed.

Mr. Webb. Good evening, Bill.

Constable Warren. Evenin', Mr. Webb.

Mr. Webb. Quite a moon!

Constable Warren. Yepp.

Mr. Webb. All quiet tonight?

Constable Warren. Simon Stimson is rollin' around a little. Just saw his wife movin' out to hunt for him so I looked the other way—there he is now.

[SIMON STIMSON *comes down Main Street from the left, only a trace of unsteadiness in his walk.*]

Mr. Webb. Good evening, Simon. . . .Town seems to have settled down for the night pretty well. . . .

[SIMON STIMSON *comes up to him and pauses a moment.*]

Good evening. . . .Yes, most of the town's settled down for the night, Simon. . . . I guess we better do the same. Can I walk along a ways with you?

[SIMON STIMSON *continues on his way without a word and disappears at the right.*]

Good night.

Constable Warren. I don't know how that's goin' to end, Mr. Webb.

Mr. Webb. Well, he's seen a peck of trouble, one thing after another. . . . Oh, Bill . . . if you see my boy smoking cigarettes, just give him a word, will you? He thinks a lot of you, Bill.

Constable Warren. I don't think he smokes no cigarettes, Mr. Webb. Leastways, not more'n two or three a year. He don't belong to that crowd that hangs out down by the gully.

Mr. Webb. Hm . . . I hope not—— Well, good night, Bill.

Constable Warren. Good night, Mr. Webb. (*Exit.*)

Mr. Webb. Who's that up there? Is that you, Myrtle?

Emily. No, it's me, Papa.

Mr. Webb. Why aren't you in bed?

Emily. I don't know. I just can't sleep yet, Papa. The moonlight's so *won*-derful. And the smell of Mrs. Gibbs's heliotrope. Can you smell it?

Mr. Webb. Hm . . . Yes. Haven't any troubles on your mind, have you, Emily?

Emily. *Troubles*, Papa. *No.*

Mr. Webb. Well, enjoy yourself, but don't let your mother catch you. Good night, Emily.

Emily. Good night, Papa.

[MR. WEBB *crosses into the house, whistling "Blessed Be the Tie That Binds" and disappears.*]

Rebecca. I never told you about that letter Jane Crofut got from her minister when she was sick. The minister of her church in the town she was in before she came here. He wrote Jane a letter and on the envelope the address was like this: It said "Jane Crofut, The Crofut Farm, Grover's Corners, Sutton County, New Hampshire, United States of America."

George. What's funny about that?

Rebecca. But listen, it's not finished: "the United States of America, Continent of North America, Western Hemisphere,

the Earth, the Solar System, the Universe, the Mind of God"—
that's what it said on the envelope.

George. What do you know!

Rebecca. And the postman brought it just the same.

George. What do you know!

Stage Manager. That's the end of the first act, friends. You can
go and smoke now, those that smoke.

Act Two˚

The tables and chairs of the two kitchens are still on the stage.

   The ladders have been withdrawn.

   The STAGE MANAGER *has been at his accustomed place watching
the audience return to its seats.*

Stage Manager. Three years have gone by. Yes, the sun's come
up over a thousand times. Summers and winters have cracked
the mountains a little bit more and the rains have brought
down some of the dirt. Some babies that weren't even born
before have begun talking regular sentences already, and a
number of people who thought they were right young and spry
have noticed that they can't bound up a flight of stairs like they
used to, without their heart fluttering a little. Some older sons
are sitting at the head of the table, and some people I know
are having their meat cut up for them—— All that can happen
in a thousand days. Nature's been pushing and contriving in
other ways, too: A number of young people fell in love and got
married. Yes, the mountain got bit away a few fractions of an
inch, millions of gallons of water went by the mill, and here
and there a new home was set up under a roof. Almost everybody in the world gets married—you know what I mean? In
our town there aren't hardly any exceptions. Most everybody
in the world climbs into their graves married. The first act was
called the Daily Life. This act is called Love and Marriage.
There's another act coming after this: I reckon you can guess

what that's about. So: It's three years later. It's 1904. It's July 7th, just after high school commencement. That's the time most of our young people jump up and get married. Soon as they've passed their last examinations in solid geometry and Cicero's orations, looks like they suddenly feel themselves fit to be married. It's early morning. Only this time it's been raining. It's been pouring and thundering. Mrs. Gibbs's garden, and Mrs. Webb's here: drenched. All those beanpoles and pea vines: drenched. All yesterday over there on Main Street, the rain looked like curtains being blown along. Hm . . . it may begin again any minute. There! You can hear the 5:45 for Boston. And here comes Howie Newsome delivering the milk. And there's Si Crowell delivering the papers like his brother before him—you remember about his brother?—all that education he's going to get and that'll be wasted. And there's Mrs. Gibbs and Mrs. Webb come down to make breakfast, just as though it were an ordinary day. I don't have to point out to the women in my audience that those ladies they see before them, both those ladies cooked three meals a day—one of 'em for twenty years, the other for forty—and no summer vacation. They brought up two children apiece, washed, cleaned the house—and never a nervous breakdown. Never thought themselves hard used, either. It's like what one of those Middle West poets said: You've got to love life to have life, and you've got to have life to love life. . . . It's what they call a vicious circle.

[SI CROWELL *has entered hurling imaginary newspapers into doorways;* HOWIE NEWSOME *has come along Main Street with* BESSIE.]

Howie Newsome. Git-ap, Bessie.
Si Crowell. Morning, Howie.
Howie Newsome. Morning, Si—— Anything in the papers I ought to know?
Si Crowell. Nothing much, except we're losing about the best baseball pitcher Grover's Corners ever had.
Howie Newsome. Reckon he was. He's been standing off the whole of south New Hampshire singlehanded, looks like.

Si Crowell. He could hit and run bases, too.

Howie Newsome. Yep. Mighty fine ball player—— Bessie! I guess I can stop and talk if I've a mind to!

Si Crowell. I don't see how he could give up a thing like that just to get married. Would you, Howie?

Howie Newsome. Can't tell, Si. Never had no talent that way.

[CONSTABLE WARREN *enters. They exchange mornings.*]

You're up early, Bill.

Constable Warren. Seein' if there's anything I can do to prevent a flood. River's been risin' all night.

Howie Newsome. Si Crowell's all worked up here about George Gibbs retiring from baseball.

Constable Warren. Yes, sir; that's the way it goes. Back in '84 we had a player, Si—even George Gibbs couldn't touch him. Name of Hank Todd. Went down to Maine and become a parson. Wonderful ball player—— Howie, how did the weather look to you?

Howie Newsome. No, 'tain't bad. Think maybe it'll clear up for good.

[CONSTABLE WARREN *and* SI CROWELL *continue on their way.* HOWIE NEWSOME *brings the milk first to* MRS. GIBBS's *house. She meets him by the trellis.*]

Mrs. Gibbs. Good morning, Howie. Do you think it's going to rain again?

Howie Newsome. Morning, Mrs. Gibbs. It rained so heavy, I think maybe it'll clear up.

Mrs. Gibbs. Certainly hope it will.

Howie Newsome. How much did you want today?

Mrs. Gibbs. I guess I'll need three a milk and two a cream, Howie. I'm going to have a house full of relations.

Howie Newsome. My wife says to tell you we both hope they'll be very happy, Mrs. Gibbs. Know they *will*.

Mrs. Gibbs. Thanks a lot, Howie. Tell your wife I hope she gits there to the wedding.

Howie Newsome. Yes, she'll be there; she'll be there if she kin. (HOWIE NEWSOME *crosses to* MRS. WEBB'*s house.*) Morning, Mrs. Webb.

Mrs. Webb. Oh, good morning, Mr. Newsome. I told you four quarts of milk, but I hope you can spare me another.

Howie Newsome. Yes'm . . . and the two of cream.

Mrs. Webb. Will it rain all day, Mr. Newsome?

Howie Newsome. No'm. Just sayin' to Mrs. Gibbs as how it may lighten up. Mrs. Newsome told me to tell you as how we hope they'll both be very happy, Mrs. Webb. Know they *will*.

Mrs. Webb. Thank you, and thank Mrs. Newsome and we hope to see you all at the wedding.

Howie Newsome. Yes, Mrs. Webb. We hope to git there. Couldn't miss that. Chck! Bessie!

[*Exit* HOWIE NEWSOME. DR. GIBBS *descends in shirt-sleeves and sits down at his breakfast table.*]

Dr. Gibbs. Well, Ma, the day has come. You're losin' one of your chicks.

Mrs. Gibbs. Frank Gibbs, don't you say another word. I feel like crying every minute. Sit down and drink your coffee.

Dr. Gibbs. The groom's up shaving himself. Whistling and singing, like he's glad to leave us—— Every now and then he says "I do" to the mirror, but it don't sound convincing to me.

Mrs. Gibbs. I declare I don't know how he'll get along. I've arranged his clothes and seen to it he's put warm things on—— Frank! They're too young. Emily won't think of such things. He'll catch his death of cold within a week—— Here's something I made for you.

Dr. Gibbs. Why, Julia Hersey! French toast!

Mrs. Gibbs. 'Tain't hard to make, and I had to do something.

Dr. Gibbs. I remember my wedding morning, Julia.

Mrs. Gibbs. Now don't start that, Frank Gibbs. I tell you I can't stand it.

Dr. Gibbs. I was the scaredest young fella in the state of New Hampshire. I thought I'd made a mistake for sure. And when I saw you comin' down that aisle, I thought you were the prettiest girl I'd ever seen, but the only trouble was that I'd never seen you before. There I was in the Congregational Church marryin' a total stranger.

Mrs. Gibbs. And how do you think I felt!—— Did you hear Rebecca stirring about upstairs?

Dr. Gibbs. Only morning in the year she hasn't been managing everybody's business. She's shut up in her room. I got the impression that maybe she's crying.

Mrs. Gibbs. Good Lord! This has got to stop—— Rebecca! Rebecca! Everything's getting cold down here.

[GEORGE *comes rattling down the stairs very brisk.*]

George. Good morning, everybody. Only five more hours to live. (*Makes the gesture of cutting his throat.*)

Mrs. Gibbs. Where are you going?

George. Just stepping across the grass to see my girl.

Mrs. Gibbs. Now, George! You take an umbrella or I won't let you out of this house.

George. Aw, Ma. It's just a *step*!

Mrs. Gibbs. From tomorrow on you can kill yourself in all weathers, but while you're in my house, you live wisely, thank you. There are your overshoes right there in the hall. And here's an umbrella.

George. Aw, Ma!

Dr. Gibbs. George, do as you mother tells you.

Mrs. Gibbs. Maybe Mrs. Webb isn't used to callers at seven in the morning. Take a cup a coffee first.

George. Be back in a minute. (*He crosses the stage, leaping over the puddles.*) Good morning, Mother Webb.

Mrs. Webb. Goodness! You frightened me!—— Now, George, you can come in a minute out of the wet, but you know I can't ask you in.

George. Why not—?

Mrs. Webb. George, you know's well as I do: The groom can't see his bride on his wedding day, not until he sees her in church.

George. Aw!—that's just a superstition.

[*Enter* MR. WEBB.]

Mr. Webb. Good morning, George.

George. Mr. Webb, you don't believe in that superstition, do you?

Mr. Webb. There's a lot of common sense in some superstitions, George.

Mrs. Webb. Millions have folla'd it, George, and you don't want to be the first to fly in the face of custom.

George. How is Emily?

Mrs. Webb. She hasn't waked up yet. I haven't heard a sound out of her.

George. Emily's *asleep*!!!

Mrs. Webb. No wonder! We were up till all hours—sewing and packing. I'll tell you what I'll do; you set down here a minute with Mr. Webb and drink this cup of coffee, and I'll go upstairs and see she doesn't come down and surprise you. There's some bacon, too, but don't be long about it.

[*Exit* MRS. WEBB. *Embarrassed silence.*]

Mr. Webb. Well, George, how are you?

George. Oh, fine, I'm fine. (*Pause*) Mr. Webb, what sense could there be in a superstition like that?

Mr. Webb. Well, you see—on her wedding morning a girl's head's apt to be full of ... clothes and things like that. Don't you think that's probably it?

George. Ye-e-s. I never thought of that.

Mr. Webb. A girl's apt to be a mite nervous on her wedding day.

[*Pause.*]

George. I wish a fellow could get married without all that marching up and down.

Mr. Webb. Well, every man that's ever lived has felt that way about it, George, but it hasn't done much good. It's the women that have built up weddings, my boy. From now on they have

it pretty much as they like. . . . All those good women standing shoulder to shoulder making sure that the knot's tied in a
mighty public way.

George. But . . . you *believe* in it, don't you, Mr. Webb?

Mr. Webb. Oh, yes; oh, yes. Don't you misunderstand me, my
boy. Marriage is a wonderful thing—wonderful thing. And
don't you forget that, George.

George. No, sir—— Mr. Webb, how old were you when you
got married?

Mr. Webb. Well, you see: I'd been to college and I'd taken a
little time to get settled. But Mrs. Webb—she wasn't much older
than what Emily is. Oh, age hasn't much to do with it, George—
not compared to other things.

George. What were you going to say, Mr. Webb?

Mr. Webb. Oh, I don't know—was I going to say something?
(*Pause*) George, I was thinking the other night of some advice
my father gave me when I got married. "Charles," he said,
"Charles, start out early showing who's boss," he said. "Best
thing to do is to give an order, even if it don't make sense, just
so she'll learn to obey." And he said, "If anything about your
wife irritates you—her conversation, or anything—just get up
and leave the house. That'll make it clear to her," he said. And,
oh, yes! He said, "Never, *never* let your wife know how much
money you have, never."

George. Well, Mr. Webb . . . I don't think I could . . .

Mr. Webb. So I took the opposite of my father's advice and
I've been happy ever since. And let that be a lesson to you,
George, never to ask advice on personal matters—— George,
are you going to raise chickens on your farm?

George. What?

Mr. Webb. Are you going to raise chickens on your farm?

George. Uncle Luke's never been much interested, but I
thought——

Mr. Webb. A book came into my office the other day, George,
on the Philo system of raising chickens. I want you to read it.
I'm thinking of beginning in a small way in the back yard, and
I'm going to put an incubator in the cellar——

[*Enter* MRS. WEBB.]

Mrs. Webb. Charles, are you talking about that old incubator again? I thought you two'd be talking about things worthwhile.
Mr. Webb. Well, Myrtle, if you want to give the boy some good advice, I'll go upstairs and leave you alone with him.
Mrs. Webb. Now, George, I'm sorry, but I've got to send you away so that Emily can come down and get some breakfast. She told me to tell you that she sends you her love but that she doesn't want to lay eyes on you. So goodbye, George.

[GEORGE *crosses the stage to his own home and disappears.*]

Mr. Webb. Myrtle, I guess you don't know about that older superstition.
Mrs. Webb. What do you mean, Charles?
Mr. Webb. Since the cavemen: The groom shouldn't be left alone with his father-in-law on the day of the wedding, or near it. Now don't forget that!
Stage Manager. Thank you. Thank you, everybody. Now I have to interrupt again here. You see, we want to know how all this began—this wedding, this plan to spend a lifetime together. I'm awfully interested in how big things like that begin. You know how it is: You're twenty-one or twenty-two and you make some decisions; then whisssh! you're seventy; you've been a lawyer for fifty years, and that white-haired lady at your side has eaten over fifty thousand meals with you. How do such things begin? George and Emily are going to show you now the conversation they had when they first knew that ... that ... as the saying goes ... they were meant for one another. But before they do it, I want you to try and remember what it was like when you were young, when you were fifteen or sixteen. For some reason it is very hard to do—those days when even the little things in life could be almost too exciting to bear. And particularly the days when you were first in love, when you were like a person sleepwalking, and you didn't quite see the street you were in, and didn't quite hear everything that was said to you. You're just a little bit crazy.

Will you remember that, please? Now they'll be coming out of high school at three o'clock. George has just been elected president of the junior class, and as it's June; that means he'll be president of the senior class all next year. And Emily's just been elected secretary and treasurer. I don't have to tell you how important that is. (*He places a board across the backs of two chairs, parallel to the footlights, and places two high stools behind it. This is the counter of* MR. MORGAN's *drugstore.*) All ready!

[EMILY, *carrying an armful of—imaginary—schoolbooks, comes along Main Street from the left.*]

Emily. I can't, Louise. I've got to go home. Goodbye. Oh, Ernestine! Ernestine! Can you come over tonight and do algebra? I did the first and third in study hall. No, they're not hard. But, Ernestine, that Caesar's awful hard. I don't see why we have to do a thing like that. Come over about seven. Tell your mother you *have* to. G'by. G'by, Helen. G'by, Fred.

[GEORGE, *also carrying books, catches up with her.*]

George. Can I carry your books home for you, Emily?
Emily (*coldly*). Thank you. (*She gives them to him.*)
George. Excuse me a minute, Emily—— Say, Bob, get everything ready. I'll be there in a quarter of an hour. If I'm a little late, start practice anyway. And give Herb some long, high ones. His eye needs a lot of practice. Seeya later.
Emily. Goodbye, Lizzy.
George. Goodbye, Lizzy—I'm awfully glad you were elected, too, Emily.
Emily. Thank you.

[*They have been standing on Main Street, almost against the back wall.* GEORGE *is about to take the first steps toward the audience when he stops again and says*]

George. Emily, why are you mad at me?

Emily. I'm not mad at you.

George. You . . . you treat me so funny.

Emily. Well, I might as well say it right out, George. I don't like the whole change that's come over you in the last year. I'm sorry if that hurts your feelings, but I've just got to tell the truth and shame the devil.

George. I'm awfully sorry, Emily. Wha-a-what do you mean?

Emily. Well, up to a year ago I used to like you a lot. And I used to watch you as you did everything . . . because we'd been friends so long . . . and then you began spending all your time at baseball . . . and you never even spoke to anybody anymore; not even to your own family you didn't . . . and, George, it's a fact, you've got awful conceited and stuck-up, and all the girls say so. They may not say so to your face, but that's what they say about you behind your back, and it hurts me to hear them say it, but I've got to agree with them a little. I'm sorry if it hurts your feelings . . . but I can't be sorry I said it.

George. I . . . I'm glad you said it, Emily. I never thought that such a thing was happening to me. I guess it's hard for a fella not to have faults creep into his character.

[*They take a step or two in silence, then stand still in misery.*]

Emily. I always expect a man to be perfect and I think he should be.

George. Oh . . . I don't think it's possible to be perfect, Emily.

Emily. Well, my father is, and as far as I can see your father is. There's no reason on earth why you shouldn't be, too.

George. Well, Emily . . . I feel it's the other way round. That men aren't naturally good, but girls are. Like you and your mother and my mother.

Emily. Well, you might as well know right now that I'm not perfect. It's not as easy for a girl to be perfect as a man, because we girls are more nervous—— Now I'm sorry I said all that about you. I don't know what made me say it.

George. No, no—I guess if it's the truth you ought to say it. You stick to it, Emily.

Emily. I don't know if it's the truth or not. And I suddenly feel that it isn't important at all.

George. Emily, would you like an ice-cream soda, or something, before you go home?

Emily. Well, thank you. . . . I would.

[*They come into the drugstore and seat themselves on the stools.*]

Stage Manager (*as* MR. MORGAN). Hello, George. Hello, Emily. What'll you have? Why, Emily Webb, what've you been crying about?

George (*he gropes for an explanation*). She . . . she just got an awful scare, Mr. Morgan. She almost got run over by that hardware-store wagon. Everybody always says that Tom Huckins drives like a crazy man.

Stage Manager. Here, take a drink of water, Emily. You look all shook up. There!—— Now, what'll you have?

Emily. I'll have a strawberry phosphate, thank you, Mr. Morgan.

George. No, no. You go and have an ice-cream soda with me, Emily—— Two strawberry ice-cream sodas, Mr. Morgan.

Stage Manager (*working the faucets*). Yes, sir. I tell you, you've got to look both ways before you cross Main Street these days. Gets worse every year. There are a hundred and twenty-five horses in Grover's Corner this minute I'm talking to you. State inspector was in here yesterday. And now they're bringing in these auto-mo-biles, the best thing to do is to just stay home. Why, I can remember the time when a dog could lie down all day in the middle of Main Street and nothing would come to disturb him—— Yes, Miss Ellis, be with you in a minute. Here are your sodas. Enjoy 'em. (*He goes off.*)

Emily. They're so expensive.

George. No, no—don't you think of that. We're celebrating. First, we're celebrating our election. And then do you know what else I'm celebrating?

Emily. No.

George. I'm celebrating because I've got a friend who tells me all the things that ought to be told me.

Emily. George, *please* don't think of that. I don't know why I said it. It's not true. You're——

George. No, you stick to it, Emily. I'm glad you spoke to me like you did. But you'll see: I'm going to change so quick—you bet I'm going to change. And, Emily, I want to ask you a favor.

Emily. What?

George. Emily, if I go away to state agriculture college next year, will you write me a letter once in a while?

Emily. I certainly will. I certainly will, George. . . . (*Pause*) It certainly seems like being away three years you'd get out of touch with things.

George. No, no. I mustn't do that. You see I'm not only going to be just a farmer. After a while maybe I'll run for something to get elected. So your letters'll be very important to me—you know, telling me what's going on here and everything. . . .

Emily. Just the same, three years is a long time. Maybe letters from Grover's Corners wouldn't be so interesting after a while. Grover's Corners isn't a very important place when you think of all New Hampshire, but I think it's a very nice town.

George. The day wouldn't come when I wouldn't want to know everything that's happening here. I know *that's* true, Emily.

Emily. Well, I'll try to make my letters interesting.

[*Pause.*]

George. Y'know, Emily, whenever I meet a farmer, I ask him if he thinks it's important to go to agriculture school to be a good farmer.

Emily. Why, George——

George. Yeah, and some of them say that it's even a waste of time. You can get all those things, anyway, out of the pamphlets the government sends out. And Uncle Luke's getting old—he's about ready for me to start in taking over his farm tomorrow, if I could.

Emily. My!

George. And, like you say, being gone all that time . . . in other places and meeting other people . . . If anything like that can happen, I don't want to go away. I guess new people aren't any better than old ones. I'll bet they almost never are. Emily . . . I feel that you're as good a friend as I've got. I don't need to go and meet the people in other towns.

Emily. But, George, maybe it's very important for you to go and learn all that about cattle judging and soils and those things. And if you're going into politics, maybe you ought to meet people from other parts of the state. . . . Of course, I don't know.

George (*after a pause*). Emily, I'm going to make up my mind right now. I won't go. I'll tell Pa about it tonight.

Emily. Why, George, I don't see why you have to decide right now. It's a whole year away.

George. Emily, I'm glad you spoke to me about that . . . that fault in my character. And what you said was right, but there was *one* thing wrong in it, and that was when you said that for a year I wasn't noticing people, and . . . you, for instance. Listen, Emily, . . . you say you were watching me when I did everything. . . . Why, I was doing the same about you all the time. Why, sure—I always thought about you as one of the chief people I thought about. I always made sure where you were sitting on the bleachers, and who you were with. And we've always had lots of talks . . . and joking, in the halls, and they always meant a lot to me. Of course, they weren't as good as the talk we're having now. Lately I'd been noticing that you'd been acting kind of funny to me, and for three days I've been trying to walk home with you, but something's always got in the way. Yesterday I was standing over against the wall waiting for you, and you walked home with Miss Corcoran.

Emily. George! . . . Life's awful funny! How could I have known that? Why, I thought——

George. Listen, Emily, I'm going to tell you why I'm not going to agriculture school. I think that once you've found a person that you're very fond of . . . I mean a person who's fond of you, too—at least enough to be interested in your character . . . Well, I think that's just as important as college is, and even more so. That's what I think.

Emily. I think it's awfully important, too.

George. Emily.

Emily. Yes, George.

George. Emily, if I improve and make a big change, . . . would you be . . . I mean: *Could* you be . . .

Emily. I . . . I am now; I always have been.

George (*pause*). So I guess this is an important talk we've been having.

Emily. Yes.

George (*takes a deep breath and straightens his back*). Wait just a minute and I'll take you home.

[*He rises and goes to the* STAGE MANAGER, *who appears and comes toward him.*]

Mr. Morgan, I'll have to go home and get the money to pay you for this. It'll only take me a minute.

Stage Manager. What's that? George Gibbs, do you mean to tell me—!

George. Yes, but I had reasons, Mr. Morgan—— Look, here's my gold watch to keep until I come back with the money.

Stage Manager. That's all right. Keep your watch. I'll trust you.

George. I'll be back in five minutes.

Stage Manager. I'll trust you ten years, George—not a day more—— Got all over your shock, Emily?

Emily. Yes, thank you, Mr. Morgan. It was nothing.

George (*taking up the books from the counter*). I'm ready.

[*They walk in grave silence down the stage, turn, and pass through the trellis at the Webbs' back door and disappear.*]

Stage Manager. Thank you, Emily. Thank you, George. Now before we go on to the wedding, there are still some more things we ought to know about this—about this marriage. I want to know some more about how the parents took it, but what I want to know most of all is: Oh, you know what I mean—what Grover's Corners thought about marriage any-way. You know's well as I do: People are never able to say right out what they think of money, or death, or fame, or marriage.

You've got to catch it between the lines; you've got to *over*-hear it. Oh, Doctor! Mrs. Gibbs!

[*They appear at their side of the stage and exchange a glance of understanding with him. The* STAGE MANAGER *lays the same plank across two chairs that served as a drugstore counter, and it has now become* MRS. GIBBS's *ironing board.* DR. GIBBS *sits down in a rocker and smokes.* MRS. GIBBS *irons a moment in silence, then goes to the foot of the stairs and calls*]

Mrs. Gibbs. Rebecca! It's time you turned out your light and went to sleep. George, you'd better get some sleep, too.
Rebecca's Voice. Ma, I haven't finished my English.
Mrs. Gibbs. What? Well, I bet you haven't been working, Rebecca. You've been reading that Sears, Roebuck catalog, that's what you've been doing—— All right, I'll give you ten more minutes. If you haven't finished by then, you'll just have to fail the course and be a disgrace to your father and me—— George, what are you doing?
George's Voice (*hurt*). I'm doing history.
Mrs. Gibbs. Well, you'd better go to bed. You're probably sleeping at the desk as it is. (*She casts an amused eye at her husband and returns to her ironing.*)
Dr. Gibbs. I had a long talk with the boy today.
Mrs. Gibbs. Did you?
Dr. Gibbs. I tell you, Mrs. G, there's nothing so terrifying in the world as a son. The relation of a father to a son is the damnedest, awkwardest—I always come away feeling like a soggy sponge of hypocrisy.
Mrs. Gibbs. Well, a mother and a daughter's no picnic, let me tell you.
Dr. Gibbs. George is set on it: He wants to marry Emily soon as school's out and take her right on to the farm. (*Pause*) He says he can sit up nights and learn agriculture from government pamphlets, without going to college for it.
Mrs. Gibbs. He always was crazy about farming. Gets that from my people.

Dr. Gibbs. At a pinch, I guess he could start in farming—but I swear I think he's too young to get married. Julia, he's just a green, half-grown kid. He isn't ready to be a family man.

Mrs. Gibbs. No, he ain't. You're right—— But he's a good boy and I wouldn't like to think of him being alone out there . . . coming into town Satiddy nights, like any old farmhand, tuckered out from work and looking for excitement. He might get into bad ways. It wouldn't be enough fun for him to come and sit by our stove—and holding hands with Emily for a year mightn't be enough either. He might lose interest in her.

Dr. Gibbs. Hm.

Mrs. Gibbs. Frank, I been watching her. George is a lucky boy when you think of all the silly girls in the world.

Dr. Gibbs. But, Julia—George *married*. That great gangling, selfish nincompoop.

Mrs. Gibbs. Yes, I know. (*She takes up a collar and examines it.*) Frank, what do you do to your collars? Do you gnaw 'em? I never saw such a man for collars.

Dr. Gibbs. Julia, when I married you, do you know what one of my terrors was in getting married?

Mrs. Gibbs. Pshaw! Go on with you!

Dr. Gibbs. I was afraid we weren't going to have material for conversation more'n 'ld last us a few weeks. I was afraid we'd run out and eat our meals in silence, that's a fact. You and I've been conversing for twenty years now without any noticeable barren spells.

Mrs. Gibbs. Well, good weather, bad weather, 'tain't very choice, but I always manage to find something to say.

[*Pause.*]

Dr. Gibbs. What do you think? What do you think, Julia? Shall we tell the boy he can go ahead and get married?

Mrs. Gibbs. Seems like it's up to us to decide. Myrtle and Charles Webb are willing. They think it's a good idea to throw the young people into the sea and let'm sink or swim, as soon as they're ready.

Dr. Gibbs. What does that mean? Must we decide right now? This minute?

Mrs. Gibbs. There you go putting the responsibility on me!

Dr. Gibbs. Here it is, almost April—— I'll go up and say a word to him right now before he goes to bed. (*He rises.*) You're sure, Julia? You've nothing more to add?

Mrs. Gibbs (*stops ironing a moment*). I don't know what to say. Seems like it's too much to ask, for a big outdoor boy like that to go and get shut up in classrooms for three years. And once he's on the farm, he might just as well have a companion, seeing he's found a fine girl like Emily. . . . People are meant to live two by two in this world. . . . Yes, Frank, go up and tell him it's all right.

Dr. Gibbs (*crosses and is about to call when——*).

Mrs. Gibbs (*her hands on her cheeks, staring into the audience, in sharp alarm*). Wait a minute! Wait a minute—— (*Then resuming her ironing*) No—go and tell him.

Dr. Gibbs. Why did you stop then, Julia?

Mrs. Gibbs. Oh, you know: I thought of all those times we went through in the first years when George and Rebecca were babies—you walking up and down with them at three in the morning, the whooping-cough, the time George fell off the porch. You and I were twenty-five years old, and more. It's wonderful how one forgets one's troubles, like that—— Yes, Frank, go upstairs and tell him. . . . It's worth it.

Dr. Gibbs. Yes, they'll have a lot of troubles, but that's none of our business. Let'm. Everybody has a right to his own troubles—— You ought to be present, Julia—important occasion like that. I'll call him—— George! Oh, George!

George's Voice. Yes, Pa.

Dr. Gibbs. Can you come down a minute? Your mother and I want to speak to you.

George. Yeah, sure.

Mrs. Gibbs (*putting her arm through her husband's*). Lord, what a fool I am: I'm trembling all over. There's nothing to tremble about.

Stage Manager. Thank you! Thank you! Now we're ready to go on with the wedding.

[*While he talks, the actors remove the chair and tables and trellises from the Gibbs and Webb homes. They arrange the pews for the church in the back of the stage. The congregation will sit facing the back wall. The aisle of the church is in the middle of the scene. A small platform is placed against the back wall on which the* STAGE MANAGER *as minister can stand.*]

There are a lot of things to be said about a wedding; there are a lot of thoughts that go on during a wedding. We can't get them all into one wedding, naturally, and especially not into a wedding at Grover's Corners, where they're awfully plain and short. In this wedding I play the minister. That gives me the right to say a few more things about it. For a while now, the play gets pretty serious. Y'see, some churches say that marriage is a sacrament. I don't quite know what that means, but I can guess. Like Mrs. Gibbs said a few minutes ago: People were made to live two by two. This is a good wedding, but people are so put together that even at a good wedding there's a lot of confusion way down deep in people's minds and we thought that that ought to be in our play, too. The real hero of this scene isn't on the stage at all, and you know who that is. It's like what one of those European fellas said: Every child born into the world is Nature's attempt to make a perfect human being. Well, we've seen Nature pushing and contriving for some time now. We all know that Nature's interested in quantity, but I think she's interested in quality, too—that's why I'm in the ministry— — Maybe she's trying to make another good governor for New Hampshire. And don't forget the other witnesses at this wedding—the ancestors. Millions of them. Most of them set out to live two by two, also. Millions of them. Well, that's all my sermon. 'Twan't very long, anyway.

[*The organ starts playing Handel's "Largo." The congregation streams into the church and sits in silence.* MRS. WEBB, *on the way to her place, turns back and speaks to the audience.*]

Mrs. Webb. I don't know why on earth I should be crying. I suppose there's nothing to cry about. It came over me at breakfast this morning; there was Emily eating her breakfast as she's done for seventeen years and now she's going off to eat it in someone else's house. I suppose that's it. And Emily! She suddenly said, "I can't eat another mouthful," and she put her head down on the table and *she* cried. (*She starts toward her seat in the church but turns back and adds*) Oh, I've got to say it: You know, there's something downright cruel about sending our girls out into marriage this way. I hope some of her girl-friends have told her a thing or two. It's cruel, I know, but I couldn't bring myself to say anything. I went into it blind as a bat myself. The whole world's wrong, that's what's the matter. There they come.

[*She hurries to her place in the pew.* GEORGE *starts to come down the right aisle of the theater, through the audience. Suddenly three members of his baseball team appear by the right proscenium pillar and start whistling and catcalling to him. They are dressed for the ball field.*]

The Baseball Players. Eh, George, George! Hsst—yaow! If things don't go right, call us in. We know what to do. Eh, fellas? Yaow! George, don't look so innocent, you old geezer. We know what you're thinking. Don't disgrace the team, big boy. Whoo-oo-oo.
Stage Manager. All right! All right! That'll do. That's enough of that.

[*Smiling, he pushes them off the stage. They lean back to shout a few more catcalls.*]

There used to be an awful lot of that kind of thing at weddings in the old days—Rome, and later. We're more civilized now—so they say.

[*The choir starts singing "Love divine, all love excelling . . ."* GEORGE *has reached the stage. He stares at the congregation a moment, then takes a few steps of withdrawal, toward the right proscenium pillar.*]

George (*darkly, to himself*). I wish I were back at school. . . . I don't want to get married.

[*His mother has left her seat and comes toward him. She stops, look-ing at him anxiously.*]

Mrs. Gibbs. George, what's the matter?
George. Ma, I don't want to grow *old*. Why's everybody push-ing me so?
Mrs. Gibbs. Why, George, . . . you wanted it.
George. Why do I have to get married at all? Listen, Ma, for the last time I ask you——
Mrs. Gibbs. No, no, George, . . . you're a man now.
George. Listen, Ma, you never listen to me. All I want to do is to be a fella. . . . Why do——
Mrs. Gibbs. George! If anyone should hear you! Now stop. Why, I'm ashamed of you!
George (*passing his hand over his forehead*). What's the matter? I've been dreaming. Where's Emily?
Mrs. Gibbs. Gracious! You gave me such a turn.
George. Cheer up, Ma. What are you looking so funny for? Cheer up; I'm getting married.
Mrs. Gibbs. Let me catch my breath a minute.
George. Now, Ma, you save Thursday nights. Emily and I are coming over to dinner every Thursday night . . . you'll see. Ma, what are you crying for? Come on; we've got to get ready for this.

[*In the meantime,* EMILY, *in white and wearing her wedding veil, has come through the audience and mounted onto the stage. She too draws back when she sees the congregation in the church. The choir begins: "Blessed Be the Tie That Binds."*]

Emily. I never felt so alone in my whole life. And George over there, looking so . . . ! I *hate* him. I wish I were dead. Papa! Papa!
Mr. Webb (*leaves his seat in the pews and comes toward her anx-iously*). Emily! Emily! Now don't get upset. . . .
Emily. But, Papa—I don't want to get married. . . .
Mr. Webb. Sh-sh—Emily. Everything's all right.
Emily. Why can't I stay for a while just as I am? Let's go away.
Mr. Webb. No, no, Emily. Now stop and think.

Emily. Don't you remember that you used to say—all the time you used to say that I was *your* girl. There must be lots of places we can go to. Let's go away. I'll work for you. I could keep house.
Mr. Webb. Sh. . . . You mustn't think of such things. You're just nervous, Emily. Now, now—you're marrying the best young fellow in the world. George is a fine fellow.
Emily. But, Papa——
Mr. Webb. George! George!

[MRS. GIBBS *returns to her seat.* GEORGE *hears* MR. WEBB *and looks up.* MR. WEBB *beckons to him. They move to the center of the stage.*]

I'm giving away my daughter, George. Do you think you can take care of her?
George. Mr. Webb, I want to . . . I want to try. Emily, I'm going to do my best. I love you, Emily. I need you.
Emily. Well, if you love me, help me. All I want is someone to love me.
George. I will, Emily.
Emily. If ever I'm sick or in trouble, that's what I mean.
George. Emily, I'll try. I'll try.
Emily. And I mean for *ever*. Do you hear? For ever and ever.

[*They fall into each other's arms. The march from* Lohengrin *is heard.*]

Mr. Webb. Come, they're waiting for us. Now you know it'll be all right. Come, quick.

[GEORGE *slips away and takes his place beside the* STAGE MANAGER–CLERGYMAN. EMILY *proceeds up the aisle on her father's arm.*]

Stage Manager. Do you, George, take this woman, Emily, to be your wedded wife, to have . . .

[MRS. SOAMES *has been sitting in the last row of the congregation. She now turns to her neighbors, and in a shrill voice says*]

Mrs. Soames. Perfectly lovely wedding! Loveliest wedding I ever saw. Oh, I do love a good wedding, don't you? Doesn't she make a lovely bride?

George. I do.

Stage Manager. Do you, Emily, take this man, George, to be your wedded husband——

Mrs. Soames. Don't know *when* I've seen such a lovely wedding. But I always cry. Don't know why it is, but I always cry. I just like to see young people happy, don't you? Oh, I think it's lovely.

[*The ring. The kiss. The stage is suddenly arrested into silent tableau. The* STAGE MANAGER, *his eyes on the distance, says to the audience*]

I've married two hundred couples in my day. Do I believe in it? I don't know. M—— marries N—— millions of them. The cottage, the go-cart, the Sunday afternoon drives in the Ford, the first rheumatism, the grandchildren, the second rheumatism, the deathbed, the reading of the will—— Once in a thousand times it's interesting. Well, let's have Mendelssohn's "Wedding March"!

[*The organ picks up the march. The bride and groom come down the aisle, radiant but trying to be very dignified.*]

Mrs. Soames. Aren't they a lovely couple? Oh, I've never been to such a nice wedding. I'm sure they'll be happy. I always say: *Happiness*, that's the great thing! The important thing is to be happy.

[*The bride and groom reach the steps leading into the audience. A bright light is thrown upon them. They descend into the auditorium and run up the aisle joyously.*]

Stage Manager. That's all the second act. Ten minutes' intermission, folks.

Act Three

*During the intermission the audience has seen the actors arranging
the stage. On the right-hand side, a little right of the center, ten or
twelve ordinary chairs have been placed in three openly spaced rows
facing the audience.*

These are graves in the cemetery.

*Toward the end of the intermission the actors enter and take their
places. The front row contains, toward the center of the stage, an empty
chair; then* MRS. GIBBS, SIMON STIMSON. *The second row contains,
among others,* MRS. SOAMES. *The third row has* WALLY WEBB.

*The dead sit in a quiet without stiffness, and in a patience with-
out listlessness.*

The STAGE MANAGER *takes his accustomed place and waits for the
houselights to go down.*

Stage Manager. This time nine years have gone by, friends—
summer—1913. Gradual changes in Grover's Corners. Horses
are getting rarer. Farmers coming into town in Fords. Chief difference is in the young people, far as I can see. They want to
go to the moving pictures all the time. They want to wear
clothes like they see there . . . want to be citified. Everybody
locks their house doors now at night. Ain't been any burglars
in town yet, but everybody's heard about 'em. But you'd be
surprised though—on the whole, things don't change much at
Grover's Corners. Guess you want to know what all these
chairs are here fur. Smarter ones have guessed it already. I don't
know how you feel about such things, but this certainly is a
beautiful place. It's on a hilltop—a windy hilltop—lots of sky,
lots of clouds—often lots of sun and moon and stars. You come
up here on a fine afternoon and you can see range on range of
hills—awful blue they are—up there by Lake Sunapee and
Lake Winnipesaukee . . . and way up, if you've got a glass, you
can see the White Mountains and Mount Washington—where
North Conway and Conway is. And, of course, our favorite
mountain, Mount Monadnock's right here—and all around it
lie these towns—Jaffrey, 'n' East Jaffrey, 'n' Peterborough, 'n'
Dublin and (*then pointing down in the audience*) there, quite a

ways down, is Grover's Corners. Yes, beautiful spot up here. Mountain laurel and li-lacks. I often wonder why people like to be buried in Woodlawn and Brooklyn when they might pass the same time up here in New Hampshire. Over in that corner— (*pointing to stage left*) are the old stones—1670, 1680. Strong-minded people that come a long way to be independent. Summer people walk around there laughing at the funny words on the tombstones . . . it don't do any harm. And genealogists come up from Boston—get paid by city people for looking up their ancestors. They want to make sure they're Daughters of the American Revolution and of the *Mayflower*. . . . Well, I guess that don't do any harm, either. Wherever you come near the human race, there's layers and layers of nonsense. . . . Over there are some Civil War veterans too. Iron flags on their graves. . . . New Hampshire boys . . . had a notion that the Union ought to be kept together, though they'd never seen more than fifty miles of it themselves. All they knew was the name, friends—the United States of America. The United States of America. And they went and died about it. This here is the new part of the cemetery. Here's your friend Mrs. Gibbs. 'N' let me see—— Here's Mr. Stimson, organist at the Congregational Church. And over there's Mrs. Soames, who enjoyed the wedding so—you remember? Oh, and a lot of others. And editor Webb's boy, Wallace, whose appendix burst while he was on a Boy Scout trip to Crawford Notch. Yes, an awful lot of sorrow has sort of quieted down up here. People just wild with grief have brought their relatives up to this hill. We all know how it is . . . and then time . . . and sunny days . . . and rainy days . . . 'n' snow . . . tz-tz-tz. We're all glad they're in a beautiful place and we're coming up here ourselves when our fit's over. This certainly is an important part of Grover's Corners. A lot of thoughts come up here, night and day, but there's no post office. Now I'm going to tell you some things you know already. You know'm as well as I do, but you don't take'm out and look at'm very often. I don't care what they say with their mouths—everybody knows that *something* is eternal. And it ain't houses and it ain't names, and it ain't earth, and it ain't even the stars . . . everybody knows in their bones that *something* is eternal, and that something has to do with human beings. All the greatest people ever lived have been telling us that for five thousand years and yet you'd be surprised how people are always losing hold of it. There's something way down deep that's eternal about every human being. (*Pause*) You know as well as I do that the dead don't stay interested in us living people for very long. Gradually, gradually, they let hold of the earth . . . and the ambitions they had . . . and the pleasures they had . . . and the things they suffered . . . and the people they loved. They get weaned away from earth—that's the way I put it—weaned away. Yes, they stay here while the earth part of 'em burns away, burns out, and all the time they slowly get indifferent to what's goin' on in Grover's Corners. They're waitin'. They're waitin' for something that they feel is comin'. Something important and great. Aren't they waitin' for the eternal part in them to come out clear? Some of the things they're going to say maybe'll hurt your feelings—but that's the way it is: Mother 'n' daughter . . . husband 'n' wife . . . enemy 'n' enemy . . . money 'n' miser . . . all those terribly important things kind of grow pale around here. And what's left? What's left when memory's gone, and your identity, Mrs. Smith? (*He looks at the audience a minute, then turns to the stage.*) Well! There are some *living* people. There's Joe Stoddard, our undertaker, supervising a newmade grave. And here comes a Grover's Corners boy that left town to go out West.

[JOE STODDARD *has hovered about in the background.* SAM CRAIG *enters left, wiping his forehead from the exertion. He carries an umbrella and strolls front.*]

Sam Craig. Good afternoon, Joe Stoddard.
Joe Stoddard. Good afternoon, good afternoon. Let me see now: Do I know you?
Sam Craig. I'm Sam Craig.
Joe Stoddard. Gracious sakes alive! Of all people! I should'a knowed you'd be back for the funeral. You've been away a long time, Sam.

Sam Craig. Yes, I've been away over twelve years. I'm in business out in Buffalo now, Joe. But I was in the East when I got news of my cousin's death, so I thought I'd combine things a little and come and see the old home. You look well.

Joe Stoddard. Yes, yes, can't complain. Very say, our journey today, Samuel.

Sam Craig. Yes.

Joe Stoddard. Yes, yes. I always say, I hate to supervise when a young person is taken. I see you brought your umbrella. It's going to rain and make it sadder still, seems like. They'll be here in a few minutes now. I had to come here early today— my son's supervisin' at the home.

Sam Craig (*reading stones*). Old farmer McCarty, I used to do chores for him—after school. He had the lumbago.

Joe Stoddard. Yes, we brought farmer McCarty here a number of years ago now.

Sam Craig (*staring at* MRS. GIBBS's *knees*). Why, this is my Aunt Julia. . . . I'd forgotten that she'd . . . of course, of course.

Joe Stoddard. Yes, Doc Gibbs lost his wife two, three years ago . . . about this time. And today's another pretty bad blow for him, too.

Mrs. Gibbs (*to* SIMON STIMSON *in an even voice*). That's my sister Carey's boy, Sam. . . . Sam Craig.

Simon Stimson. I'm always uncomfortable when *they're* around.

Mrs. Gibbs. Simon.

Simon Stimson. They and their nonsense and their damned glee at being alive . . .

Mrs. Gibbs. Simon, be patient. . . .

Sam Craig. Do they choose their own verses much, Joe?

Joe Stoddard. No . . . not usual. Mostly the bereaved pick a verse.

Sam Craig. Doesn't sound like Aunt Julia. There aren't many of those Hersey sisters left now. Let me see: Where are . . . I wanted to look at my father's and mother's . . .

Joe Stoddard. Over there with the Craigs . . . Avenue F.

Sam Craig (*reading* SIMON STIMSON's *epitaph*). He was organist at church, wasn't he?—— Hm, drank a lot, we used to say.

Joe Stoddard. Nobody was supposed to know about it. He'd seen a peck of trouble. Those musical fellas ain't like the rest of us, I reckon. (*Behind his hand*) Took his own life, y' know?

Sam Craig. Oh, did he?

Joe Stoddard. Hung himself in the attic. They tried to hush it up, but of course it got around. His wife's just married Senator Barstow. Many a time I've seen her, eleven o'clock at night, goin' around the streets huntin' for her husband. Think o' that! Now she's married to Senator Barstow over at Manchester. He chose his own epytaph. You can see it there. It ain't a verse exactly.

Sam Craig. Why, it's just some notes of music—what is it?

Joe Stoddard. Oh, I wouldn't know. It was wrote up in the Boston papers at the time.

Sam Craig. Joe, what did she die of?

Joe Stoddard. Who?

Sam Craig. My cousin.

Joe Stoddard. Oh, didn't you know? Had some trouble bringing a baby into the world. Let's see, today's Friday—'twas almost a week ago now.

Sam Craig (*putting up his umbrella*). Did the baby live?

Joe Stoddard (*raising his coat collar*). No. 'Twas her second, though. There's a little boy 'bout four years old.

Sam Craig. The grave's going to be over there?

Joe Stoddard. Yes, there ain't much more room over here among the Gibbses, so they're opening up a whole new Gibbs section over by Avenue B. You'll excuse me now. I see they're comin'.

The Dead (*not lugubrious, and strongly New England in accent*). Rain'll do a lot of good—— Yes, reckon things were gettin' downright parched. Don't look like it's goin' to last long, though—— Lemuel, you remember the floods of '79? Carried away all the bridges but one.

[*From left to right, at the back of the stage, comes a procession. Four men carry a casket, invisible to us. All the rest are under umbrellas. One can vaguely see* DR. GIBBS, GEORGE, *the* WEBBS, *etc. They gather about a grave in the back center of the stage, a little to the left of center.*]

Mrs. Soames. Who is it, Julia?

Mrs. Gibbs (*without raising her eyes*). My daughter-in-law, Emily Webb.

Mrs. Soames (*a little surprised, but no emotion*). Well, I declare! The road up here must have been awful muddy. What did she die of, Julia?

Mrs. Gibbs. In childbirth.

Mrs. Soames. Childbirth. (*Almost with a laugh*) I'd forgotten all about that! My, wasn't life awful—(*with a sigh*) and wonderful?

Simon Stimson (*with a sideways glance*). Wonderful, was it?

Mrs. Gibbs. Simon! Now, remember!

Mrs. Soames. I remember Emily's wedding. Wasn't it a lovely wedding? And I remember her reading the class poem at graduation exercises. Emily was one of the brightest girls ever graduated from high school. I've heard principal Wilkins say so time after time. I called on them at their new farm, just before I died. Perfectly beautiful farm.

A Woman from Among the Dead. It's on the same road we lived on.

A Man Among the Dead. Yes, just near the Elks' picnic grounds. Remember, Joe? By the lake where we always used to go Fourth of July? Right smart farm.

[*They subside. The group by the grave starts singing "Blessed Be the Tie That Binds."*]

A Woman Among the Dead. I always liked that hymn. I was hopin' they'd sing a hymn.

A Man Among the Dead. My wife—my second wife—knows all the verses of about every hymn there is. It just beats the Dutch. . . . She can go through them all by heart.

[*Pause. Suddenly* EMILY *appears from among the umbrellas. She is wearing a white dress. Her hair is down her back and tied by a white ribbon like a little girl. She comes slowly, gazing wonderingly at the dead, a little dazed. She stops halfway and smiles faintly.*]

Emily. Hello.

Voices Among the Dead. Hello, Emily. H'lo, M's. Gibbs.

Emily. Hello, Mother Gibbs.

Mrs. Gibbs. Emily.

Emily. Hello. (*The hymn continues.* EMILY *looks back at the funeral. She says dreamily*) It's raining.

Mrs. Gibbs. Yes. . . . They'll be gone soon, dear. Just rest yourself.

[EMILY *sits down in the empty chair by* MRS. GIBBS.]

Emily. It seems thousands and thousands of years since I . . . How stupid they all look. They don't have to look like that!

Mrs. Gibbs. Don't look at them now, dear. They'll be gone soon.

Emily. Oh, I wish I'd been here a long time. I don't like being new here—— How do you do, Mr. Stimson?

Simon Stimson. How do you do, Emily?

[EMILY *continues to look about her with a wan and wondering smile, but for a moment her eyes do not return to the funeral group. As though to shut out from her mind the thought of that group, she starts speaking to* MRS. GIBBS *with a touch of nervousness.*]

Emily. Mother Gibbs, George and I have made that farm into just the best place you ever saw. We thought of you all the time. We wanted to show you the new barn and a great long ce-ment drinking fountain for the stock. We bought that out of the money you left us.

Mrs. Gibbs. I did?

Emily. Don't you remember, Mother Gibbs—the legacy you left us? Why, it was over three hundred and fifty dollars.

Mrs. Gibbs. Yes, yes, Emily.

Emily. Well, there's a patent device on this drinking fountain so that it never overflows, Mother Gibbs, and it never sinks below a certain mark they have there. It's fine. (*Her voice trails off and her eyes return to the funeral group.*) It won't be the same

to George without me, but it's a lovely farm. (*Suddenly she looks directly at* MRS. GIBBS.) Live people don't understand, do they?
Mrs. Gibbs. No, dear—not very much.
Emily. They're sort of shut up in little boxes, aren't they? I feel as though I knew them last a thousand years ago. . . . My boy is spending the day at Mrs. Carter's. (*She sees* MR. CARTER *among the dead.*) Oh, Mr. Carter, my little boy is spending the day at your house.
Mr. Carter Is he?
Emily. Yes, he loves it there—— Mother Gibbs, we have a Ford, too. Never gives any trouble. I don't drive, though. Mother Gibbs, when does this feeling go away?—— Of being . . . one of *them*? How long does it . . . ?
Mrs. Gibbs. Sh! dear. Just wait and be patient.
Emily (*with a sigh*). I know—— Look, they're finished. They're going.
Mrs. Gibbs. Sh——

[*The umbrellas leave the stage.* DR. GIBBS *comes over to his wife's grave and stands before it a moment.* EMILY *looks up at his face.* MRS. GIBBS *does not raise her eyes.*]

Emily. Look! Father Gibbs is bringing some of my flowers to you. He looks just like George, doesn't he? Oh, Mother Gibbs, I never realized before how troubled and how . . . how in the dark live persons are. From morning till night, that's all they are—troubled.

[DR. GIBBS *goes off.*]

The Dead. Little cooler than it was—— Yes, that rain's cooled it off a little. Those northeast winds always do the same thing, don't they? If it isn't a rain, it's a three-day blow—— Reckon it may clear up before night; often does.

[*A patient calm falls on the stage. The* STAGE MANAGER *appears at his proscenium pillar, smoking.* EMILY *sits up abruptly with an idea.*]

Emily. But, Mother Gibbs, one can go back; one can go back there again . . . into living. I feel it. I know it. Why, just then for a moment I was thinking about . . . about the farm . . . and for a minute I *was* there, and my baby was on my lap as plain as day.

Mrs. Gibbs. Yes, of course you can.

Emily. I can go back there and live all those days over again . . . why not?

Mrs. Gibbs. All I can say is, Emily, don't.

Emily (*takes a few steps toward the* STAGE MANAGER). But it's true, isn't it? I can go and live . . . back there . . . again.

Stage Manager. Yes, some have tried—but they soon come back here.

Mrs. Gibbs. Don't do it, Emily.

Mrs. Soames. Emily, don't. It's not what you think it'd be.

Emily. But I won't live over a sad day. I'll choose a happy one—— I'll choose the day I first knew that I loved George. Why should that be painful?

[*They are silent. Her question turns to the* STAGE MANAGER.]

Stage Manager. You not only live it, but you watch yourself living it.

Emily. Yes.

Stage Manager. And as you watch it, you see the thing that they—down there—never know. You see the future. You know what's going to happen afterwards.

Emily. But is that—painful? Why?

Mrs. Gibbs. That's not the only reason why you shouldn't do it, Emily. When you've been here longer, you'll see that our life here is our hope that soon we'll forget all that, and think only of what's ahead, and be ready for what's ahead. When you've been here longer, you'll understand.

Emily (*softly*). But Mother Gibbs, how can I ever forget that life? It's all I know. It's all I had.

[MRS. GIBBS *does not answer.*]

Mr. Stimson, did you go back?

Simon Stimson (*sharply*). No.

Emily. Did you, Mrs. Soames?

Mrs. Soames. Oh, Emily. It isn't wise. Really, it isn't. All we can do is just warn you. It won't be what you expect.

Emily (*slowly*). But it's a thing I must know for myself. I'll choose a happy day, anyway.

Mrs. Gibbs. No. At least, choose an unimportant day. Choose the least important day in your life. It will be important enough.

Emily (*to the* STAGE MANAGER). Then it can't be since I was married, or since the baby was born. I can choose a birthday at least, can't I—— I choose my twelfth birthday.

Stage Manager. All right. February 11th, 1899. A Tuesday—— Do you want any special time of day?

Emily. Oh, I want the whole day.

Stage Manager. We'll begin at dawn. You remember it had been snowing for several days, but it had stopped the night before, and they had begun clearing the roads. The sun's coming up.

Emily (*with a cry*). There's Main Street ... why, that's Mr. Morgan's drugstore before he changed it! ... And there's the livery stable. (*She walks toward the back of the stage.*)

Stage Manager. Yes, it's 1899. This is fourteen years ago.

Emily. Oh, that's the town I knew as a little girl. And, look, there's the old white fence that used to be around our house. Oh, I'd forgotten that! Oh, I love it so! Are *they* inside?

Stage Manager. Yes, your mother'll be coming downstairs in a minute to make breakfast.

Emily (*softly*). Will she?

Stage Manager. And you remember: Your father had been away for several days; he came back on the early morning train.

Emily. No ... ?

Stage Manager. He'd been back to his college to make a speech—in western New York, at Clinton.

Emily. Look! There's Howie Newsome. There's our policeman. But he's *dead*; he *died*.

[*The* STAGE MANAGER *retires to his corner. The voices of* HOWIE NEW-SOME, CONSTABLE WARREN, *and* JOE CROWELL, JR., *are heard at the left of the stage.*]

Howie Newsome. Whoa, Bessie!—Bessie! Morning, Bill.
Bill. Morning, Howie.
Howie Newsome. You're up early.
Bill. Been rescuin' a party; darn near froze to death, down by Polish Town thar. Got drunk and lay out in the snowdrifts. Thought he was in bed when I shook'm.
Emily. Why, there's Joe Crowell. . . .
Joe Crowell. Good morning, Mr. Warren. Morning, Howie.

[MRS. WEBB *has appeared in her kitchen, but* EMILY *does not see her until she calls.*]

Mrs. Webb. Chil-*dren*! Wally! Emily! . . . Time to get up.
Emily. Mama, here I am! Oh! how young Mama looks! I didn't know Mama was ever that young. Oh!
Mrs. Webb. You can come and dress by the kitchen fire if you like, but hurry.

[HOWIE NEWSOME *has entered along Main Street and brings the milk to* MRS. WEBB's *door.*]

Good morning, Mr. Newsome. Whhhh—it's cold.
Howie Newsome. Ten below by my barn, Mrs. Webb.
Mrs. Webb. Think of it! Keep yourself wrapped up. (*She takes her bottles in, shuddering.*)
Emily (*with an effort*). Mama, I can't find my blue hair ribbon anywhere.
Mrs. Webb. Just open your eyes, dear, that's all. I laid it out for you special—on the dresser, there. If it were a snake it would bite you.
Emily. Yes, yes. . . .

[*She puts her hand on her heart.* MR. WEBB *comes along Main Street, where he meets* CONSTABLE WARREN.]

Mr. Webb. Good morning, Bill.

Bill. Good morning, Mr. Webb. You're up early.

Mr. Webb. Yes, just been back to my old college in New York State. Been any trouble here?

Bill. Well, I was called up this mornin' to rescue a Polish fella— darn near froze to death he was.

Mr. Webb. We must get it in the paper.

Bill. 'Twan't much.

Emily (*whispers*). Papa.

[MR. WEBB *shakes the snow off his feet and enters his house.*]

Mr. Webb. Good morning, Mother.

Mrs. Webb. How did it go, Charles?

Mr. Webb. Oh, fine, I guess. I told'm a few things.

Mrs. Webb. Did you sit up on the train all night?

Mr. Webb. Yes. Never could sleep on a Pullman anyway.

Mrs. Webb. Charles, seems to me—we're rich enough so that you could sleep in a train once in a while.

Mr. Webb. Everything all right here?

Mrs. Webb. Yes—can't think of anything that's happened, special. Been right cold. Howie Newsome says it's ten below over to his barn.

Mr. Webb. Yes, well, it's colder than that at Hamilton College. Students' ears are falling off. It ain't Christian—— Paper have any mistakes in it?

Mrs. Webb. None that I noticed. Coffee's ready when you want it.

[*He starts upstairs.*]

Charles! Don't forget, it's Emily's birthday. Did you remember to get her something?

Mr. Webb (*patting his pocket*). Yes, I've got something here.

Mrs. Webb. Goodness sakes! I hope she likes what I got for her. I hunted hard enough for it. Child*ren*! Hurry up! Hurry up!

Mr. Webb. Where's my girl? Where's my birthday girl? (*He goes off left.*)

Mrs. Webb. Don't interrupt her now, Charles. You can see her at breakfast. She's slow enough as it is. Hurry up, children! It's seven o'clock. Now, I don't want to call you again.

Emily (*softly, more in wonder than in grief*). I can't bear it. They're so young and beautiful. Why did they ever have to get old? Mama, I'm here. I'm grown up. I love you all, everything—— I can't look at everything hard enough. There's the butternut tree. (*She wanders up Main Street.*) There's Mr. Morgan's drugstore. And there's the high school, forever and ever, and ever. And there's the Congregational Church, where I got married. Oh, dear. Oh, dear. Oh, dear! (*The* STAGE MANAGER *beckons partially to her. He points to the house. She says a breathless "yes" and goes to the house.*) Good morning, Mama.

Mrs. Webb (*at the foot of the stairs, kissing her in a matter-of-fact way*). Well, now, dear, a very happy birthday to my girl and many happy returns. There are some surprises waiting for you on the kitchen table.

Emily. Oh, Mama, you *shouldn't* have. (*She throws an anguished glance at the* STAGE MANAGER.) I can't—I can't.

Mrs. Webb (*facing the audience, over her stove*). But birthday or no birthday, I want you to eat your breakfast good and slow. I want you to grow up and be a good, strong girl. (*She goes to the stairs and calls*) Wally! Wally, wash yourself good. Everything's getting cold down here. (*She returns to the stove with her back to* EMILY. EMILY *opens her parcels.*) That in the blue paper is from your Aunt Carrie and I reckon you can guess who brought the postcard album. I found it on the doorstep when I brought in the milk—George Gibbs . . . must have come over in the cold pretty early . . . right nice of him.

Emily (*to herself*). Oh, George! I'd forgotten that. . . .

Mrs. Webb. Chew that bacon slow. It'll help keep you warm on a cold day.

Emily (*beginning softly but urgently*). Oh, Mama, just look at me one minute as though you really saw me. Mama, fourteen years have gone by. I'm dead. You're a grandmother, Mama. I married George Gibbs, Mama. Wally's dead, too. Mama, his appendix burst on a camping trip to North Conway. We felt just terrible about it—don't you remember? But, just for a moment now we're all together. Mama, just for a moment we're happy. Let's look at one another.

Mrs. Webb. That in the yellow paper is something I found in the attic among your grandmother's things. You're old enough to wear it now, and I thought you'd like it.

Emily. And this is from you. Why, Mama, it's just lovely and it's just what I wanted. It's beautiful! (*She flings her arms around her mother's neck. Her mother goes on with her cooking, but is pleased.*)

Mrs. Webb. Well, I hoped you'd like it. Hunted all over. Your Aunt Norah couldn't find one in Concord, so I had to send all the way to Boston. (*Laughing*) Wally has something for you, too. He made it at manual training class and he's very proud of it. Be sure you make a big fuss about it—— Your father has a surprise for you, too; don't know what it is myself. Sh—here he comes.

Mr. Webb (*offstage*). Where's my girl? Where's my birthday girl?

Emily (*in a loud voice to the* STAGE MANAGER). I can't. I can't go on. Oh! Oh. It goes so fast. We don't have time to look at one another. (*She breaks down sobbing. At a gesture from the* STAGE MANAGER, MRS. WEBB *disappears.*) I didn't realize. So all that was going on and we never noticed. Take me back—up the hill—to my grave. But first: Wait! One more look. Goodbye, good-bye, world. Goodbye, Grover's Corners . . . Mama and Papa. Goodbye to clocks ticking . . . and Mama's sunflowers. And food and coffee. And new-ironed dresses and hot baths . . . and sleeping and waking up. Oh, earth, you're too wonderful for anybody to realize you. (*She looks toward the* STAGE MANAGER *and asks abruptly, through her tears*) Do any human beings ever real-ize life while they live it?—every, every minute?

Stage Manager. No. (*Pause*) The saints and poets, maybe—they do some.

Emily. I'm ready to go back. (*She returns to her chair beside* MRS. GIBBS.) Mother Gibbs, I should have listened to you. Now I want to be quiet for a while—— Oh, Mother Gibbs, I saw it all. I saw your garden.

Mrs. Gibbs. Did you, dear?

Emily. That's all human beings are!—just blind people.

Mrs. Gibbs. Look, it's clearing up. The stars are coming out.

Emily. Oh, Mr. Stimson, I should have listened to them.

Simon Stimson (*with mounting violence, bitingly*). Yes, now you know. Now you know! That's what it was to be alive. To move about in a cloud of ignorance, to go up and down trampling on the feelings of those . . . of those about you. To spend and waste time as though you had a million years. To be always at the mercy of one self-centered passion, or another. Now you know—that's the happy existence you wanted to go back and see. Did you shout to 'em? Did you call to 'em?

Emily. Yes, I did.

Simon Stimson. Now you know them as they are: in ignorance and blindness.

Mrs. Gibbs (*spiritedly*). Simon Stimson, that ain't the whole truth and you know it.

[*The dead have begun to stir.*]

The Dead. Lemuel, wind's coming up, seems like—— Oh dear—— I keep remembering things tonight—— It's right cold for June, ain't it?

Mrs. Gibbs. Look what you've done, you and your rebellious spirit stirring us up here—— Emily, look at that star. I forget its name.

The Dead. I'm getting to know them all, but I don't know their names—— My boy Joel was a sailor—knew 'em all. He'd set on the porch evenings and tell 'em all by name. Yes, sir, it was wonderful—— A star's mighty good company—— Yes, yes—— Yes, 'tis.

Simon Stimson. Here's one of *them* coming.

The Dead. That's funny. 'Tain't no time for one of them to be here—— Goodness sakes.

Emily. Mother Gibbs, it's George.

Mrs. Gibbs. Sh, dear. You just rest yourself.

Emily. It's George.

[GEORGE *enters from the left, and slowly comes toward them.*]

A Man from Among the Dead. And my boy Joel, who knew the stars—he used to say it took millions of years for that speck o' light to git to the earth. Don't seem like a body could believe it, but that's what he used to say—millions of years.
Another. That's what they say.

[GEORGE *flings himself on* EMILY'*s grave.*]

The Dead. Goodness! That ain't no way to behave!—— He ought to be home.
Emily. Mother Gibbs?
Mrs. Gibbs. Yes, Emily?
Emily. They don't understand much, do they?
Mrs. Gibbs. No, dear, not very much.

[*The* STAGE MANAGER *appears at the right, one hand on a dark curtain which he slowly draws across the scene. In the distance a clock is heard striking the hour very faintly.*]

Stage Manager. Most everybody's asleep in Grover's Corners. There are a few lights on: Shorty Hawkins, down at the depot, has just watched the Albany train go by. And at the livery stable somebody's setting up late and talking—— Yes, it's clearing up. There are the stars—doing their old, old crisscross journeys in the sky. Scholars haven't settled the matter yet, but they seem to think there are no living beings up there. They're just chalk . . . or fire. Only this one is straining away, straining away all the time to make something of itself. The strain's so bad that every sixteen hours everybody lies down and gets a rest. (*He winds his watch.*) Hm. . . . Eleven o'clock in Grover's Corners—— You get a good rest, too. Good night.

Dorothy Parker
(1893–1967)

When an interviewer once asked Dorothy Parker what the source for her writing had been, she replied, "Need of money, dear." Like much of Parker's famous dark humor, that comment was both bitter in tone and at least partly true. Parker's mother died when she was only four, and she didn't get along well with her father and stepmother. When her father died, in 1913, Parker was left alone in New York City, a young woman with no means of support. She sold her first poem, less than a year later, to the publisher of *Vogue*, who then hired her as a copy-writer. In 1917, she transferred to the trendy magazine *Vanity Fair*, where she soon replaced the British writer P. G. Wodehouse (1881–1975) as drama critic.

The editors' choices of Parker and Wodehouse—the latter still famous for his comic portrayals of English high society—suggest that they were looking for a clever critic with a sophisticated sense of humor. But Parker turned out to be a bit too clever. After several Broadway plays fizzled following harsh reviews in *Vanity Fair*, the shows' producers complained, and Parker was fired. (Parker, in a typically scathing review, once wrote that an actress "ran the gamut of emotions from A to B.")

The New Yorker magazine, which later hired Parker to write book reviews under the pen name Constant Reader, proved more tolerant of her sarcasm. Here is a sample: "This is not a book to be lightly tossed aside. It should be thrown aside with great force."

One lasting result of Parker's stint at *Vanity Fair* was her twenty-year friendship with the humorist Robert Benchley (1889–1945). The two often lunched at New York's Algonquin Hotel, where, with a group of literary friends, they made up what came to be known as the Algonquin Round Table. Newspaper columnists reported their witty remarks, and Parker, one of the quickest wits, became a celebrity. ("Most of us become writers because we can never think of the apt thing to say till the moment to say it has passed," the British writer W. Somerset Maugham (1874–1965) once wrote, whereas Parker seemed "to carry a hammer in her handbag to hit the appropriate nail on the head.") Soon it appeared that any clever or sarcastic remark heard in New York City was attributed to Dorothy Parker.

Parker's fame did not depend solely on lunchtime wise-cracking. All three of her books of verse were best-sellers. Her short stories, with their cynical portrayals of male-female relations—drawing, no doubt, on her two tempestuous marriages and many unhappy love affairs—continue to be popular. In the 1930s, she collaborated on a number of successful screenplays, including *A Star Is Born* (1937).

Throughout her life, Parker was deeply involved with issues of social justice. Before she died, in 1967, she willed her entire estate to civil rights causes. A 1994 film about her life, *Mrs. Parker and the Vicious Circle*, starred Jennifer Jason Leigh.

But in the end, Parker considered her verse dated, her stories inferior because they relied on dialogue rather than narrative, and her writing for Hollywood shallow and empty. In an ironic twist that Parker herself might have invented, the only work she felt truly proud of, a play called *The Ladies of the Corridor* (1953), turned out to be a flop.

Here We Are
Dorothy Parker

Scene: A compartment in a Pullman car. He is storing the suitcases in the rack and hanging up coats. She is primping. He finishes disposing of the luggage and sits.

He. Well!

She. Well!

He. Well, here we are.

She. Here we are, aren't we?

He. Eeyop. I should say we are. Here we are.

She. Well!

He. Well! Well! How does it feel to be an old married lady?

She. Oh, it's too soon to ask me that. At least—I mean. Well, I mean, goodness, we've only been married about three hours, haven't we?

He. We have been married exactly two hours and twenty-six minutes.

She. My, it seems like longer.

He. No, it isn't hardly half-past six yet.

She. It seems like later. I guess it's because it starts getting dark so early.

He. It does, at that. The nights are going to be pretty long from now on. I mean. I mean—well, it starts getting dark early.

She. I didn't have any idea what time it was. Everything was so mixed up, I sort of don't know where I am, or what it's all about. Getting back from the church, and then all those people, and then changing all my clothes, and then everybody throwing things, and all. Goodness, I don't see how people do it every day.

He. Do what?

She. Get married. When you think of all the people, all over the world, getting married just as if it was nothing. Chinese people and everybody. Just as if it wasn't anything.

He. Well, let's not worry about people all over the world. Let's don't think about a lot of Chinese. We've got something better to think about. I mean. I mean—well, what do we care about them?

She. I know, but I just sort of got to thinking of them, all of them, all over everywhere, doing it all the time. At least, I mean—getting married, you know. And it's—well, it's sort of such a big thing to do, it makes you feel queer. You think of them, all of them, all doing it just like it wasn't anything. And how does anybody know what's going to happen next?

He. Let them worry, we don't have to. We know darn well what's going to happen next. I mean—well, we know it's going to be great. Well, we know we're going to be happy. Don't we?

She. Oh, of course. Only you think of all the people, and you have to sort of keep thinking. It makes you feel funny. An awful lot of people that get married, it doesn't turn out so well. And I guess they all must have thought it was going to be great.

He. Aw, come on, now, this is no way to start a honeymoon, with all this thinking going on. Look at us—all married and everything done. I mean. The wedding all done and all.

She. Ah, it was nice, wasn't it? Did you really like my veil?

He. You looked great, just great.

She. Oh, I'm terribly glad. Ellie and Louise looked lovely, didn't they? I'm terribly glad they did finally decide on pink. They looked perfectly lovely.

He. Listen, I want to tell you something. When I was standing up there in that old church waiting for you to come up, and I saw those two bridesmaids, I thought to myself, I thought, "Well, I never knew Louise could look like that!" I thought she'd have knocked anybody's eye out.

She. Oh, really? Funny. Of course, everybody thought her dress and hat were lovely, but a lot of people seemed to think she looked sort of tired. People have been saying that a lot, lately. I tell them I think it's awfully mean of them to go around saying that about her. I tell them they've got to remember that

Louise isn't so terribly young any more, and they've got to expect her to look like that. Louise can say she's twenty-three all she wants to, but she's a good deal nearer twenty-seven.

He. Well, she was certainly a knockout at the wedding. Boy!

She. I'm terribly glad you thought so. I'm glad someone did. How did you think Ellie looked?

He. Why, I honestly didn't get a look at her.

She. Oh, really? Well, I certainly think that's too bad. I don't suppose I ought to say it about my own sister, but I never saw anybody look as beautiful as Ellie looked today. And always so sweet and unselfish, too. And you didn't even notice her. But you never pay attention to Ellie, anyway. Don't think I haven't noticed it. It makes me feel just terrible. It makes me feel just awful that you don't like my own sister.

He. I do so like her! I'm crazy for Ellie. I think she's a great kid.

She. Don't think it makes any difference to Ellie! Ellie's got enough people crazy about her. It isn't anything to her whether you like her or not. Don't flatter yourself she cares! Only, the only thing is, it makes it awfully hard for me you don't like her, that's the only thing. I keep thinking, when we come back and get in the apartment and everything, it's going to be awfully hard for me that you won't want all my family around. I know how you feel about my family. Don't think I haven't seen it. Only, if you don't ever want to see them, that's your loss. Not theirs. Don't flatter yourself!

He. Oh, now, come on! What's all this talk about not wanting your family around? Why, you know how I feel about your family. I think your old lady—I think your mother's swell. And Ellie. And your father. What's all this talk?

She. Well, I've seen it. Don't think I haven't. Lots of people they get married, and they think it's going to be great and everything, and then it all goes to pieces because people don't like people's families, or something like that. Don't tell me! I've seen it happen.

He. Honey, what is all this? What are you getting all angry about? Hey, look, this is our honeymoon. What are you trying to start a fight for? Ah, I guess you're just feeling sort of nervous.

She. Me? What have I got to be nervous about? I mean. I mean, goodness, I'm not nervous.

He. You know, lots of times, they say that girls get kind of nervous and yippy on account of thinking about—I mean. I mean—well, it's like you said, things are all so sort of mixed up and everything, right now. But afterwards, it'll be all right. I mean. I mean—well, look, honey, you don't look any too comfortable. Don't you want to take your hat off? And let's don't ever fight, ever. Will we?

She. Ah, I'm sorry I was cross. I guess I did feel a little bit funny. All mixed up, and then thinking of all those people all over everywhere, and then being sort of 'way off here, all alone with you. It's so sort of different. It's sort of such a big thing. You can't blame a person for thinking, can you? Yes, don't let's ever, ever fight. We won't be like a whole lot of them. We won't fight or be nasty or anything. Will we?

He. You bet your life we won't.

She. I guess I will take this darned old hat off. It kind of presses. Just put it up on the rack, will you, dear? Do you like it, sweetheart?

He. Looks good on you.

She. No, but I mean, do you really like it?

He. Well, I'll tell you, I know this is the new style and everything like that, and it's probably great. I don't know anything about things like that. Only I like the kind of a hat like that blue hat you had. Gee, I like that hat.

She. Oh, really? Well, that's nice. That's lovely. The first thing you say to me, as soon as you get me off on a train away from my family and everything, is that you don't like my hat. The first thing you say to your wife is you think she has terrible taste in hats. That's nice, isn't it?

He. Now, honey, I never said anything like that. I only said——

She. What you don't seem to realize is this hat cost twenty-two dollars. Twenty-two dollars. And that horrible old blue thing you think you're so crazy about, that cost three ninety-five.

He. I don't give a darn what they cost. I only said—I said I liked that blue hat. I don't know anything about hats. I'll be crazy about this one as soon as I get used to it. Only it's kind of not like your other hats. I don't know about the new styles. What do I know about women's hats?

She. It's too bad you didn't marry somebody that would get the kind of hats you'd like. Hats that cost three ninety-five. Why didn't you marry Louise? You always think she looks so beautiful. You'd love her taste in hats. Why didn't you marry her?

He. Ah, now, honey, for heaven's sakes!

She. Why didn't you marry her? All you've done, ever since we got on this train, is talk about her. Here I've sat and sat, and just listened to you saying how wonderful Louise is. I suppose that's nice, getting me off here all alone with you, and then raving about Louise right in front of my face. Why didn't you ask her to marry you? I'm sure she would have jumped at the chance. There aren't so many people asking her to marry them. It's too bad you didn't marry her. I'm sure you'd have been much happier.

He. Listen, baby, while you're talking about things like that, why didn't you marry Joe Brooks? I suppose he could have given you all the twenty-two-dollar hats you wanted, I suppose!

She. Well, I'm not so sure I'm not sorry I didn't. There! Joe Brooks wouldn't have waited until he got me all off alone and then sneered at my taste in clothes. Joe Brooks wouldn't ever hurt my feelings. Joe Brooks has always been fond of me.

He. Yeah, he's fond of you. He was so fond of you he didn't even send a wedding present. That's how fond of you he was.

She. I happen to know for a fact that he was away on business, and as soon as he comes back he's going to give me anything I want for the apartment.

He. Listen, I don't want anything he gives you in our apartment. Anything he gives you, I'll throw right out the window. That's what I think of your friend Joe Brooks. And how do you know where he is and what he's going to do, anyway? Has he been writing to you?

She. I suppose my friends can correspond with me. I didn't hear there was any law against that.

He. Well, I suppose they can't! And what do you think of that? I'm not going to have my wife getting a lot of letters from cheap traveling salesmen!

She. Joe Brooks is not a cheap traveling salesman! He is not! He gets a wonderful salary.

He. Oh yeah? Where did you hear that?

She. He told me so himself.

He. Oh, he told you so himself. I see. He told you so himself.

She. You've got a lot of right to talk about Joe Brooks. You and your friend Louise. All you ever talk about is Louise.

He. Oh, for heaven's sakes! What do I care about Louise? I just thought she was a friend of yours, that's all. That's why I ever noticed her.

She. Well, you certainly took an awful lot of notice of her today. On our wedding day! You said yourself when you were standing there in the church you just keep thinking of her. Right up at the altar. Oh, right in the presence of God! And all you thought about was Louise.

He. Listen, honey, I never should have said that. How does anybody know what kind of crazy things come into their heads when they're standing there waiting to get married? I was just telling you that because it was so kind of crazy. I thought it would make you laugh.

She. I know, I've been all sort of mixed up today, too. I told you that. Everything so strange and everything. And me all the time thinking about all those people all over the world, and now us here all alone, and everything. I know you get all mixed up. Only I did think, when you kept talking about how beautiful Louise looked, you did it with malice and forethought.

He. I never did anything with malice and forethought! I just told you that about Louise because I thought it would make you laugh.

She. Well, it didn't.

He. No, I know it didn't. It certainly did not. Ah, baby, and we ought to be laughing, too. Hell, honey lamb, this is our honeymoon. What's the matter?

She. I don't know. We used to squabble a lot when we were going together and then engaged and everything, but I thought everything would be so different as soon as you were married. And now I feel so sort of strange and everything. I feel so sort of alone.

He. Well, you see, sweetheart, we're not really married yet. I mean. I mean—well, things will be different afterwards. Oh, hell. I mean, we haven't been married very long.

She. No.

He. Well, we haven't got much longer to wait now. I mean—well, we'll be in New York in about twenty minutes. Then we can have dinner, and sort of see what we feel like doing. Or, I mean—is there anything special you want to do tonight?

She. What?

He. What I mean to say, would you like to go to a show or something?

She. Why, whatever you like. I sort of didn't think people went to theaters and things on their—I mean, I've got a couple of letters I simply must write. Don't let me forget.

He. Oh, you're going to write letters tonight?

She. Well, you see, I've been perfectly terrible. What with all the excitement and everything. I never did thank poor old Mrs. Sprague for her berry spoon, and I never did a thing about those book ends the McMasters sent. It's just too awful of me. I've got to write them this very night.

He. And when you've finished writing your letters, maybe I could get you a magazine or a bag of peanuts.

She. What?

He. I mean, I wouldn't want you to be bored.

She. As if I could be bored with you! Silly! Aren't we married? Bored!

He. What I thought, I thought when we got in, we could go right up to the Biltmore and anyway leave our bags, and maybe have a little dinner in the room, kind of quiet, and then do whatever we wanted. I mean. I mean—well, let's go right up there from the station.

She. Oh, yes, let's. I'm so glad we're going to the Biltmore. I just love it. The twice I've stayed in New York we've always stayed there, Papa and Mamma and Ellie and I, and I was crazy about it. I always sleep so well there. I go right off to sleep the minute I put my head on the pillow.

He. Oh, you do?

She. At, least, I mean, 'way up high it's so quiet.

He. We might go to some show or other tomorrow night instead of tonight. Don't you think that would be better?

She. Yes, I think it might.

He. Do you really have to write those letters tonight?

She. Well, I don't suppose they'd get there any quicker than if I wrote them tomorrow.

He. And we won't ever fight any more, will we?

She. Oh, no. Not ever! I don't know what made me do like that. It all got so sort of funny, sort of like a nightmare, the way I got thinking of all those people getting married all the time; and so many of them, everything spoils on account of fighting and everything. I got all mixed up thinking about them. Oh, I don't want to be like them. But we won't be, will we?

He. Sure we won't.

She. We won't go all to pieces. We won't fight. It'll all be different, now we're married. It'll all be lovely. Reach me down my hat, will you, sweetheart? It's time I was putting it on. Thanks. Ah, I'm sorry you don't like it.

He. I do so like it!

She. You said you didn't. You said you thought it was perfectly terrible.

He. I never said any such thing. You're crazy.

She. All right, I may be crazy. Thank you very much. But that's what you said. Not that it matters—it's just a little thing. But it makes you feel pretty funny to think you've gone and married somebody that says you have perfectly terrible taste in hats. And then goes and says you're crazy, besides.

He. Now, listen here, nobody said any such thing. Why, I love that hat. The more I look at it the better I like it. I think it's great.

She. That isn't what you said before.

He. Honey, stop it, will you? What do you want to start all this for? I love the damned hat. I mean, I love your hat. I love anything you wear. What more do you want me to say?

She. Well, I don't want you to say it like that.

He. I said I think it's great. That's all I said.

She. Do you really? Do you honestly? Ah, I'm so glad. I'd hate you not to like my hat. It would be—I don't know, it would be sort of such a bad start.

He. Well, I'm crazy for it. Now we've got that settled, for heaven's sakes. Ah, baby. Baby lamb. We're not going to have any bad starts. Look at us—we're on our honeymoon. Pretty soon we'll be regular old married people. I mean. I mean, in a few minutes we'll be getting in to New York, and then we'll be going to the hotel, and then everything will be all right. I mean—well, look at us! Here we are married! Here we are!

She. Yes, here we are, aren't we?

CURTAIN

Anton Chekhov
(1860–1904)

Anton Chekhov is one of the two playwrights who have most influenced modern drama. The other is the Norwegian writer Henrik Ibsen (1828–1906), whose best-known plays often deal with the social problems of his time and are constructed in the form of what has been called the well-made play. Chekhov's major plays, on the other hand, are often called slices of life; they meander rather than march. They are concerned more with psychological insights than with a well-crafted plot. Most modern American playwrights have followed Ibsen's model, not Chekhov's. Those who have tried to write slice-of-life plays have generally failed because, by and large, American audiences are not attuned to plays that chart the ebb and flow of moods and subtly shifting relationships.

Chekhov was born in a small seaport in southern Russia, the grandson of a serf and the son of an unsuccessful shopkeeper. As a young man he supported his mother, father, four brothers, and sister by writing short stories and sketches for humor magazines. At the same time he was studying medicine at the University of Moscow.

Chekhov received his medical degree but did not practice medicine for long. Instead, he fell back on his literary work to earn a living. Over the course of his short life, he produced hundreds of short stories and four major plays. *A Marriage Proposal* is one of several one-act comedies ("jokes") that he wrote early in his career. Though those little comedies do not match the achievement of his later plays—and Chekhov himself considered them unimportant "vaudevilles"—the public loved them.

In the last years of his life, Chekhov wrote five serious full-length plays, four of which are considered masterpieces: *The Sea Gull*, *Uncle Vanya*, *Three Sisters*, and *The Cherry Orchard*. Those new plays were different from the kind of drama audiences were used to, and the first production of *The Sea Gull* was a failure. The audience hissed, and Chekhov left the theater vowing never again to write a play. Fortunately, he did not keep his vow. Later *The Sea Gull* was restaged in Moscow and was a smashing success.

Chekhov died of tuberculosis when he was only forty-four years old.

The Bear
A Farce in One Act
Anton Chekhov

Characters

Mrs. Helen Popov, a young widow with dimpled cheeks;
  a landowner
Gregory Smirnov, a landowner in early middle age
Luke, Mrs. Popov's old servant

The action takes place in the drawing room of Mrs. Popov's country house.

Scene 1

MRS. POPOV, *in deep mourning, with her eye fixed on a snapshot, and* LUKE.

Luke. This won't do, madam; you're just making your life a misery. Cook's out with the maid picking fruit, every living creature's happy, and even our cat knows how to enjoy herself—she's parading round the yard trying to pick up a bird or two. But here you are cooped up inside all day like you was in a convent cell—you never have a good time. Yes, it's true. Nigh on twelve months it is since you last set foot outdoors.
Mrs. Popov. And I'm never going out again; why should I? My life's finished. He lies in his grave; I've buried myself inside these four walls—we're both dead.
Luke. There you go again! I don't like to hear such talk, I don't. Your husband died and that was that—God's will be done, and may he rest in peace. You've shed a few tears and that'll do;

it's time to call it a day—you can't spend your whole life a-moaning and a-groaning. The same thing happened to me once, when my old woman died, but what did I do? I grieved a bit, shed a tear or two for a month or so, and that's all she's getting. Catch me wearing sackcloth and ashes for the rest of my days; it'd be more than the old girl was worth! (*Sighs*) You've neglected all the neighbors—won't go and see them or have them in the house. We never get out and about, lurking here like dirty great spiders, saving your presence. The mice have been at my livery too. And it's not for any lack of nice people either—the country's full of 'em, see. There's the regiment stationed at Ryblovo, and them officers are a fair treat; a proper sight for sore eyes they are. They have a dance in camp of a Friday, and the brass band plays most days. This ain't right, missus. You're young, and pretty as a picture with that peaches-and-cream look, so make the most of it. Them looks won't last forever, you know. If you wait another ten years to come out of your shell and lead them officers a dance, you'll find it's too late.

Mrs. Popov (*decisively*). Never talk to me like that again, please. When Nicholas died, my life lost all meaning, as you know. You may think I'm alive, but I'm not really. I swore to wear this mourning and shun society till my dying day, do you hear? Let his departed spirit see how I love him! Yes, I realize you know what went on—that he was often mean to me, cruel and, er, unfaithful even; but I'll be true to the grave and show him how much I can love. And he'll find me in the next world just as I was before he died.

Luke. Don't talk like that—walk round the garden instead. Or else have Toby or Giant harnessed and go and see the neighbors.

Mrs. Popov. Oh dear! (*Weeps*)

Luke. Missus! Madam! What's the matter? For heaven's sake!

Mrs. Popov. He was so fond of Toby—always drove him when he went over to the Korchagins' place and the Vlasovs'. He drove so well too! And he looked so graceful when he pulled hard on the reins, remember? Oh Toby, Toby! See he gets an extra bag of oats today.

Luke. Very good, madam.

[*A loud ring.*]

Mrs. Popov (*shudders*). Who is it? Tell them I'm not at home.
Luke. Very well, madam. (*Goes out*)

Scene 2

MRS. POPOV *alone.*

Mrs. Popov (*looking at the snapshot*). Now you shall see how I can love and forgive, Nicholas. My love will only fade when I fade away myself, when this poor heart stops beating. (*Laughs through tears*) Well, aren't you ashamed of yourself? I'm your good, faithful little wifey; I've locked myself up, and I'll be faithful to the grave, while you—aren't you ashamed, you naughty boy? You deceived me, and you used to make scenes and leave me alone for weeks on end.

Scene 3

MRS. POPOV *and* LUKE.

Luke (*comes in agitatedly*). Someone's asking for you, madam. Wants to see you——
Mrs. Popov. Then I hope you told them I haven't received visitors since the day my husband died.
Luke. I did, but he wouldn't listen—his business is very urgent, he says.
Mrs. Popov. *I am not at home!*
Luke. So I told him, but he just swears and barges straight in, drat him. He's waiting in the dining room.
Mrs. Popov (*irritatedly*). All right, ask him in here then. Aren't people rude?

[LUKE *goes out.*]

Mrs. Popov. Oh, aren't they all a bore? What do they want with me; why must they disturb my peace? (*Sighs*) Yes, I see I really shall have to get me to a nunnery. (*Reflects*) I'll take the veil; that's it.

Scene 4

MRS. POPOV, LUKE, *and* SMIRNOV.

Smirnov (*coming in, to* LUKE). You're a fool, my talkative friend. An ass. (*Seeing* MRS. POPOV, *with dignity*) May I introduce myself, madam? Gregory Smirnov, landed gentleman and lieutenant of artillery retired. I'm obliged to trouble you on most urgent business.

Mrs. Popov (*not holding out her hand*). What do you require?

Smirnov. I had the honor to know your late husband. He died owing me twelve hundred rubles—— I have his two IOUs. Now I've some interest due to the land bank tomorrow, madam, so may I trouble you to let me have the money today?

Mrs. Popov. Twelve hundred rubles—— How did my husband come to owe you that?

Smirnov. He used to buy his oats from me.

Mrs. Popov (*sighing, to* LUKE). Oh yes—Luke, don't forget to see Toby has his extra bag of oats. (LUKE *goes out. To* SMIRNOV.) Of course I'll pay if Nicholas owed you something, but I've nothing on me today, sorry. My manager will be back from town the day after tomorrow, and I'll get him to pay you whatever it is then, but for the time being I can't oblige. Besides, it's precisely seven months today since my husband died, and I am in no fit state to discuss money.

Smirnov. Well, I'll be in a fit state to go bust with a capital *B* if I can't pay that interest tomorrow. They'll have the bailiffs in on me.

Mrs. Popov. You'll get your money the day after tomorrow.

Smirnov. I don't want it the day after tomorrow; I want it now.

Mrs. Popov. I can't pay you now, sorry.

Smirnov. And I can't wait till the day after tomorrow.

Mrs. Popov. Can I help it if I've no money today?

Smirnov. So you can't pay then?

Mrs. Popov. Exactly.

Smirnov. I see. And that's your last word, is it?

Mrs. Popov. It is.

Smirnov. Your last word? You really mean it?

Mrs. Popov. I do.

Smirnov (*sarcastic*). Then I'm greatly obliged to you; I'll put it in my diary! (*Shrugs*) And people expect me to be cool and collected! I met the local excise man on my way here just now. "My dear Smirnov," says he, "why are you always losing your temper?" But how can I help it, I ask you? I'm in desperate need of money! Yesterday morning I left home at crack of dawn. I call on everyone who owes me money, but not a soul forks out. I'm dog tired. I spend the night in some God-awful place. Then I fetch up here, fifty miles from home, hoping to see the color of my money, only to be fobbed off with this "no fit state" stuff! How *can* I keep my temper?

Mrs. Popov. I thought I'd made myself clear. You can have your money when my manager gets back from town.

Smirnov. It's not your manager I'm after; it's you. What the blazes, pardon my language, do I want with your manager?

Mrs. Popov. I'm sorry, my dear man, but I'm not accustomed to these peculiar expressions and to this tone. I have closed my ears. (*Hurries out*)

Scene 5

SMIRNOV, *alone.*

Smirnov. Well, what price that! "In no fit state!" Her husband died seven months ago, if you please! Now have I got my interest to pay or not? I want a straight answer—yes or no? All right, your husband's dead, you're in no fit state and so on and so forth, and your blasted manager's hopped it. But what am I supposed to do? Fly away from my creditors by balloon, I take it! Or go and bash the old brain box against a brick wall? I call on Gruzdev—not at home. Yaroshevich is in hiding. I have a real old slanging match with Kuritsyn and almost chuck him out of the window. Mazutov has the bellyache, and this creature's "in no fit state." Not one of the swine will pay. This is what comes of being too nice to them and behaving like some sniveling no-hoper or old woman. It doesn't pay to wear kid gloves with this lot! All right, just you wait—I'll give you something to remember me by! You don't make a monkey out of me, blast you! I'm staying here—going to stick around till she coughs up. Pah! I feel well and truly riled today. I'm shaking like a leaf, I'm so furious—choking I am. Phew, my God, I really think I'm going to pass out! (*shouts*) Hey, you there!

Scene 6

SMIRNOV *and* LUKE.

Luke (*comes in*). What is it?
Smirnov. Bring me some kvass or water, will you?

[LUKE *goes out.*]

Smirnov. What a mentality, though! You need money so bad you could shoot yourself, but she won't pay, being "in no fit state to discuss money," if you please! There's female logic for you and no mistake! That's why I don't like talking to women. Never have. Talk to a woman—why, I'd rather sit on top of a powder magazine! Pah! It makes my flesh creep, I'm so fed up with her, her and that great trailing dress! Poetic creatures they call 'em! Why, the very sight of one gives me cramp in both legs, I get so aggravated.

Scene 7

SMIRNOV *and* LUKE.

Luke (*comes in and serves some water*). Madam's unwell and won't see anyone.
Smirnov. You clear out!

[LUKE *goes out.*]

Smirnov. "Unwell and won't see anyone." All right then, don't! I'm staying put, chum, and I don't budge one inch till you unbelt. Be ill for a week, and I'll stay a week; make it a year, and a year I'll stay. I'll have my rights, lady! As for your black dress and dimples, you don't catch me that way—we know all about those dimples! (*Shouts through the window*) Unhitch, Simon; we're here for some time—I'm staying put. Tell the stable people to give my horses oats. And you've got that animal tangled in the reins again, you great oaf! (*Imitates him*) "I don't care." I'll give you don't care! (*Moves away from the window*) How ghastly—it's unbearably hot, no one will pay up, I had a bad night, and now here's this female with her long black dress and her states. I've got a headache. How about a glass of vodka? That might be an idea. (*Shouts*) Hey, you there!
Luke (*comes in*). What is it?
Smirnov. Bring me a glass of vodka.

[LUKE *goes out.*]

Smirnov. Phew! (*Sits down and looks himself over*) A fine specimen I am, I must say—dust all over me, my boots dirty, unwashed, hair unbrushed, straw on my waistcoat. I bet the little woman took me for a burglar. (*Yawns*) It's not exactly polite to turn up in a drawing room in this rig! Well, anyway, I'm not a guest here; I'm collecting money. And there's no such thing as correct wear for the well-dressed creditor.

Luke (*comes in and gives him the vodka*). This is a liberty, sir.

Smirnov (*angrily*). What!

Luke. I, er, it's all right, I just——

Smirnov. Who do you think you're talking to? You hold your tongue!

Luke (*aside*). Now we'll never get rid of him, botheration take it! It's an ill wind brought him along. (LUKE *goes out.*)

Smirnov. Oh, I'm so furious! I could pulverize the whole world, I'm in such a rage. I feel quite ill. (*Shouts*) Hey, you there!

Scene 8

MRS. POPOV *and* SMIRNOV.

Mrs. Popov (*comes in, with downcast eyes*). Sir, in my solitude I have grown unaccustomed to the sound of human speech, and I can't stand shouting. I must urgently request you not to disturb my peace.

Smirnov. Pay up and I'll go.

Mrs. Popov. As I've already stated quite plainly, I've no ready cash. Wait till the day after tomorrow.

Smirnov. I've also had the honor of stating quite plainly that I need the money today, not the day after tomorrow. If you won't pay up now, I'll have to put my head in a gas oven tomorrow.

Mrs. Popov. Can I help it if I've no cash in hand? This is all rather odd.

Smirnov. So you won't pay up now, eh?

Mrs. Popov. I can't.

Smirnov. In that case I'm not budging; I'll stick around here till I do get my money. (*Sits down*) You'll pay the day after tomorrow, you say? Very well, then I'll sit here like this till the day after tomorrow. I'll just stay put exactly as I am. (*Jumps up*) I ask you—have I got that interest to pay tomorrow or haven't I? Think I'm trying to be funny, do you?

Mrs. Popov. Kindly don't raise your voice at me, sir—we're not in the stables.

Smirnov. I'm not discussing stables; I'm asking whether my interest falls due tomorrow. Yes or no?

Mrs. Popov. You don't know how to treat a lady.

Smirnov. Oh yes I do.

Mrs. Popov. Oh no you don't. You're a rude, ill-bred person. Nice men don't talk to ladies like that.

Smirnov. Now, this *is* a surprise! How do you want me to talk then? In French, I suppose? (*In an angry, simpering voice*) *Madame, je voo pree.* You won't pay me—how perfectly delightful. Oh, *pardong*, I'm sure—sorry you were troubled! Now isn't the weather divine today? And that black dress looks too, too charming! (*Bows and scrapes*)

Mrs. Popov. That's silly. And not very clever.

Smirnov (*mimics her*). "Silly, not very clever." I don't know how to treat a lady, don't I? Madam, I've seen more women in my time than you have house sparrows. I've fought three duels over women. There have been twenty-one women in my life. Twelve times it was me broke it off; the other nine got in first. Oh yes! Time was I made an ass of myself, slobbered, mooned around, bowed and scraped and practically crawled on my belly. I loved; I suffered; I sighed at the moon; I languished; I melted; I grew cold. I loved passionately, madly, in every conceivable fashion, damn me, burbling nineteen to the dozen about women's emancipation and wasting half my substance on the tender passion. But now—no thank you very much! I can't be fooled anymore; I've had enough. Black eyes, passionate looks, crimson lips, dimpled cheeks, moonlight, "Whispers, passion's bated breathing"—I don't give a tinker's cuss for the lot now, lady. Present company excepted, all women, large or small, are simpering, mincing, gossipy creatures. They're great haters. They're eyebrow deep in lies. They're futile; they're trivial; they're cruel; they're outrageously illogical. And as for having anything upstairs (*taps his forehead*)—I'm sorry to be so blunt, but the very birds in the trees can run rings round your average bluestocking. Take any one of these poetical creations. Oh, she's all froth and fluff, she is; she's half divine; she sends you into a million raptures. But you take a peep inside her mind, and what do you see? A common or garden crocodile! (*Clutches the back of a chair, which cracks and breaks*) And yet this crocodile somehow thinks its great lifework, privilege and monopoly is the tender passion—that's what really gets me! But damn and blast it, and crucify me upside down on that wall if I'm wrong—does a woman know how to love any living creature apart from lap dogs? Her love gets no further than sniveling and slobbering. The man suffers and makes sacrifices, while she just twitches the train of her dress and tries to get him squirming under her thumb; that's what her love adds up to! You must know what women are like, seeing you've the rotten luck to be one. Tell me frankly, did you ever see a sincere, faithful, true woman? You know you didn't. Only the old and ugly ones are true and faithful. You'll never find a constant woman, not in a month of Sundays you won't, not once in a blue moon!

Mrs. Popov. Well, I like that! Then who is true and faithful in love to your way of thinking? Not men by any chance?

Smirnov. Yes, madam. Men.

Mrs. Popov. *Men!* (*Gives a bitter laugh*) Men true and faithful in love! That's rich, I must say. (*Vehemently*) What right have you to talk like that? Men true and faithful! If it comes to that, the best man I've ever known was my late husband, I may say. I loved him passionately, with all my heart as only an intelligent young woman can. I gave him my youth, my happiness, my life, my possessions. I lived only for him. I worshiped him as an idol. And—what do you think? This best of men was shamelessly deceiving me all along the line! After his death I found a drawer in his desk full of love letters, and when he was alive—oh, what a frightful memory!—he used to leave me on my own for weeks on end, he carried on with other girls before my very eyes, he was unfaithful to me, he spent my money like water, and he joked about my feelings for him. But I loved him all the same, and I've been faithful to him. What's more, I'm still faithful and true now that he's dead. I've buried myself alive inside these four walls, and I shall go round in these widow's weeds till my dying day.

Smirnov (*with a contemptuous laugh*). Widow's weeds! Who do you take me for? As if I didn't know why you wear this fancy dress and bury yourself indoors! Why, it sticks out a mile! Mysterious and romantic, isn't it? Some army cadet or hack poet may pass by your garden, look up at your windows and think: "There dwells Tamara, the mysterious princess, the one who buried herself alive from love of her husband." Who do you think you're fooling?

Mrs. Popov (*flaring up*). *What!* You dare to take that line with me!

Smirnov. Buries herself alive—but doesn't forget to powder her nose!

Mrs. Popov. You dare adopt that tone!

Smirnov. Don't you raise your voice to me, madam; I'm not one of your servants. Let me call a spade a spade. Not being a woman, I'm used to saying what I think. So stop shouting, pray.

Mrs. Popov. It's you who are shouting, not me. Leave me alone, would you mind?

Smirnov. Pay up, and I'll go.

Mrs. Popov. You'll get nothing out of me.

Smirnov. Oh yes I shall.

Mrs. Popov. Just to be awkward, you won't get one single kopeck. And you can leave me alone.

Smirnov. Not having the pleasure of being your husband or fiancé, I'll trouble you not to make a scene. (*Sits down*) I don't like it.

Mrs. Popov (*choking with rage*). Do I see you sitting down?

Smirnov. You most certainly do.

Mrs. Popov. Would you mind leaving?

Smirnov. Give me my money. (*Aside*) Oh, I'm in such a rage! Furious I am!

Mrs. Popov. I've no desire to bandy words with cads, sir. Kindly clear off! (*Pause*) Well, are you going or aren't you?

Smirnov. No.
Mrs. Popov. No?
Smirnov. No!
Mrs. Popov. Very well then! (*rings*)

Scene 9

The above and LUKE.

Mrs. Popov. Show this gentleman out, Luke.
Luke (*goes up to* SMIRNOV). Be so good as to leave, sir, when you're told, sir. No point in——
Smirnov (*jumping up*). You hold your tongue! Who do you think you're talking to? I'll carve you up in little pieces.
Luke (*clutching at his heart*). Heavens and saints above us! (*Falls into an armchair*) Oh, I feel something terrible—fair took my breath away, it did.
Mrs. Popov. But where's Dasha? Dasha! (*Shouts*) Dasha! Pelegeya! Dasha! (*Rings*)
Luke. Oh, they've all gone fruit picking. There's no one in the house. I feel faint. Fetch water.
Mrs. Popov. Be so good as to clear out!
Smirnov. Couldn't you be a bit more polite?
Mrs. Popov (*clenching her fists and stamping*). You uncouth oaf! You have the manners of a bear! Think you own the place? Monster!
Smirnov. What! You say that again!
Mrs. Popov. I called you an ill-mannered oaf, a monster!
Smirnov (*advancing on her*). Look here, what right have you to insult me?
Mrs. Popov. All right, I'm insulting you. So what? Think I'm afraid of you?
Smirnov. Just because you look all romantic, you can get away with anything—is that your idea? This is dueling talk!
Luke. Heavens and saints above us! Water!
Smirnov. Pistols at dawn!

Mrs. Popov. Just because you have big fists and the lungs of an ox, you needn't think I'm scared, see? Think you own the place, don't you!

Smirnov. We'll shoot it out! No one calls me names and gets away with it, weaker sex or no weaker sex.

Mrs. Popov (*trying to shout him down*). You coarse lout!

Smirnov. Why should it only be us men who answer for our insults? It's high time we dropped that silly idea. If women want equality, let them damn well have equality! I challenge you, madam!

Mrs. Popov. Want to shoot it out, eh? Very well.

Smirnov. This very instant!

Mrs. Popov. Most certainly! My husband left some pistols; I'll fetch them instantly. (*Moves hurriedly off and comes back*) I'll enjoy putting a bullet through that thick skull, damn your infernal cheek! (*Goes out*)

Smirnov. I'll pot her like a sitting bird. I'm not one of your sentimental young puppies. She'll get no chivalry from me!

Luke. Kind sir! (*Kneels*) Grant me a favor; pity an old man and leave this place. First you frighten us out of our wits; now you want to fight a duel.

Smirnov (*not listening*). A duel! There's true women's emancipation for you! That evens up the sexes with a vengeance! I'll knock her off as a matter of principle. But what a woman! (*Mimics her*) "Damn your infernal cheek! I'll put a bullet through that thick skull." Not bad, eh? Flushed all over, flashing eyes, accepts my challenge! You know, I've never seen such a woman in my life.

Luke. Go away, sir, and I'll say prayers for you till the day I die.

Smirnov. There's a regular woman for you, something I do appreciate! A proper woman—not some namby-pamby, wishy-washy female, but a really red-hot bit of stuff, a regular pistol-packing little spitfire. A pity to kill her, really.

Luke (*weeps*). Kind sir—do leave. Please!

Smirnov. I definitely like her. Definitely! Never mind her dimples; I like her. I wouldn't mind letting her off what she owes me, actually. And I don't feel angry anymore. Wonderful woman!

Scene 10

The above and MRS. POPOV.

Mrs. Popov (*comes in with the pistols*). Here are the pistols. But before we start would you mind showing me how to fire them? I've never had a pistol in my hands before.

Luke. Lord help us! Mercy on us! I'll go and find the gardener and coachman. What have we done to deserve this? (*Goes out*)

Smirnov (*examining the pistols*). Now, there are several types of pistol. There are Mortimer's special dueling pistols with percussion caps. Now, yours here are Smith and Wessons, triple action with extractor, center fired. They're fine weapons, worth a cool ninety rubles the pair. Now, you hold a revolver like this. (*Aside*) What eyes, what eyes! She's hot stuff all right.

Mrs. Popov. Like this?

Smirnov. Yes, that's right. Then you raise the hammer and take aim like this. Hold your head back a bit; stretch your arm out properly. Right. And then with this finger you press this little gadget; and that's it. But the great thing is—don't get excited, and do take your time about aiming. Try and see your hand doesn't shake.

Mrs. Popov. All right. We can't very well shoot indoors; let's go in the garden.

Smirnov. Very well. But I warn you, I'm firing in the air.

Mrs. Popov. Oh, this is the limit! Why?

Smirnov. Because, because—— That's my business.

Mrs. Popov. Got cold feet, eh? I see. Now don't shilly-shally, sir. Kindly follow me. I shan't rest till I've put a bullet through your brains, damn you. Got the wind up, have you?

Smirnov. Yes.

Mrs. Popov. That's a lie. Why won't you fight?

Smirnov. Because, er, because you, er, I like you.

Mrs. Popov (*with a vicious laugh*). He likes me! He dares to say he likes me! (*Points to the door*) I won't detain you.

Smirnov (*puts down the revolver without speaking, picks up his peaked cap, and moves off; near the door he stops, and for about half* *a minute the two look at each other without speaking; then he speaks, going up to her hesitantly).* Listen. Are you still angry? I'm absolutely furious myself, but you must see—how can I put it? The fact is that, er, it's this way, actually—— (*Shouts*) Anyway, can I help it if I like you? (*Clutches the back of a chair, which cracks and breaks*) Damn fragile stuff, furniture! I like you! Do you understand? I, er, I'm almost in love.

Mrs. Popov. Keep away from me; I loathe you.

Smirnov. God, what a woman! Never saw the like of it in all my born days. I'm sunk! Without trace! Trapped like a mouse!

Mrs. Popov. Get back or I shoot.

Smirnov. Shoot away. I'd die happily with those marvelous eyes looking at me; that's what you can't see—die by that dear little velvet hand. Oh, I'm crazy! Think it over and make your mind up now, because once I leave this place we shan't see each other again. So make your mind up. I'm a gentleman and a man of honor, I've ten thousand a year, I can put a bullet through a coin in midair and I keep a good stable. Be my wife.

Mrs. Popov (*indignantly brandishes the revolver*). A duel! We'll shoot it out!

Smirnov. I'm out of my mind! Nothing makes any sense. (*Shouts*). Hey, you there—water!

Mrs. Popov (*shouts*). We'll shoot it out!

Smirnov. I've lost my head, fallen for her like some damfool boy! (*Clutches her hand. She shrieks with pain.*) I love you! (*Kneels*) I love you as I never loved any of my twenty-one other women—twelve times it was me broke it off; the other nine got in first. But I never loved anyone as much as you. I've gone all sloppy, soft and sentimental. Kneeling like an imbecile, offering my hand! Disgraceful! Scandalous! I haven't been in love for five years, I swore not to, and here I am crashing head over heels, hook, line, and sinker! I offer you my hand. Take it or leave it. (*Gets up and hurries to the door*)

Mrs. Popov. Just a moment.

Smirnov (*stops*). What is it?

Mrs. Popov. Oh, never mind, just go away. But wait. No, go, go away. I hate you. Or no—don't go away. Oh, if you knew

how furious I am! (*Throws the revolver on the table*) My fingers
are numb from holding this beastly thing. (*Tears a handkerchief
in her anger*) Why are you hanging about? Clear out!
Smirnov. Goodbye.
Mrs. Popov. Yes, yes, go away! (*Shouts*) Where are you going?
Stop. Oh, go away then. I'm so furious! Don't you come near
me, I tell you.
Smirnov (*going up to her*). I'm so fed up with myself! Falling
in love like a schoolboy! Kneeling down! It's enough to give
you the willies! (*Rudely*) I love you! Oh, it's just what the doctor ordered, this is! There's my interest due in tomorrow, hay
making's upon us—and *you* have to come along! (*Takes her by
the waist*) I'll never forgive myself.
Mrs. Popov. Go away! You take your hands off me! I, er, hate
you! We'll sh-shoot it out!

[*A prolonged kiss.*]

Scene 11

The above, LUKE *with an ax, the gardener with a rake, the coachman
with a pitchfork, and some workmen with sundry sticks and staves.*

Luke (*seeing the couple kissing*). Mercy on us! (*Pause*)
Mrs. Popov (*lowering her eyes*). Luke, tell them in the stables—
Toby gets no oats today.

CURTAIN

Translated by Ronald Hingley

Lucille Fletcher
(1912–2000)

Lucille Fletcher was a master of suspense and dramatic surprises. Her plays and novels, as well as the movies based on her work, still keep audiences holding their breath, guessing—and fearing—what will happen next.

Fletcher was born in Brooklyn, the daughter of a marine draftsman and his wife. In 1933, at the height of the Great Depression, she graduated from Vassar College. For the next five years she worked for CBS radio as a music librarian, a copyright clerk, and a publicity writer. In 1939, she married Bernard Herrmann (1911–1975), who would become enormously successful as a composer of soundtracks for such movies as Alfred Hitchcock's *Vertigo* (1958) and *Psycho* (1960). In 1934, the same year Fletcher was hired, Herrmann joined CBS as conductor of the CBS Symphony Orchestra and as a composer of soundtracks for weekly radio adaptations of literary works. In 1949, after Herrmann and Fletcher divorced, she married John Douglass Wallop III, a writer.

When Fletcher began a serious writing career, she focused on radio drama, a medium whose techniques she knew well from her years at CBS. Unlike drama on television, radio drama depends solely on dialogue, sound effects, and music; setting, action, and the way the characters look and dress are left entirely to the audience's imagination. In 1940, *My Client Curley*, the first of Fletcher's radio plays, was broadcast, followed in 1941 by her popular suspense drama *Hitchhiker*. Weekly drama-suspense series kept faithful listeners glued to their radios. Fletcher wrote for all the popular shows—*Suspense*, *The Mercury Theatre on the Air*, *Lights Out*, and *Chrysler Theatre*. Many of her radio plays were transformed into movies, novels, and television plays.

Sorry, Wrong Number was first broadcast in 1943, with Agnes Moorehead (1900–1974, known to TV audiences mainly as Endora on *Bewitched*) as Mrs. Stevenson. Barbara Stanwyck (1907–1990) played Mrs. Stevenson with a riveting, Academy Award–nominated performance in the 1948 movie version, which also starred Burt Lancaster and Wendell Corey. In 1948, Fletcher also adapted her radio play for television. The following year, she collaborated with Allan Ullman to publish *Sorry, Wrong Number* as a novel. The latest incarnation of *Sorry, Wrong Number* is a one-act opera, with music by the American composer Jack Beeson and lyrics by Sheldon Harnick. In May 1999, the opera premiered at the Hunter College Playhouse in New York City. Stephen King, the popular horror-suspense writer, has written a fantasy that pays homage to Fletcher's famous play; he calls it *Sorry, Right Number*.

The one-act adaptation used here has additions made by the author for the stage, which are placed in brackets and labeled "SCENE."

Sorry, Wrong Number
Lucille Fletcher

Characters

Mrs. Stevenson	5th Operator
1st Operator	Information
1st Man	Hospital Receptionist
2nd Man (George)	Western Union
Chief Operator	Sergeant Duffy
2nd Operator	A Lunch Room Counter
3rd Operator	Attendant
4th Operator	

[SCENE: *As curtain rises, we see a divided stage, only the center part of which is lighted and furnished as* MRS. STEVENSON's *bedroom. Expensive, rather fussy furnishings. A large bed, on which* MRS. STEVENSON, *clad in bed jacket, is lying. A night table close by, with phone, lighted lamp, and pill bottles. A mantel, with clock, right. A closed door, right. A window, with curtains closed, rear. The set is lit by one lamp on night table. It is enclosed by three flats. Beyond this central set, the stage, on either side, is in darkness.*

MRS. STEVENSON *is dialing a number on phone as curtain rises. She listens to phone, slams down receiver in irritation. As she does so, we hear sound of a train roaring by in the distance. She reaches for her pill bottle, pours herself a glass of water, shakes out pill, swallows it, then reaches for phone again, dials number nervously.*]
SOUND: *Number being dialed on phone: busy signal.*

Mrs. Stevenson (*a querulous, self-centered neurotic*). Oh—dear! (*Slams down receiver. Dials operator*)

117

[SCENE: *A spotlight, left of side flat, picks up out of peripheral darkness figure of* 1ST OPERATOR, *sitting with headphones at small table. If spotlight not available, use flashlight, clicked on by* 1ST OPERATOR, *illumining her face.*]

Operator. Your call, please?

Mrs. Stevenson. Operator? I've been dialing Murray Hill 4-0098 now for the last three quarters of an hour, and the line is always busy. But I don't see how it *could* be busy that long. Will you try it for me, please?

Operator. Murray Hill 4-0098? One moment, please. [SCENE: *She makes gesture of plugging in call through a switchboard.*]

Mrs. Stevenson. I don't see how it could be busy all this time. It's my husband's office. He's working late tonight, and I'm all alone here in the house. My health is very poor—and I've been feeling so nervous all day. . . .

Operator. Ringing Murray Hill 4-0098. . . . (SOUND: *Phone buzz. It rings three times. Receiver is picked up at other end.*)

[SCENE: *Spotlight picks up figure of a heavyset man, seated at desk with phone on right side of dark periphery of stage. He is wearing a hat. Picks up phone, which rings three times*]

Man. Hello.

Mrs. Stevenson. Hello . . . ? (*A little puzzled*) Hello. Is Mr. Stevenson there?

Man (*into phone, as though he had not heard*). Hello. . . . (*Louder*) Hello.

[SCENE: *Spotlight on left now moves from* OPERATOR *to another man,* GEORGE. *A killer type, also wearing hat, but standing as in a phone booth. A three-sided screen may be used to suggest this.*]

2nd Man (*slow, heavy quality, faintly foreign accent*). Hello.

1st Man. Hello. George?

George. Yes, sir.

Mrs. Stevenson (*louder and more imperious, to phone*). Hello. Who's this? What number am I calling, please?

1st Man. We have heard from our client. He says the coast is clear for tonight.

George. Yes, sir.

1st Man. Where are you now?

George. In a phone booth.

1st Man. OK. You know the address. At eleven o'clock the private patrolman goes around to the bar on Second Avenue for a beer. Be sure that all the lights downstairs are out. There should be only one light visible from the street. At eleven-fifteen a subway train crosses the bridge. It makes a noise in case her window is open and she should scream.

Mrs. Stevenson (*shocked*). Oh—HELLO! What number is this, please?

George. OK. I understand.

1st Man. Make it quick. As little blood as possible. Our client does not wish to make her suffer long.

George. A knife OK, sir?

1st Man. Yes. A knife will be OK. And remember—remove the rings and bracelets and the jewelry in the bureau drawer. Our client wishes it to look like simple robbery.

George. OK—I get—— [SCENE: *Spotlight suddenly goes out on* GEORGE.] (SOUND: *A bland buzzing signal*)

[SCENE: *Spotlight goes off on* 1ST MAN.]

Mrs. Stevenson (*clicking phone*). Oh . . . ! (*Bland buzzing signal continues. She hangs up.*) How awful! How unspeakably . . . [SCENE: *She lies back on her pillow, overcome for a few seconds, then suddenly pulls herself together, reaches for phone.*] (SOUND: *Dialing. Phone buzz*)

[SCENE: *Spotlight goes on at* 1ST OPERATOR's *switchboard.* 1ST *and* 2ND MAN *exit as unobtrusively as possible in darkness.*]

Operator. Your call, please?

Mrs. Stevenson. (*unnerved and breathless, into phone*). Operator. I—I've just been cut off.

Operator. I'm sorry, madam. What number were you calling?

Mrs. Stevenson. Why—it was supposed to be Murray Hill 4-0098, but it wasn't. Some wires must have crossed—I was cut into a wrong number—and—I've just heard the most dreadful thing—a—a murder—and—— (*Imperiously*) Operator, you'll simply have to retrace that call at once.

Operator. I beg your pardon, madam—I don't quite——

Mrs. Stevenson. Oh—I know it was a wrong number, and I had no business listening—but these two men—they were cold-blooded fiends—and they were going to murder somebody—some poor innocent woman—who was all alone—in a house near a bridge. And we've got to stop them—we've got to——

Operator (*patiently*). What number were you calling, madam?

Mrs. Stevenson. That doesn't matter. This was a *wrong* number. And *you* dialed it. And we've got to find out what it was—immediately!

Operator. But—madam——

Mrs. Stevenson. Oh—why are you so stupid? Look—it was obviously a case of some little slip of the finger. I told you to try Murray Hill 4-0098 for me—you dialed it—but your finger must have slipped—and I was connected with some other number—and I could hear them, but they couldn't hear me. Now, I simply fail to see why you couldn't make that same mistake again—on purpose—why you couldn't *try* to dial Murray Hill 4-0098 in the same careless sort of way. . . .

Operator (*quickly*). Murray Hill 4-0098? I will try to get it for you, madam.

Mrs. Stevenson (*sarcastically*). *Thank* you. [SCENE: *She bridles, adjusts herself on her pillows, reaches for handkerchief, wipes forehead, glancing uneasily for a moment toward window, while still holding phone.*] (*Sound of ringing: busy signal*)

Operator. I am sorry. Murray Hill 4-0098 is busy.

Mrs. Stevenson (*frantically clicking receiver*). Operator. Operator.

Operator. Yes, madam.

Mrs. Stevenson (*angrily*). You *didn't* try to get that wrong number at all. I asked explicitly. And all you did was dial correctly.

Operator. I am sorry. What number were you calling?

Mrs. Stevenson. Can't you, for once, forget what number I was calling and do something specific? Now I want to trace that call. It's my civic duty—it's *your* civic duty—to trace that call . . . and to apprehend those dangerous killers—and if *you* won't . . .

Operator [SCENE: *Glancing around wearily*]. I will connect you with the chief operator.

Mrs. Stevenson. *Please!* (*Sound of ringing*)

[SCENE: OPERATOR *puts hand over mouthpiece of phone, gestures into darkness. A half whisper*]

[SCENE: **Operator.** Miss Curtis. Will you pick up on 17, please?

[MISS CURTIS, *chief operator, enters. Middle-aged, efficient type, pleasant. Wearing headphones*]

Miss Curtis. Yes, dear. What's the trouble?

Operator. Somebody wanting a call traced. I can't make head nor tail of it. . . .

Miss Curtis (*sitting down at desk as* OPERATOR *gets up*). Sure, dear. 17? (*She makes gesture of plugging in her headphone.*)]

Chief Operator (*coolly and professionally*). This is the chief operator.

Mrs. Stevenson. Chief operator? I want you to trace a call. A telephone call. Immediately. I don't know where it came from, or who was making it, but it's absolutely necessary that it be tracked down. Because it was about a murder. Yes, a terrible, cold-blooded murder of a poor innocent woman—tonight—at eleven-fifteen.

Chief Operator. I see.

Mrs. Stevenson (*high-strung, demanding*). Can you trace it for me? Can you track down those men?

Chief Operator. It depends, madam.

Mrs. Stevenson. Depends on what?

Chief Operator. It depends on whether the call is still going on. If it's a live call, we can trace it on the equipment. If it's been disconnected, we can't.

Mrs. Stevenson. Disconnected?

Chief Operator. If the parties have stopped talking to each other.

Mrs. Stevenson. Oh—but—but of course they must have stopped talking to each other by *now*. That was at least five minutes ago—and they didn't sound like the type who would make a long call.

Chief Operator. Well, I can try tracing it. [SCENE: *She takes pencil out of her hairdo.*] Now—what is your name, madam?

Mrs. Stevenson. Mrs. Stevenson. Mrs. Elbert Stevenson. But—listen——

Chief Operator [SCENE: *writing it down*]. And your telephone number?

Mrs. Stevenson (*more irritated*). Plaza 4-2295. But if you go on wasting all this time—— [SCENE: *She glances at clock on mantel.*]

Chief Operator. And what is your reason for wanting this call traced?

Mrs. Stevenson. My reason? Well—for heaven's sake—isn't it obvious? I overhear two men—they're killers—they're planning to murder this woman—it's a matter for the police.

Chief Operator. Have you told the police?

Mrs. Stevenson. No. How could I?

Chief Operator. You're making this check into a private call purely as a private individual?

Mrs. Stevenson. Yes. But meanwhile——

Chief Operator. Well, Mrs. Stevenson—I seriously doubt whether we could make this check for you at this time just on your say-so as a private individual. We'd have to have something more official.

Mrs. Stevenson. Oh—for heaven's sake! You mean to tell me I can't report a murder without getting tied up in all this red tape? Why—it's perfectly idiotic. All right, then. I *will* call the police. (*She slams down receiver.*)

[SCENE: *Spotlight goes off on two* OPERATORS.]

Ridiculous! (*Sound of dialing*)

[SCENE: MRS. STEVENSON *dials number on phone as two* OPERATORS *exit unobtrusively in darkness.* (*On right of stage, spotlight picks up a* 2ND OPERATOR, *seated like first, with headphones at table* [*same one vacated by* 1ST MAN].)]

2nd Operator. Your call, please?
Mrs. Stevenson (*very annoyed*). The Police Department—*please.*
2nd Operator. Ringing the Police Department. (*Ring twice. Phone is picked up.*)

[SCENE: *Left stage, at table vacated by* 1ST *and* CHIEF OPERATOR, *spotlight now picks up* SERGEANT DUFFY, *seated in a relaxed position. Just entering beside him is a young man in cap and apron, carrying a large brown paper parcel, delivery boy for a local lunch counter. Phone is ringing.*]

[SCENE: **Young Man.** Here's your lunch, Sarge. They didn't have no jelly doughnuts, so I give you French crullers. OK, Sarge?
Sgt. Duffy. French crullers. I got ulcers. Whyn't you make it apple pie? (*Picks up phone, which has rung twice*)]
Duffy. Police Department. Precinct 43. Duffy speaking.
[SCENE: **Lunchroom Attendant** (*anxiously*). We don't have no apple pie, either, Sarge——]
Mrs. Stevenson. Police Department? Oh. This is Mrs. Stevenson—Mrs. Elbert Smythe Stevenson of 53 North Sutton Place. I'm calling up to report a murder.

[SCENE: DUFFY *has been examining lunch but double-takes suddenly on above.*]

Duffy. Eh?
Mrs. Stevenson. I mean—the murder hasn't been committed yet. I just overheard plans for it over the telephone . . . over a wrong number that the operator gave me.

[SCENE: DUFFY *relaxes, sighs, starts taking lunch from bag.*]

I've been trying to trace down the call myself, but everybody is so stupid—and I guess in the end you're the only people who could *do* anything.

Duffy (*not too impressed*). [SCENE: *pays* ATTENDANT, *who exits*]. Yes, ma'am.

Mrs. Stevenson (*trying to impress him*). It was a perfectly *definite* murder. I heard their plans distinctly.

[SCENE: DUFFY *begins to eat sandwich, phone at his ear.*]

Two men were talking, and they were going to murder some woman at eleven-fifteen tonight—she lived in a house near a bridge.

Duffy. Yes, ma'am.

Mrs. Stevenson. And there was a private patrolman on the street. He was going to go around for a beer on Second Avenue. And there was some third man—a client, who was paying to have this poor woman murdered—they were going to take her rings and bracelets—and use a knife . . . well, it's unnerved me dreadfully—and I'm not well. . . .

Duffy. I see. [SCENE: *Having finished sandwich, he wipes mouth with paper napkin.*] When was all this, ma'am?

Mrs. Stevenson. About eight minutes ago. Oh . . . (*Relieved*) then you *can* do something? You *do* understand——

Duffy. And what is your name, ma'am? [SCENE: *He reaches for pad.*]

Mrs. Stevenson (*impatiently*). Mrs. Stevenson. Mrs. Elbert Stevenson.

Duffy. And your address?

Mrs. Stevenson. 53 North Sutton Place. *That's* near a bridge. The Queensboro Bridge, you know—and *we* have a private patrolman on *our* street—and Second Avenue——

Duffy. And what was that number you were calling?

Mrs. Stevenson. Murray Hill 4-0098.

[SCENE: DUFFY *writes it down.*]

But—that wasn't the number I overheard. I mean Murray Hill 4-0098 is my husband's office.

[SCENE: DUFFY, *in exasperation, holds pencil poised.*]

He's working late tonight, and I was trying to reach him to ask him to come home. I'm an invalid, you know—and it's the maid's night off—and I *hate* to be alone—even though he says I'm perfectly safe as long as I have the telephone right beside my bed.
Duffy (*stolidly*). [SCENE: *he has put pencil down, pushes pad away*]. Well—we'll look into it, Mrs. Stevenson—and see if we can check it with the telephone company.
Mrs. Stevenson (*getting impatient*). But the telephone company said they couldn't check the call if the parties had stopped talking. I've already taken care of *that*.
Duffy. Oh—yes? [SCENE: *He yawns slightly.*]
Mrs. Stevenson (*highhanded*). Personally, I feel you ought to do something far more immediate and drastic than just check the call. What good does checking the call do if they've stopped talking? By the time you track it down, they'll already have committed the murder.
Duffy [SCENE: *he reaches for paper cup of coffee*]. Well—we'll take care of it, lady. Don't worry. [SCENE: *He begins to take off paper top of coffee container.*]
Mrs. Stevenson. I'd say the whole thing calls for a search—a complete and thorough search of the whole city.

[SCENE: DUFFY *puts down phone for a moment, to work on cap, as her voice continues.*]

I'm very near a bridge, and I'm not far from Second Avenue. And I know *I'd* feel a whole lot better if you sent around a radio car to *this* neighborhood at once.
Duffy [SCENE: *picks up phone again, drinks coffee*]. And what makes you think the murder's going to be committed in your neighborhood, ma'am?
Mrs. Stevenson. Oh—I don't know. The coincidence is so horrible. Second Avenue—the patrolman—the bridge . . .

Duffy [SCENE: *he sips coffee*]. Second Avenue is a very long street, ma'am. And do you happen to know how many bridges there are in the city of New York alone? Not to mention Brooklyn, Staten Island, Queens, and the Bronx? And how do you know there isn't some little house out on Staten Island—on some little Second Avenue you've never heard about? [SCENE: *A long gulp of coffee*] How do you know they were even talking about New York at all?

Mrs. Stevenson. But I heard the call on the New York dialing system.

Duffy. How do you know it wasn't a long-distance call you overheard? Telephones are funny things. [SCENE: *He sets down coffee.*] Look, lady, why don't you look at it this way? Supposing you hadn't broken in on that telephone call? Supposing you'd got your husband the way you always do? Would this murder have made any difference to you then?

Mrs. Stevenson. I suppose not. But it's so inhuman—so cold-blooded . . .

Duffy. A lot of murders are committed in this city every day, ma'am. If we could do something to stop 'em, we would. But a clue of this kind that's so vague isn't much more use to us than no clue at all.

Mrs. Stevenson. But surely——

Duffy. Unless, of course, you have some reason for thinking this call is phony—and that someone may be planning to murder *you*?

Mrs. Stevenson. *Me*? Oh—no—I hardly think so. I—I mean—why should anybody? I'm alone all day and night—I see nobody except my maid Eloise—she's a big two-hundred-pounder—she's too lazy to bring up my breakfast tray—and the only other person is my husband Elbert—he's crazy about me—adores me—waits on me hand and foot—he's scarcely left my side since I took sick twelve years ago——

Duffy. Well—then—there's nothing for you to worry about, is there?

[SCENE: LUNCH COUNTER ATTENDANT *has entered. He is carrying a piece of apple pie on a plate. Points it out to* DUFFY *triumphantly*]

And now—if you'll just leave the rest of this to us——

Mrs. Stevenson. But what will you *do*? It's so late—it's nearly eleven o'clock.

Duffy (*firmly*). [SCENE: *he nods to* ATTENDANT, *pleased*]. We'll take care of it, lady.

Mrs. Stevenson. Will you broadcast it all over the city? And send out squads? And warn your radio cars to watch out—especially in suspicious neighborhoods like mine?

[SCENE: ATTENDANT, *in triumph, has put pie down in front of* DUFFY. *Takes fork out of his pocket, stands at attention, waiting*]

Duffy (*more firmly*). Lady, I *said* we'd take care of it. [SCENE: *Glances at pie*] Just now I've got a couple of other matters here on my desk that require my immediate——

Mrs. Stevenson. Oh! (*She slams down receiver hard.*) Idiot.

[SCENE: DUFFY, *listening at phone, hangs up. Shrugs. Winks at* ATTENDANT *as though to say,* "What a crazy character!" *Attacks his pie as spotlight on him fades out*]

[SCENE: MRS. STEVENSON, *in bed, looking at phone nervously*] Now—why did I do that? Now—he'll think I *am* a fool. [SCENE: *She sits there tensely, then throws herself back against pillows, lies there a moment, whimpering with self-pity.*] Oh—why doesn't Elbert come home? *Why* doesn't he? [SCENE: *We hear sound of train roaring by in the distance. She sits up, reaching for phone.*] (*Sound of dialing operator*)

[SCENE: *Spotlight picks up* 2ND OPERATOR, *seated right.*]

Operator. Your call, please?

Mrs. Stevenson. Operator—for heaven's sake—will you ring that Murray Hill 4-0098 number again? I can't think what's keeping him so long.

Operator. Ringing Murray Hill 4-0098. (*Rings. Busy signal*) The line is busy. Shall I——

Mrs. Stevenson (*nastily*). I can hear it. You don't have to tell me. I know it's busy. (*Slams down receiver*)

[SCENE: *Spotlight fades off on* 2ND OPERATOR.]

[SCENE: MRS. STEVENSON *sinks back against pillows again, whimpering to herself fretfully. She glances at clock, then, turning, punches her pillows up, trying to make herself comfortable. But she isn't. Whimpers to herself as she squirms restlessly in bed*] If I could only get out of this bed for a little while. If I could get a breath of fresh air—or just lean out the window—and see the street. . . . [SCENE: *She sighs, reaches for pill bottle, shakes out a pill. As she does so*] (*The phone rings. She darts for it instantly.*) Hello. Elbert? Hello. Hello. Hello. Oh—what's the *matter* with this phone? HELLO? HELLO? (*Slams down receiver*) [SCENE: *She stares at it, tensely.*] (*The phone rings again. Once. She picks it up.*) Hello? Hello. . . . Oh—for heaven's sake—who *is* this? Hello. Hello. HELLO. (*Slams down receiver. Dials operator*)

[SCENE: *Spotlight comes on left, showing* 3RD OPERATOR, *at spot vacated by* DUFFY.]

3rd Operator. Your call, please?

Mrs. Stevenson (*very annoyed and imperious*). Hello. Operator. I don't know what's the matter with this telephone tonight, but it's positively driving me crazy. I've never seen such inefficient, miserable service. Now, look. I'm an invalid, and I'm very nervous, and I'm *not* supposed to be annoyed. But if this keeps on much longer . . .

3rd Operator (*a young, sweet type*). What seems to be the trouble, madam?

Mrs. Stevenson. Well—everything's wrong. The whole world could be murdered, for all you people care. And now—my phone keeps ringing. . . .

Operator. Yes, madam?

Mrs. Stevenson. Ringing and ringing and ringing every five seconds or so, and when I pick it up, there's no one there.

Operator. I am sorry, madam. If you will hang up, I will test it for you.

Mrs. Stevenson. I don't want you to test it for me. I want you to put through that call—whatever it is—at once.

Operator (*gently*). I am afraid that is not possible, madam.

Mrs. Stevenson (*storming*). Not possible? And why—may I ask?

Operator. The system is automatic, madam. If someone is trying to dial your number, there is no way to check whether the call is coming through the system or not—unless the person who is trying to reach you complains to his particular operator——

Mrs. Stevenson. Well, of all the stupid, complicated . . . ! And meanwhile *I've* got to sit here in my bed, *suffering* every time that phone rings—imagining everything.

Operator. I will try to check it for you, madam.

Mrs. Stevenson. Check it! Check it! That's all anybody can do. Of all the stupid, idiotic . . . ! (*She hangs up.*) Oh—what's the use . . .

[SCENE: 3RD OPERATOR *fades out of spotlight as*]

(*Instantly* MRS. STEVENSON's *phone rings again. She picks up receiver. Wildly*) Hello. HELLO. Stop ringing, do you hear me? Answer me? What do you want? Do you realize you're driving me crazy?

[SCENE: *Spotlight goes on right. We see a* MAN *in eyeshade and shirt sleeves, at desk with phone and telegrams.*]

Stark, staring . . .

Man (*dull, flat voice*). Hello. Is this Plaza 4-2295?

Mrs. Stevenson (*catching her breath*). Yes. Yes. This is Plaza 4-2295.

Western Union. This is Western Union. I have a telegram here for Mrs. Elbert Stevenson. Is there anyone there to receive the message?

Mrs. Stevenson (*trying to calm herself*). I am Mrs. Stevenson.

Western Union (*reading flatly*). The telegram is as follows: "Mrs. Elbert Stevenson. 53 North Sutton Place, New York, New York. Darling. Terribly sorry. Tried to get you for last hour, but line busy. Leaving for Boston eleven P.M. tonight on urgent business. Back tomorrow afternoon. Keep happy. Love. Signed. Elbert."

Mrs. Stevenson (*breathlessly, aghast, to herself*). Oh . . . no . . .
Western Union. That is all, madam. Do you wish us to deliver
a copy of the message?
Mrs. Stevenson. No—no, thank you.
Western Union. Thank you, madam. Good night. (*He hangs up
phone.*) [SCENE: *Spotlight on* WESTERN UNION *immediately out*]
Mrs. Stevenson (*mechanically, to phone*). Good night. (*She hangs
up slowly. Suddenly bursting into*) No—no—it isn't true! He
couldn't do it! Not when he knows I'll be all alone. It's some
trick—some fiendish . . . [SCENE: *We hear sound of train roaring
by outside. She half rises in bed, in panic, glaring toward curtains.
Her movements are frenzied. She beats with her knuckles on bed, then
suddenly stops and reaches for phone.*] (*She dials operator.*)

[SCENE: *Spotlight picks up* 4TH OPERATOR, *seated left.*]

Operator (*coolly*). Your call, please?
Mrs. Stevenson. Operator—try that Murray Hill 4-0098 number for me just once more, please.
Operator. Ringing Murray Hill 4-0098. (*Call goes through. We
hear ringing at other end. Ring after ring*) [SCENE: *If telephone noises
are not used visually, have* OPERATOR *say after a brief pause: "They
do not answer."*]
Mrs. Stevenson. He's gone. Oh—Elbert, how could you? How
could you . . . ? (*She hangs up phone, sobbing pityingly to herself,
turning restlessly.*)

[SCENE: *Spotlight goes out on* 4TH OPERATOR.]

Mrs. Stevenson. But I can't be alone tonight. I can't. If I'm
alone one more second . . . [SCENE: *She runs hand wildly through
hair.*] I don't care what he says—or what the expense is—I'm
a sick woman—I'm entitled . . . [SCENE: *With trembling fingers,
she picks up receiver again.*] (*She dials Information.*)

[SCENE: *The spotlight picks up* INFORMATION OPERATOR, *seated right.*]

Information. This is Information.
Mrs. Stevenson. I want the telephone number of Henchley
Hospital.

Information. Henchley Hospital? Do you have the address, madam?

Mrs. Stevenson. No. It's somewhere in the 70s, though. It's a very small, private, and exclusive hospital where I had my appendix out two years ago. Henchley. H-E-N-C——

Information. One moment, please.

Mrs. Stevenson. Please—hurry. And please—what *is* the time?

Information. I do not know, madam. You may find out the time by dialing Meridian 7-1212.

Mrs. Stevenson (*irritated*). Oh—for heaven's sake! Couldn't you—?

Information. The number of Henchley Hospital is Butterfield 7-0105, madam.

Mrs. Stevenson. Butterfield 7-0105. (*She hangs up before she finishes speaking and immediately dials number as she repeats it.*)

[SCENE: *Spotlight goes out on* INFORMATION.]

[*Phone rings.*]

[SCENE: *Spotlight picks up a* WOMAN *in nurse's uniform, seated at desk, left.*]

Woman (*middle-aged, solid, firm, practical*). Henchley Hospital, good evening.

Mrs. Stevenson. Nurses' Registry.

Woman. Who was it you wished to speak to, please?

Mrs. Stevenson (*highhanded*). I want the Nurses' Registry at once. I want a trained nurse. I want to hire her immediately. For the night.

Woman. I see. And what is the nature of the case, madam?

Mrs. Stevenson. Nerves. I'm very nervous. I need soothing—and companionship. My husband is away—and I'm——

Woman. Have you been recommended to us by any doctor in particular, madam?

Mrs. Stevenson. No. But I really don't see why all this catechizing is necessary. I want a trained nurse. I was a patient in your hospital two years ago. And after all, I *do* expect to *pay* this person——

Woman. We quite understand that, madam. But registered nurses are very scarce just now—and our superintendent has asked us to send people out only on cases where the physician in charge feels it is absolutely necessary.

Mrs. Stevenson. (*growing hysterical*). Well—it *is* absolutely necessary. I'm a sick woman. I—I'm very upset. Very. I'm alone in this house—and I'm an invalid—and tonight I overheard a telephone conversation that upset me dreadfully. About a murder—a poor woman who was going to be murdered at eleven-fifteen tonight—in fact, if someone doesn't come at once—I'm afraid I'll go out of my mind. . . . (*Almost off handle by now*)

Woman. (*calmly*). I see. Well—I'll speak to Miss Phillips as soon as she comes in. And what is your name, madam?

Mrs. Stevenson. Miss Phillips. And when do you expect her in?

Woman. I really don't know, madam. She went out to supper at eleven o'clock.

Mrs. Stevenson. Eleven o'clock. But it's not eleven yet. (*She cries out.*) Oh, my clock *has* stopped. I thought it was running down. What time is it?

[SCENE: WOMAN *glances at wristwatch.*]

Woman. Just fourteen minutes past eleven. . . .

[*Sound of phone receiver being lifted on same line as* MRS. STEVENSON's. *A click*]

Mrs. Stevenson (*crying out*). What's *that*?

Woman. What was what, madam?

Mrs. Stevenson. That—that click just now—in my own telephone? As though someone had lifted the receiver off the hook of the extension phone downstairs. . . .

Woman. I didn't hear it, madam. Now—about this . . .

Mrs. Stevenson (*scared*). But I *did*. There's someone in this house. Someone downstairs in the kitchen. And they're listening to me now. They're . . . [SCENE: *She puts hand over her mouth.*] (*Hangs up phone*) [SCENE: *She sits there, in terror, frozen, listening.*] (*In a suffocated voice*) I won't pick it up. I won't let them hear me. I'll be quiet—and they'll think . . . (*With growing terror*) But if I don't call someone now—while they're still down there— there'll be no time. . . . (*She picks up receiver. Bland buzzing signal. She dials operator. Ring twice*)

[SCENE: *On second ring, spotlight goes on right. We see* 5TH OPERATOR.]

Operator (*fat and lethargic*). Your call, please?
Mrs. Stevenson (*a desperate whisper*). Operator—I—I'm in desperate trouble . . . I——
Operator. I cannot hear you, madam. Please speak louder.
Mrs. Stevenson (*still whispering*). I don't dare. I—there's someone listening. Can you hear me now?
Operator. Your call, please? What number are you calling, madam?
Mrs. Stevenson (*desperately*). You've got to hear me. Oh— please. You've got to help me. There's someone in this house. Someone who's going to murder me. And you've got to get in touch with . . . (*Click of receiver being put down in* MRS. STEVENSON's *line. Bursting out wildly*) Oh—there it is . . . he's put it down . . . he's put down the extension . . . he's coming . . . (*She screams.*) he's coming up the stairs. . . . [SCENE: *She thrashes in bed, phone cord catching in lamp wire. Lamp topples, goes out. Darkness*] (*Hoarsely*) Give me the Police Department. . . .

[SCENE: *We see on the dark center stage the shadow of door opening.*]

(*Screaming*) The police! . . .

[SCENE: *Onstage, swift rush of a shadow, advancing to bed—sound of her voice is choked out as*]

Operator. Ringing the Police Department.

[*Phone is rung. We hear sound of a train beginning to fade in. On second ring,* MRS. STEVENSON *screams again, but roaring of train drowns out her voice. For a few seconds we hear nothing but roaring of train, then dying away, phone at police headquarters ringing.*]

[SCENE: *Spotlight goes on* DUFFY, *left stage.*]

Duffy. Police Department. Precinct 43. Duffy speaking. (*Pause*)

[SCENE: *Nothing visible but darkness on center stage*]

Police Department. Duffy speaking.

[SCENE: *A flashlight goes on, illuminating open phone to one side of* MRS. STEVENSON's *bed. Nearby, hanging down, is her lifeless hand. We see the second man,* GEORGE, *in black gloves, reach down and pick up phone. He is breathing hard.*]

George. Sorry. Wrong number. (*Hangs up*)

[SCENE: *He replaces receiver on hook quietly, exits as* DUFFY *hangs up with a shrug, and curtain falls.*]

Susan Glaspell
(1882–1948)

Trifles was first performed in an unusual theater—a tiny fish house at the end of a wharf in Provincetown, Massachusetts.

Susan Glaspell and her husband, George Cram Cook (1873–1924), known as Jig, were part of a group of artists, writers, and leftist radicals from New York City who spent their summers in Provincetown, on the tip of Cape Cod. Glaspell and Cook wanted to create a new kind of theater, one that would be true to real life and real problems. They had co-written a satirical one-act play about Freudian psychology (then a relatively new subject), called *Suppressed Desires* (1915), but even the Washington Square Players, an experimental theater company in New York City's Greenwich Village, turned it down as too "esoteric." Glaspell and her husband performed their play for friends in their Village apartment instead.

In the summer of 1915, they got together with a group of Provincetown friends, several of whom had also written scripts, and put on their plays for their neighbors. For a stage they built a set in the fish house, which one of the couples in the group used as a studio. "There was a fog," Glaspell later wrote, describing one of their performances on the wharf; "the tide was in, and it washed under us and around, spraying through the holes in the floor, giving us the rhythm and the flavor of the sea."

The fish-house performances were a great success. Back home in New York, Glaspell and Cook were so enthusiastic about this new community theater that the next summer a larger group of New Yorkers went out to Cape Cod. But the new theater needed more material.

Susan Glaspell wrote *Trifles* in a little more than a week. "I looked a long time at that bare little stage," she wrote. "After a time the stage became a kitchen. . . . I saw just where the stove was, the table, and the steps going upstairs. The door at the back opened, and the people all bundled up came in."

Although *Trifles* was the first play she wrote by herself, Glaspell had had years of experience as a writer. Back in Iowa, where she was born and grew up, she was a brilliant journalism student at Drake University and then became a reporter for the *Des Moines Daily News*. On one of her assignments, she covered the murder trial of a farm woman who had killed her husband with a hatchet as he slept—in fact, she mentioned visiting the woman's home. That experience presumably inspired *Trifles*.

In the fall of 1916, the group moved from their summer theater on the wharf to year-round quarters in Greenwich Village, where they transformed a former stable into the Playwright's Theatre and adopted the name the Provincetown Players. It was there that the young Edna St. Vincent Millay (1892–1950) auditioned as an actress and later saw her first play produced.

The Provincetown Players provided a venue not just for the playwriting efforts of Glaspell and her friends but also for other talent. When they were looking for more material, a friend of Glaspell's told her that he had a roommate with a "whole trunkful of plays." Glaspell invited her friend's roommate to read one of his plays that evening in her Provincetown home. He was too shy to read himself, so he sat in another room while Glaspell and the rest of the group read his play aloud. The shy roommate was the twenty-eight-year-old Eugene O'Neill (1888–1953), who would one day be recognized as one of America's greatest playwrights.

In 1931, Glaspell won the Pulitzer Prize for drama for *Alison's House*, a play based on the life of the American poet Emily Dickinson (1830–1886).

Trifles

Susan Glaspell

Characters

Mr. Peters, the sheriff
Mr. Henderson, the county attorney
Mr. Hale, a neighbor
Mrs. Hale, wife of Mr. Hale
Mrs. Peters, wife of Sheriff Peters

Scene: The kitchen in the now abandoned farmhouse of JOHN WRIGHT, *a gloomy kitchen, and left without having been put in order—unwashed pans under the sink, a loaf of bread outside the breadbox, a dish towel on the table—other signs of uncompleted work. At the rear the outer door opens, and the* SHERIFF *comes in, followed by the* COUNTY ATTORNEY *and* HALE. *The* SHERIFF *and* HALE *are men in middle life; the* COUNTY ATTORNEY *is a young man; all are much bundled up and go at once to the stove. They are followed by the two women—the* SHERIFF'S WIFE *first; she is a slight, wiry woman, with a thin, nervous face.* MRS. HALE *is larger and would ordinarily be called more comfortable-looking, but she is disturbed now and looks fearfully about as she enters. The women have come in slowly and stand close together near the door.*

County Attorney (*rubbing his hands*). This feels good. Come up to the fire, ladies.
Mrs. Peters (*takes a step forward and look around*). I'm not—cold.
Sheriff (*unbuttoning his overcoat and stepping away from the stove as if to mark the beginning of official business*). Now, Mr. Hale, before we move things about, you explain to Mr. Henderson just what you saw when you came here yesterday morning.
County Attorney. By the way, has anything been moved? Are things just as you left them yesterday?

Sheriff (*looking about*). It's just the same. When it dropped below zero last night, I thought I'd better send Frank out this morning to make a fire for us—no use getting pneumonia with a big case on; but I told him not to touch anything except the stove—and you know Frank.

County Attorney. Somebody should have been left here yesterday.

Sheriff. Oh—yesterday. When I had to send Frank to Morris Center for that man who went crazy—I want you to know I had my hands full yesterday. I knew you could get back from Omaha by today, and as long as I went over everything here myself——

County Attorney. Well, Mr. Hale, tell just what happened when you came here yesterday morning.

Hale. Harry and I had started to town with a load of potatoes. We came along the road from my place; and as I got here, I said, "I'm going to see if I can't get John Wright to go in with me on a party telephone." I spoke to Wright about it once before, and he put me off, saying folks talked too much anyway, and all he asked was peace and quiet—I guess you know about how much he talked himself; but I thought maybe if I went to the house and talked about it before his wife, though I said to Harry that I didn't know as what his wife wanted made much difference to John——

County Attorney. Let's talk about that later, Mr. Hale. I do want to talk about that, but tell now just what happened when you got to the house.

Hale. I didn't hear or see anything; I knocked at the door, and still it was all quiet inside. I knew they must be up; it was past eight o'clock. So I knocked again, and I thought I heard somebody say, "Come in." I wasn't sure, I'm not sure yet, but I opened the door—this door (*jerking a hand backward*) and there in that rocker—(*pointing to it*)—sat Mrs. Wright.

[*They all look at the rocker.*]

County Attorney. What—was she doing?

Hale. She was rockin' back and forth. She had her apron in her hand and was kind of—pleating it.

County Attorney. And how did she—look?

Hale. Well, she looked queer.

County Attorney. How do you mean—queer?

Hale. Well, as if she didn't know what she was going to do next. And kind of done up.

County Attorney. How did she seem to feel about your coming?

Hale. Why, I don't think she minded—one way or other. She didn't pay much attention. I said, "How do, Mrs. Wright, it's cold, ain't it?" And she said, "Is it?"—and went on kind of pleating at her apron. Well, I was surprised; she didn't ask me to come up to the stove, or to set down, but just sat there, not even looking at me, so I said, "I want to see John." And then she—laughed. I guess you would call it a laugh. I thought of Harry and the team outside, so I said a little sharp: "Can't I see John?" "No," she says, kind o' dull like. "Ain't he home?" says I. "Yes," says she, "he's home." "Then why can't I see him?" I asked her, out of patience. "'Cause he's dead," says she. *"Dead?"* says I. She just nodded her head, not gettin' a bit excited, but rockin' back and forth. "Why—where is he?" says I, not knowing what to say. She just pointed upstairs—like that. (*Himself pointing to the room above*) I got up, with the idea of going up there. I walked from there to here—(*pointing*)—then I says, "Why, what did he die of?" "He died of a rope around his neck," says she, and just went on pleatin' at her apron. Well, I went out and called Harry. I thought I might—need help. We went upstairs, and there he was—lyin'——

County Attorney. I think I'd rather have you go into that upstairs, where you can point it all out. Just go on now with the rest of the story.

Hale. Well, my first thought was to get that rope off. I looked . . . (*stops; his face twitches*) . . . but Harry, he went up to him, and he said, "No, he's dead all right, and we'd better not touch anything." So we went back downstairs. She was still sitting that same way. "Has anybody been notified?" I asked. "No," says she, unconcerned. "Who did this, Mrs. Wright?" said Harry. He said it businesslike—and she stopped pleatin' of her apron. "I don't know," she says. "You don't *know*?" says Harry. "No," says she. "Weren't you sleepin' in the bed with him?" says Harry. "Yes," says she, "but I was on the inside." "Somebody slipped a rope round his neck and strangled him, and you didn't wake up?" says Harry. "I didn't wake up," she said after him. We must 'a looked as if we didn't see how that could be, for after a minute she said, "I sleep sound." Harry was going to ask her more questions, but I said maybe we ought to let her tell her story first to the coroner, or the sheriff, so Harry went fast as he could to Rivers' place, where there's a telephone.

County Attorney. And what did Mrs. Wright do when she knew that you had gone for the coroner?

Hale. She moved from that chair to this over here . . . (*pointing to a small chair in the corner*) . . . and just sat there with her hands held together and looking down. I got a feeling that I ought to make some conversation, so I said I had come in to see if John wanted to put in a telephone, and at that she started to laugh, and then she stopped and looked at me—scared.

[*The* COUNTY ATTORNEY, *who has had his notebook out, makes a note.*]

I dunno, maybe it wasn't scared. I wouldn't like to say it was. Soon Harry got back, and then Dr. Lloyd came, and you, Mr. Peters, and so I guess that's all I know that you don't.

County Attorney (*looking around*). I guess we'll go upstairs first—and then out to the barn and around there. (*To the* SHERIFF) You're convinced that there was nothing important here— nothing that would point to any motive?

Sheriff. Nothing here but kitchen things.

[*The* COUNTY ATTORNEY, *after again looking around the kitchen, opens the door of a cupboard closet. He gets up on a chair and looks on a shelf. Pulls his hand away, sticky*]

County Attorney. Here's a nice mess.

[*The women draw nearer.*]

Mrs. Peters (*to the other woman*). Oh, her fruit; it did freeze. (*To the* LAWYER) She worried about that when it turned so cold. She said the fire'd go out and her jars would break.

Sheriff. Well, can you beat the woman! Held for murder and worryin' about her preserves.

County Attorney (*setting his lips firmly*). I guess before we're through she may have something more serious than preserves to worry about.

Hale. Well, women are used to worrying over trifles.

[*The two women move a little closer together.*]

County Attorney (*with the gallantry of a young politician*). And yet, for all their worries, what would we do without the ladies?

[*The women do not unbend.*]

(*He goes to the sink, takes a dipperful of water from the pail, and, pouring it into a basin, washes his hands. Starts to wipe them on the roller towel, turns it for a cleaner place*) Dirty towels! (*Kicks his foot against the pans under the sink*) Not much of a housekeeper, would you say, ladies?

Mrs. Hale (*stiffly*). There's a great deal of work to be done on a farm.

County Attorney. To be sure, and yet ... (*with a little bow to her*) ... I know there are some Dickson County farmhouses which do not have such roller towels. (*He gives it a pull to expose its full length again.*)

Mrs. Hale. Those towels get dirty awful quick. Men's hands aren't always as clean as they might be.

County Attorney. Ah, loyal to your sex, I see. But you and Mrs. Wright were neighbors. I suppose you were friends, too.

Mrs. Hale (*shaking her head*). I've not seen much of her of late years. I've not been in this house—it's more than a year.

County Attorney. And why was that? You didn't like her?

Mrs. Hale. I like her well enough. Farmers' wives have their hands full, Mr. Henderson. And then——

County Attorney. Yes—?

Mrs. Hale (*looking about*). It never seemed a very cheerful place.

County Attorney. No—it's not cheerful. I shouldn't say she had the homemaking instinct.

Mrs. Hale. Well, I don't know as Wright had, either.

County Attorney. You mean that they didn't get on very well?

Mrs. Hale. No, I don't mean anything. But I don't think a place'd be any cheerfuler for John Wright's being in it.

County Attorney. I'd like to talk more of that a little later. I want to get the lay of things upstairs now.

[*Moves to stair door, followed by the two women*]

Sheriff. I suppose anything Mrs. Peters does'll be all right. She was to take in some clothes for her, you know, and a few little things. We left in such a hurry yesterday.

County Attorney. Yes, but I would like to see what you take, Mrs. Peters, and keep an eye out for anything that might be of use to us.

Mrs. Peters. Yes, Mr. Henderson.

[*The women listen to the men's steps on the stairs, then look about the kitchen.*]

Mrs. Hale. I'd hate to have men coming into my kitchen, snooping around and criticizing. (*She arranges the pans under the sink which the* COUNTY ATTORNEY *shoved out of place.*)

Mrs. Peters. Of course it's no more than their duty.

Mrs. Hale. Duty's all right, but I guess that deputy sheriff that came out to make the fire might have got a little of this on. (*Gives the roller towel a pull*) Wish I'd thought of that sooner. Seems mean to talk about her for not having things slicked up when she had to come away in such a hurry.

Mrs. Peters (*who has gone to a small table in the left rear corner of the room and lifted one end of a towel that covers a pan*). She had bread set. (*Stands still*)

Mrs. Hale (*eyes fixed on a loaf of bread beside the breadbox, which is on a low shelf at the other side of the room. Moves slowly toward* *it*). She was going to put this in there. (*Picks up loaf, then abruptly drops it. In a manner of returning to familiar things*) It's a shame about her fruit. I wonder if it's all gone. (*Gets up on the chair and looks*) I think there's some here that's all right, Mrs. Peters. Yes—here—(*holding it toward the window*)—this is cherries, too. (*Looking again*) I declare I believe that's the only one. (*Gets down, bottle in her hand. Goes to the sink and wipes it off on the outside*) She'll feel awful bad after all her hard work in the hot weather. I remember the afternoon I put up my cherries last summer. (*She puts the bottle on the big kitchen table, center of the room. With a sigh, is about to sit down in the rocking chair. Before she is seated, realizes what chair it is; with a slow look at it, steps back. The chair, which she has touched, rocks back and forth.*)

Mrs. Peters. Well, I must get those things from the front-room closet. (*She goes to the door at the right but, after looking into the other room, steps back.*) You coming with me, Mrs. Hale? You could help me carry them.

[*They go in the other room, reappear,* MRS. PETERS *carrying a dress and skirt,* MRS. HALE *following with a pair of shoes.*]

Mrs. Peters. My, it's cold in there. (*She puts the clothes on the big table and hurries to the stove.*)

Mrs. Hale (*examining the skirt*). Wright was close. I think maybe that's why she kept so much to herself. She didn't even belong to the Ladies' Aid. I suppose she felt she couldn't do her part, and then you don't enjoy things when you feel shabby. She used to wear pretty clothes and be lively when she was Minnie Foster, one of the town girls singing in the choir. But that—oh, that was thirty years ago. This all you was to take in?

Mrs. Peters. She said she wanted an apron. Funny thing to want, for there isn't much to get you dirty in jail, goodness knows. But I suppose just to make her feel more natural. She said they was in the top drawer in this cupboard. Yes, here. And then her little shawl that always hung behind the door. (*Opens stair door and looks*) Yes, here it is. (*Quickly shuts door leading upstairs*)

Mrs. Hale (*abruptly moving toward her*). Mrs. Peters?

Mrs. Peters. Yes, Mrs. Hale?

Mrs. Hale. Do you think she did it?

Mrs. Peters (*in a frightened voice*). Oh, I don't know.

Mrs. Hale. Well, I don't think she did. Asking for an apron and her little shawl. Worrying about her fruit.

Mrs. Peters (*starts to speak, glances up, where footsteps are heard in the room above. In a low voice*). Mr. Peters says it looks bad for her. Mr. Henderson is awful sarcastic in a speech, and he'll make fun of her sayin' she didn't wake up.

Mrs. Hale. Well, I guess John Wright didn't wake when they was slipping that rope under his neck.

Mrs. Peters. No, it's strange. It must have been done awful crafty and still. They say it was such a—funny way to kill a man, rigging it all up like that.

Mrs. Hale. That's just what Mr. Hale said. There was a gun in the house. He says that's what he can't understand.

Mrs. Peters. Mr. Henderson said coming out that what was needed for the case was a motive, something to show anger, or—sudden feeling.

Mrs. Hale (*who is standing by the table*). Well, I don't see any signs of anger around here. (*She puts her hand on the dish towel which lies on the table, stands looking down at the table, one half of which is clean, the other half messy.*) It's wiped to here. (*Makes a move as if to finish work, then turns and looks at loaf of bread outside the breadbox. Drops towel. In that voice of coming back to familiar things*) Wonder how they are finding things upstairs? I hope she had it a little more redd-up up there. You know, it seems kind of *sneaking*. Locking her up in town and then coming out here and trying to get her own house to turn against her!

Mrs. Peters. But, Mrs. Hale, the law is the law.

Mrs. Hale. I s'pose 'tis. (*Unbuttoning her coat*) Better loosen up your things, Mrs. Peters. You won't feel them when you go out.

[MRS. PETERS *takes off her fur tippet, goes to hang it on hook at back of room, stands looking at the underpart of the small corner table.*]

Mrs. Peters. She was piecing a quilt. (*She brings the large sewing basket, and they look at the bright pieces.*)

Mrs. Hale. It's log-cabin pattern. Pretty, isn't it? I wonder if she was goin' to quilt it or just knot it?

[*Footsteps have been heard coming down the stairs. The* SHERIFF *enters, followed by* HALE *and the* COUNTY ATTORNEY.]

Sheriff. They wonder if she was going to quilt it or just knot it.

[*The men laugh; the women look abashed.*]

County Attorney (*rubbing his hands over the stove*). Frank's fire didn't do much up there, did it? Well, let's go out to the barn and get that cleared up.

[*The men go outside.*]

Mrs. Hale (*resentfully*). I don't know as there's anything so strange, our takin' up our time with little things while we're waiting for them to get the evidence. (*She sits down at the big table, smoothing out a block with decision.*) I don't see as it's anything to laugh about.

Mrs. Peters (*apologetically*). Of course they've got awful important things on their minds. (*Pulls up a chair and joins* MRS. HALE *at the table*)

Mrs. Hale (*examining another block*). Mrs. Peters, look at this one. Here, this is the one she was working on, and look at the sewing! All the rest of it has been so nice and even. And look at this! It's all over the place! Why, it looks as if she didn't know what she was about!

[*After she has said this, they look at each other, then start to glance back at the door. After an instant* MRS. HALE *has pulled at a knot and ripped the sewing.*]

Mrs. Peters. Oh, what are you doing, Mrs. Hale?

Mrs. Hale (*mildly*). Just pulling out a stitch or two that's not sewed very good. (*Threading a needle*) Bad sewing always made me fidgety.

Mrs. Peters (*nervously*). I don't think we ought to touch things.

Mrs. Hale. I'll just finish up this end. (*Suddenly stopping and leaning forward*) Mrs. Peters?

Mrs. Peters. Yes, Mrs. Hale?

Mrs. Hale. What do you suppose she was so nervous about?

Mrs. Peters. Oh—I don't know. I don't know as she was nervous. I sometimes sew awful queer when I'm just tired.

[MRS. HALE *starts to say something, looks at* MRS. PETERS, *compresses her lips a little, then goes on sewing.*]

Well, I must get these things wrapped up. They may be through sooner than we think. (*Putting apron and other things together*) I wonder where I can find a piece of paper and string.

Mrs. Hale. In that cupboard, maybe.

Mrs. Peters (*looking in cupboard*). Why, here's a birdcage. (*Holds it up*) Did she have a bird, Mrs. Hale?

Mrs. Hale. Why, I don't know whether she did or not—I've not been here for so long. There was a man around last year selling canaries cheap, but I don't know as she took one; maybe she did. She used to sing real pretty herself.

Mrs. Peters (*glancing around*). Seems funny to think of a bird here. But she must have had one, or why should she have a cage? I wonder what happened to it?

Mrs. Hale. I s'pose maybe the cat got it.

Mrs. Peters. No, she didn't have a cat. She's got that feeling some people have about cats—being afraid of them. My cat got in her room, and she was real upset and asked me to take it out.

Mrs. Hale. My sister Bessie was like that. Queer, ain't it?

Mrs. Peters (*examining the cage*). Why, look at this door. It's broke. One hinge is pulled apart.

Mrs. Hale (*looking, too*). Looks as if someone must have been rough with it.

Mrs. Peters. Why, yes. (*She brings the cage forward and puts it on the table.*)

Mrs. Hale. I wish if they're going to find any evidence, they'd be about it. I don't like this place.

Mrs. Peters. But I'm awful glad you came with me, Mrs. Hale. It would be lonesome for me sitting here alone.

Mrs. Hale. It would, wouldn't it? (*Dropping her sewing, voice falling*) But I tell you what I do wish, Mrs. Peters. I wish I had come over sometimes when *she* was here. I—(*looking around the room*)—wish I had.

Mrs. Peters. But of course you were awful busy, Mrs. Hale—your house and your children.

Mrs. Hale. I could've come. I stayed away because it weren't cheerful—and that's why I ought to have come. I—I've never liked this place. Maybe because it's down in a hollow, and you don't see the road. I dunno what it is, but it's a lonesome place and always was. I wish I had come over to see Minnie Foster sometimes. I can see now—— (*Shakes her head*)

Mrs. Peters. Well, you mustn't reproach yourself, Mrs. Hale. Somehow we just don't see how it is with other folks until—something comes up.

Mrs. Hale. Not having children makes less work—but it makes a quiet house, and Wright out to work all day, and no company when he did come in. Did you know John Wright, Mrs. Peters?

Mrs. Peters. Not to know him; I've seen him in town. They say he was a good man.

Mrs. Hale. Yes—good; he didn't drink and kept his word as well as most, I guess, and paid his debts. But he was a hard man, Mrs. Peters. Just to pass the time of day with him. (*Shivers*) Like a raw wind that gets to the bone. (*Pauses, her eye falling on the cage*) I should think she would 'a wanted a bird. But what do you suppose went wrong with it?

Mrs. Peters. I don't know, unless it got sick and died. (*She reaches over and swings the broken door, swings it again; both women watch it.*)

Mrs. Hale. You weren't raised round here, were you?

[MRS. PETERS *shakes her head.*]

You didn't know—her?

Mrs. Peters. Not till they brought her yesterday.

Mrs. Hale. She—come to think of it, she was kind of like a bird herself—real sweet and pretty, but kind of timid and—fluttery. How—she—did—change. (*Silence; then as if struck by a happy thought and relieved to get back to everyday things*) Tell you what, Mrs. Peters, why don't you take the quilt in with you? It might take up her mind.

Mrs. Peters. Why, I think that's a real nice idea, Mrs. Hale. There couldn't possibly be any objection to it, could there? Now, just what would I take? I wonder if her patches are in here—and her things.

[*They look in the sewing basket.*]

Mrs. Hale. Here's some red. I expect this has got sewing things in it. (*Brings out a fancy box*) What a pretty box. Looks like something somebody would give you. Maybe her scissors are in here. (*Opens box. Suddenly puts her hand to her nose*) Why——

[MRS. PETERS *bends nearer, then turns her face away.*]

There's something wrapped up in this piece of silk.

Mrs. Peters. Why, this isn't her scissors.

Mrs. Hale (*lifting the silk*). Oh, Mrs. Peters—it's——

[MRS. PETERS *bends closer.*]

Mrs. Peters. It's the bird.

Mrs. Hale (*jumping up*). But, Mrs. Peters—look at it. Its neck! Look at its neck! It's all—other side *to.*

Mrs. Peters. Somebody—wrung—its neck.

[*Their eyes meet. A look of growing comprehension of horror. Steps are heard outside.* MRS. HALE *slips box under quilt pieces and sinks into her chair. Enter* SHERIFF *and* COUNTY ATTORNEY; MRS. PETERS *rises.*]

County Attorney (*as one turning from serious things to little pleasantries*). Well, ladies, have you decided whether she was going to quilt it or knot it?

Mrs. Peters. We think she was going to—knot it.

County Attorney. Well, that's interesting, I'm sure. (*Seeing the birdcage*) Has the bird flown?

Mrs. Hale (*putting more quilt pieces over the box*). We think the—cat got it.

County Attorney (*preoccupied*). Is there a cat?

[MRS. HALE *glances in a quick, covert way at* MRS. PETERS.]

Mrs. Peters. Well, not *now*. They're superstitious, you know. They leave.

County Attorney (*to* SHERIFF PETERS, *continuing an interrupted conversation*). No sign at all of anyone having come from the outside. Their own rope. Now let's go up again and go over it piece by piece. (*They start upstairs.*) It would have to have been someone who knew just the——

[MRS. PETERS *sinks into her chair. The two women sit there not looking at one another, but as if peering into something and at the same time holding back. When they talk now, it is in the manner of feeling their way over strange ground, as if afraid of what they are saying, but as if they cannot help saying it.*]

Mrs. Hale. She liked the bird. She was going to bury it in that pretty box.

Mrs. Peters (*in a whisper*). When I was a girl—my kitten—there was a boy took a hatchet, and before my eyes—and before I could get there—— (*Covers her face an instant*) If they hadn't held me back, I would have—(*catches herself, looks upstairs, where steps are heard, falters weakly*)—hurt him.

Mrs. Hale (*with a slow look around her*). I wonder how it would seem never to have had any children around. (*Pause*) No, Wright wouldn't like the bird—a thing that sang. She used to sing. He killed that, too.

Mrs. Peters (*moving uneasily*). We don't know who killed the bird.

Mrs. Hale. I knew John Wright.

Mrs. Peters. It was an awful thing was done in this house that night, Mrs. Hale. Killing a man while he slept, slipping a rope around his neck that choked the life out of him.

Mrs. Hale. His neck. Choked the life out of him. (*Her hand goes out and rests on the birdcage.*)

Mrs. Peters (*with rising voice*). We don't know who killed him. We don't *know*.

Mrs. Hale (*her own feeling not interrupted*). If there'd been years and years of nothing, then a bird to sing to you, it would be awful—still after the bird was still.

Mrs. Peters (*something within her speaking*). I know what stillness is. When we homesteaded in Dakota, and my first baby died—after he was two years old and me with no other then——

Mrs. Hale (*moving*). How soon do you suppose they'll be through looking for evidence?

Mrs. Peters. I know what stillness is. (*Pulling herself back*) The law has got to punish crime, Mrs. Hale.

Mrs. Hale (*not as if answering that*). I wish you'd seen Minnie Foster when she wore a white dress with blue ribbons and stood up there in the choir and sang. (*Suddenly looking around the room*) Oh, I *wish* I'd come over here once in a while! That was a crime! That was a crime! Who's going to punish that?

Mrs. Peters (*looking upstairs*). We mustn't—take on.

Mrs. Hale. I might have known she needed help! I know how things can be—for women. I tell you, it's queer, Mrs. Peters. We live close together, and we live far apart. We all go through the same things—it's all just a different kind of the same thing. (*Brushes her eyes, then, noticing the bottle of fruit, reaches out for it*) If I was you, I wouldn't tell her her fruit was gone. Tell her it *ain't*. Tell her it's all right. Take this in to prove it to her. She—she may never know whether it was broke or not.

Mrs. Peters (*takes the bottle, looks about for something to wrap it in, takes petticoat from the clothes brought from the other room, very nervously begins winding this around the bottle. In a false voice*). My, it's a good thing the men couldn't hear us. Wouldn't they just laugh! Getting all stirred up over a little thing like a—dead

canary. As if that could have anything to do with—with—
wouldn't they *laugh*!

[*The men are heard coming downstairs.*]

Mrs. Hale (*under her breath*). Maybe they would—maybe they
wouldn't.
County Attorney. No, Peters, it's all perfectly clear except a
reason for doing it. But you know juries when it comes to
women. If there was some definite thing. Something to show—
something to make a story about—a thing that would connect
up with this strange way of doing it.

[*The women's eyes meet for an instant. Enter* HALE *from outer door.*]

Hale. Well, I've got the team around. Pretty cold out there.
County Attorney. I'm going to stay here awhile by myself. (*To
the* SHERIFF) You can send Frank out for me, can't you? I want
to go over everything. I'm not satisfied that we can't do better.
Sheriff. Do you want to see what Mrs. Peters is going to take in?

[*The* ATTORNEY *goes to the table, picks up the apron, laughs.*]

County Attorney. Oh, I guess they're not very dangerous things
the ladies have picked up. (*Moves a few things about, disturbing
the quilt pieces which cover the box. Steps back*) No, Mrs. Peters
doesn't need supervising. For that matter, a sheriff's wife is
married to the law. Ever think of it that way, Mrs. Peters?
Mrs. Peters. Not—just that way.
Sheriff (*chuckling*). Married to the law. (*Moves toward the other
room*) I just want you to come in here a minute, George. We
ought to take a look at these windows.
County Attorney (*scoffingly*). Oh, windows!
Sheriff. We'll be right out, Mr. Hale.

[HALE *goes outside. The* SHERIFF *follows the* COUNTY ATTORNEY *into
the other room. The two women's eyes follow them. Then* MRS. HALE

rises, hands tight together, looking intensely at MRS. PETERS, *whose eyes make a slow turn, finally meeting* MRS. HALE's. *A moment* MRS. HALE *holds her; then her own eyes point the way to where the box is concealed. Suddenly* MRS. PETERS *throws back quilt pieces and tries to put the box in the bag she is wearing. It is too big. She opens box, starts to take bird out, cannot touch it, goes to pieces, stands there helpless. Sound of a knob turning in the other room.* MRS. HALE *snatches the box and puts it in the pocket of her big coat. Enter* COUNTY ATTORNEY *and* SHERIFF.]

County Attorney (*facetiously*). Well, Henry, at least we found out that she was not going to quilt it. She was going to—what is it you call it, ladies?
Mrs. Hale (*her hand against her pocket*). We call it—knot it, Mr. Henderson.

CURTAIN

John Millington Synge
(1871–1909)

John Millington Synge was born in a suburb of Dublin, Ireland, to a Protestant family that had once been wealthy and important. (Their name, pronounced "sing," had, according to legend, been given to an ancestor by the English king Henry VIII as a mark of his pleasure at the boy's performance in choir.) Synge's father died when he was a baby, and the child was raised by his mother. Their early close relationship may later have lent him a special sympathy for the grieving mother in his one-act tragedy *Riders to the Sea* (1904).

Synge grew up speaking English, as did all Irish people of his class; only peasants spoke the native tongue, Irish Gaelic, a language that the English colonists had tried to exterminate. But in college, Synge studied the Irish language and became fascinated with its rhythms and figures of speech. He even kept a diary in Irish as he traveled around Europe, trying to decide what to do with himself. It was at a student boardinghouse in Paris that he met the Irish poet W. B. Yeats (1865–1939). That meeting would change Synge's life.

Yeats had just returned from a trip to the Aran Islands, a trio of tiny windswept and rocky islands off the west coast of Ireland. He was fascinated by the culture and folklore of the Irish-speaking islanders but frustrated because he didn't speak their language. Yeats saw in their lives a source for what he dreamed of—a literature that would be authentically Irish rather than imitation English. He urged Synge to give up his studies in Paris and return home. "Go to the Aran Islands," he said. "Live there as if you were one of the people themselves; express a life that has never found expression."

Synge went to Aran, and he kept going back—every year for five years. He took a room over a pub, and every night he listened to the people talking below. He found his voice in the poetic patterns of Irish speech, and he found his subject in the people's daily struggle for existence. The fishermen of Aran made their living by going to sea in *curraghs* (fragile canvas boats), and frequently they did not return. *Riders to the Sea* was inspired by a young man whose body washed ashore while Synge was on Aran. It had to be buried in a coffin made of boards that another man had saved for two years so that he might bury his aging mother when her time came. An old woman had foreseen the young man's death, an Aran Island boy told Synge, but she remained silent, and so he went out to sea and was drowned.

Writing about the Aran Islands, Synge felt, allowed him to create a drama that was at once starkly realistic, wildly beautiful, and essentially Irish. But not everyone shared his feelings. At the first performances of his 1907 play, *The Playboy of the Western World*, Irish nationalists rioted in the theater. They took Synge's portrayal of human failings as an attack on their national character, and believed that it undercut their fight for independence. Today the play is considered his masterpiece.

Riders to the Sea
John Millington Synge

Characters

Maurya, an old woman
Bartley, her son
Cathleen, her daughter
Nora, a younger daughter
Men and Women

Scene: An island off the west of Ireland.

Cottage kitchen, with nets, oilskins, spinning wheel, some new boards standing by the wall, etc. CATHLEEN, *a girl of about twenty, finishes kneading cake and puts it down in the pot oven by the fire, then wipes her hands and begins to spin at the wheel.* NORA, *a young girl, puts her head in at the door.*

Nora (*in a low voice*). Where is she?
Cathleen. She's lying down, God help her, and maybe sleeping, if she's able.

[NORA *comes in softly and takes a bundle from under her shawl.*]

Cathleen (*spinning the wheel rapidly*). What is it you have?
Nora. The young priest is after bringing them. It's a shirt and a plain stocking were got off a drowned man in Donegal.

[CATHLEEN *stops her wheel with a sudden movement and leans out to listen.*]

Nora. We're to find out if it's Michael's they are, some time herself will be down looking by the sea.

Cathleen. How would they be Michael's, Nora? How would he go the length of that way to the far north?

Nora. The young priest says he's known the like of it. "If it's Michael's they are," says he, "you can tell herself he's got a clean burial, by the grace of God; and if they're not his, let no one say a word about them, for she'll be getting her death," says he, "with crying and lamenting."

[*The door which* NORA *half closed is blown open by a gust of wind.*]

Cathleen (*looking out anxiously*). Did you ask him would he stop Bartley going this day with the horses to the Galway fair?

Nora. "I won't stop him," says he; "but let you not be afraid. Herself does be saying prayers half through the night, and the Almighty God won't leave her destitute," says he, "with no son living."

Cathleen. Is the sea bad by the white rocks, Nora?

Nora. Middling bad, God help us. There's a great roaring in the west, and it's worse it'll be getting when the tide's turned to the wind. (*She goes over to the table with the bundle.*) Shall I open it now?

Cathleen. Maybe she'd wake up on us and come in before we'd done. (*Coming to the table*) It's a long time we'll be, and the two of us crying.

Nora (*goes to the inner door and listens*). She's moving about on the bed. She'll be coming in a minute.

Cathleen. Give me the ladder, and I'll put them up in the turf loft, the way she won't know of them at all, and maybe when the tide turns, she'll be going down to see would he be floating from the east.

[*They put the ladder against the gable of the chimney;* CATHLEEN *goes up a few steps and hides the bundle in the turf loft.* MAURYA *comes from the inner room.*]

Maurya (*looking up at* CATHLEEN *and speaking querulously*). Isn't it turf enough you have for this day and evening?

Cathleen. There's a cake baking at the fire for a short space (*throwing down the turf*), and Bartley will want it when the tide turns if he goes to Connemara.

[NORA *picks up the turf and puts it round the pot oven.*]

Maurya (*sitting down on a stool at the fire*). He won't go this day with the wind rising from the south and west. He won't go this day, for the young priest will stop him surely.
Nora. He'll not stop him, mother; and I heard Eamon Simon and Stephen Pheety and Colum Shawn saying he would go.
Maurya. Where is he itself?
Nora. He went down to see would there be another boat sailing in the week, and I'm thinking it won't be long till he's here now, for the tide's turning at the green head, and the hooker's tacking from the east.
Cathleen. I hear someone passing the big stones.
Nora (*looking out*). He's coming now, and he in a hurry.
Bartley (*comes in and looks round the room. Speaking sadly and quietly*). Where is the bit of new rope, Cathleen, was bought in Connemara?
Cathleen (*coming down*). Give it to him, Nora; it's on a nail by the white boards. I hung it up this morning, for the pig with the black feet was eating it.
Nora (*giving him a rope*). Is that it, Bartley?
Maurya. You'd do right to leave that rope, Bartley, hanging by the boards.

[BARTLEY *takes the rope.*]

It will be wanting in this place, I'm telling you, if Michael is washed up tomorrow morning or the next morning, or any morning in the week; for it's a deep grave we'll make him, by the grace of God.
Bartley (*beginning to work with the rope*). I've no halter the way I can ride down on the mare, and I must go now quickly.

This is the one boat going for two weeks or beyond it, and the fair will be a good fair for horses, I heard them saying below.

Maurya. It's a hard thing they'll be saying below if the body is washed up and there's no man in it to make the coffin, and I after giving a big price for the finest white boards you'd find in Connemara. (*She looks round at the boards.*)

Bartley. How would it be washed up, and we after looking each day for nine days, and a strong wind blowing a while back from the west and south?

Maurya. If it isn't found itself, that wind is raising the sea, and there was a star up against the moon, and it rising in the night. If it was a hundred horses, or a thousand horses, you had itself, what is the price of a thousand horses against a son where there is one son only?

Bartley (*working at the halter, to* CATHLEEN). Let you go down each day and see the sheep aren't jumping in on the rye, and if the jobber comes, you can sell the pig with the black feet if there is a good price going.

Maurya. How would the like of her get a good price for a pig?

Bartley (*to* CATHLEEN). If the west wind holds with the last bit of the moon, let you and Nora get up weed enough for another cock for the kelp. It's hard set we'll be from this day with no one in it but one man to work.

Maurya. It's hard set we'll be surely the day you're drowned with the rest. What way will I live and the girls with me, and I an old woman looking for the grave?

[BARTLEY *lays down the halter, takes off his old coat, and puts on a newer one of the same flannel.*]

Bartley (*to* NORA). Is she coming to the pier?

Nora (*looking out*). She's passing the green head and letting fall her sails.

Bartley (*getting his purse and tobacco*). I'll have half an hour to go down, and you'll see me coming again in two days, or in three days, or maybe in four days if the wind is bad.

Maurya (*turning round to the fire, and putting her shawl over her head*). Isn't it a hard and cruel man won't hear a word from an old woman, and she holding him from the sea?

Cathleen. It's the life of a young man to be going on the sea, and who would listen to an old woman with one thing, and she saying it over?

Bartley (*taking the halter*). I must go now quickly. I'll ride down on the red mare, and the gray pony 'ill run behind me. . . . The blessing of God on you. (*He goes out.*)

Maurya (*crying out as he is in the door*). He's gone now, God spare us, and we'll not see him again. He's gone now, and when the black night is falling, I'll have no son left me in the world.

Cathleen. Why wouldn't you give him your blessing, and he looking round in the door? Isn't it sorrow enough is on everyone in this house without you sending him out with an unlucky word behind him, and a hard word in his ear?

[MAURYA *takes up the tongs and begins raking the fire aimlessly without looking round.*]

Nora (*turning towards her*). You're taking away the turf from the cake.

Cathleen (*crying out*). The Son of God forgive us, Nora, we're after forgetting his bit of bread. (*She comes over to the fire.*)

Nora. And it's destroyed he'll be going till dark night, and he after eating nothing since the sun went up.

Cathleen (*turning the cake out of the oven*). It's destroyed he'll be, surely. There's no sense left on any person in a house where an old woman will be talking forever.

[MAURYA *sways herself on her stool.*]

Cathleen (*cutting off some of the bread and rolling it in a cloth; to* MAURYA). Let you go down now to the spring well and give him this and he passing. You'll see him then, and the dark word will be broken, and you can say "God speed you," the way he'll be easy in his mind.

Maurya (*taking the bread*). Will I be in it as soon as himself?

Cathleen. If you go now quickly.

Maurya (*standing up unsteadily*). It's hard set I am to walk.

Cathleen (*looking at her anxiously*). Give her the stick, Nora, or maybe she'll slip on the big stones.

Nora. What stick?

Cathleen. The stick Michael brought from Connemara.

Maurya (*taking a stick* NORA *gives her*). In the big world the old people do be leaving things after them for their sons and children, but in this place it is the young men do be leaving things behind for them that do be old.

[*She goes out slowly.* NORA *goes over to the ladder.*]

Cathleen. Wait, Nora, maybe she'd turn back quickly. She's that sorry, God help her, you wouldn't know the thing she'd do.

Nora. Is she gone round by the bush?

Cathleen (*looking out*). She's gone now. Throw it down quickly, for the Lord knows when she'll be out of it again.

Nora (*getting the bundle from the loft*). The young priest said he'd be passing tomorrow, and we might go down and speak to him below if it's Michael's they are surely.

Cathleen (*taking the bundle*). Did he say what way they were found?

Nora (*coming down*). "There were two men," says he, "and they rowing round with poteen before the cocks crowed, and the oar of one of them caught the body, and they passing the black cliffs of the north."

Cathleen (*trying to open the bundle*). Give me a knife, Nora; the string's perished with salt water, and there's a black knot on it you wouldn't loosen in a week.

Nora (*giving her a knife*). I've heard tell it was a long way to Donegal.

Cathleen (*cutting the string*). It is surely. There was a man in here a while ago—the man sold us that knife—and he said if you set off walking from the rocks beyond, it would be in seven days you'd be in Donegal.

Nora. And what time would a man take, and he floating?

[CATHLEEN *opens the bundle and takes out a bit of a shirt and a stocking. They look at them eagerly.*]

Cathleen (*in a low voice*). The Lord spare us, Nora! Isn't it a queer hard thing to say if it's his they are surely?
Nora. I'll get his shirt off the hook the way we can put the one flannel on the other. (*She looks through some clothes hanging in the corner.*) It's not with them, Cathleen, and where will it be?
Cathleen. I'm thinking Bartley put it on him in the morning, for his own shirt was heavy with the salt in it. (*Pointing to the corner*) there's a bit of a sleeve was of the same stuff. Give me that and it will do.

[NORA *brings it to her and they compare the flannel.*]

Cathleen. It's the same stuff, Nora; but if it is itself, aren't there great rolls of it in the shops of Galway, and isn't it many another man may have a shirt of it as well as Michael himself?
Nora (*who has taken up the stocking and counted the stitches, crying out*). It's Michael, Cathleen, it's Michael; God spare his soul, and what will herself say when she hears this story, and Bartley on the sea?
Cathleen (*taking the stocking*). It's a plain stocking.
Nora. It's the second one of the third pair I knitted, and I put up three score stitches, and I dropped four of them.
Cathleen (*counts the stitches*). It's that number is in it. (*Crying out*) Ah, Nora, isn't it a bitter thing to think of him floating that way to the far north, and no one to keen him but the black hags that do be flying on the sea?
Nora (*swinging herself half round and throwing out her arms on the clothes*). And isn't it a pitiful thing when there is nothing left of a man who was a great rower and fisher but a bit of an old shirt and a plain stocking?
Cathleen (*after an instant*). Tell me is herself coming, Nora? I hear a little sound on the path.

Nora (*looking out*). She is, Cathleen. She's coming up to the door.
Cathleen. Put these things away before she'll come in. Maybe it's easier she'll be after giving her blessing to Bartley, and we won't let on we've heard anything the time he's on the sea.
Nora (*helping* CATHLEEN *to close the bundle*). We'll put them here in the corner.

[*They put them into a hole in the chimney corner.* CATHLEEN *goes back to the spinning wheel.*]

Nora. Will she see it was crying I was?
Cathleen. Keep your back to the door the way the light'll not be on you.

[NORA *sits down at the chimney corner, with her back to the door.* MAURYA *comes in very slowly, without looking at the girls, and goes over to her stool at the other side of the fire. The cloth with the bread is still in her hand. The girls look at each other, and* NORA *points to the bundle of bread.*]

Cathleen (*after spinning for a moment*). You didn't give him his bit of bread?

[MAURYA *begins to keen softly, without turning round.*]

Cathleen. Did you see him riding down?

[MAURYA *goes on keening.*]

Cathleen (*a little impatiently*). God forgive you; isn't it a better thing to raise your voice and tell what you seen than to be making lamentation for a thing that's done? Did you see Bartley, I'm saying to you?
Maurya (*with a weak voice*). My heart's broken from this day.
Cathleen (*as before*). Did you see Bartley?
Maurya. I seen the fearfulest thing.
Cathleen (*leaves her wheel and looks out*). God forgive you; he's riding the mare now over the green head, and the gray pony behind him.

Maurya (*starts, so that her shawl falls back from her head and shows her white tossed hair. With a frightened voice*). The gray pony behind him . . .

Cathleen (*coming to the fire*). What is it ails you at all?

Maurya (*speaking very slowly*). I've seen the fearfulest thing any person has seen since the day Bride Dara seen the dead man with the child in his arms.

Cathleen *and* **Nora.** Uah.

[*They crouch down in front of the old woman at the fire.*]

Nora. Tell us what it is you seen.

Maurya. I went down to the spring well, and I stood there saying a prayer to myself. Then Bartley came along, and he riding on the red mare with the gray pony behind him. (*She puts up her hands, as if to hide something from her eyes.*) The Son of God spare us, Nora!

Cathleen. What is it you seen?

Maurya. I seen Michael himself.

Cathleen (*speaking softly*). You did not, Mother. It wasn't Michael you seen, for his body is after being found in the far north, and he's got a clean burial, by the grace of God.

Maurya (*a little defiantly*). I'm after seeing him this day, and he riding and galloping. Bartley came first on the red mare, and I tried to say "God speed you," but something choked the words in my throat. He went by quickly; and "the blessing of God on you," says he, and I could say nothing. I looked up then, and I crying, at the gray pony, and there was Michael upon it—with fine clothes on him, and new shoes on his feet.

Cathleen (*begins to keen*). It's destroyed we are from this day. It's destroyed, surely.

Nora. Didn't the young priest say the Almighty God won't leave her destitute with no son living?

Maurya (*in a low voice, but clearly*). It's little the like of him knows of the sea. . . . Bartley will be lost now, and let you call in Eamon and make me a good coffin out of the white boards, for I won't live after them. I've had a husband, and a husband's father, and six sons in this house—six fine men, though it was a hard birth I had with every one of them and they coming to the world—and some of them were found and some of them were not found, but they're gone now the lot of them. . . . There were Stephan and Shawn were lost in the great wind, and found after in the Bay of Gregory of the Golden Mouth, and carried up the two of them on one plank, and in by that door.

[*She pauses for a moment; the girls start as if they heard something through the door that is half-open behind them.*]

Nora (*in a whisper*). Did you hear that, Cathleen? Did you hear a noise in the northeast?

Cathleen (*in a whisper*). There's someone after crying out by the seashore.

Maurya (*continues without hearing anything*). There was Sheamus and his father, and his own father again, were lost in a dark night, and not a stick or sign was seen of them when the sun went up. There was Patch after was drowned out of a curragh that turned over. I was sitting here with Bartley, and he a baby lying on my two knees, and I seen two women, and three women, and four women coming in, and they crossing themselves and not saying a word. I looked out then, and there were men coming after them, and they holding a thing in the half of a red sail, and water dripping out of it—it was a dry day, Nora—and leaving a track to the door.

[*She pauses again with her hand stretched out toward the door. It opens softly and old women begin to come in, crossing themselves on the threshold and kneeling down in front of the stage with red petticoats over their heads.*]

Maurya (*half in a dream, to* CATHLEEN). Is it Patch, or Michael, or what is it at all?

Cathleen. Michael is after being found in the far north, and when he is found there, how could he be here in this place?

Maurya. There does be a power of young men floating round in the sea, and what way would they know if it was Michael they had, or another man like him, for when a man is nine days in the sea, and the wind blowing, it's hard set his own mother would be to say what man was in it.

Cathleen. It's Michael, God spare him, for they're after sending us a bit of his clothes from the far north.

[*She reaches out and hands* MAURYA *the clothes that belonged to Michael.* MAURYA *stands up slowly and takes them in her hands.* NORA *looks out.*]

Nora. They're carrying a thing among them, and there's water dripping out of it and leaving a track by the big stones.

Cathleen (*in a whisper to the women who have come in*). Is it Bartley it is?

One of the Women. It is, surely, God rest his soul.

[*Two younger women come in and pull out the table. Then men carry in the body of* BARTLEY, *laid on a plank, with a bit of a sail over it, and lay it on the table.*]

Cathleen (*to the women as they are doing so*). What way was he drowned?

One of the Women. The gray pony knocked him over into the sea, and he was washed out where there is a great surf on the white rocks.

[MAURYA *has gone over and knelt down at the head of the table. The women are keening softly and swaying themselves with a slow movement.* CATHLEEN *and* NORA *kneel at the other end of the table. The men kneel near the door.*]

Maurya (*raising her head and speaking as if she did not see the people around her*). They're all gone now, and there isn't anything more the sea can do to me. . . . I'll have no call now to be up crying and praying when the wind breaks from the south, and you can hear the surf is in the east, and the surf is in the west, making a great stir with the two noises, and they hitting one on the other. I'll have no call now to be going down and getting holy water in the dark nights after Samhain, and I won't care what way the sea is when the other women will be keening. (*To* NORA) Give me the holy water, Nora; there's a small sup still on the dresser.

[NORA *gives it to her.*]

Maurya (*drops Michael's clothes across* BARTLEY's *feet and sprinkles the holy water over him*). It isn't that I haven't prayed for you, Bartley, to the Almighty God. It isn't that I haven't said prayers in the dark night till you wouldn't know what I'd be saying; but it's a great rest I'll have now, and it's time, surely. It's a great rest I'll have now, and great sleeping in the long nights after Samhain, if it's only a bit of wet flour we do have to eat, and maybe a fish that would be stinking.

[*She kneels down again, crossing herself, and saying prayers under her breath.*]

Cathleen (*to an old man*). Maybe yourself and Eamon would make a coffin when the sun rises. We have fine white boards herself bought, God help her, thinking Michael would be found, and I have a new cake you can eat while you'll be working.
The Old Man (*looking at the boards*). Are there nails with them?
Cathleen. There are not, Colum; we didn't think of the nails.
Another Man. It's a great wonder she wouldn't think of the nails, and all the coffins she's seen made already.
Cathleen. It's getting old she is, and broken.

[MAURYA *stands up again very slowly and spreads out the pieces of Michael's clothes beside the body, sprinkling them with the last of the holy water.*]

Nora (*in a whisper to* CATHLEEN). She's quiet now and easy; but the day Michael was drowned you could hear her crying out from this to the spring well. It's fonder she was of Michael, and would anyone have thought that?

Cathleen (*slowly and clearly*). An old woman will be soon tired with anything she will do, and isn't it nine days herself is after crying and keening, and making great sorrow in the house?
Maurya (*puts the empty cup mouth downward on the table and lays her hands together on* BARTLEY's *feet*). They're all together this time, and the end is come. May the Almighty God have mercy on Bartley's soul, and on Michael's soul, and on the souls of Sheamus and Patch, and Stephen and Shawn (*bending her head*); and may He have mercy on my soul, Nora, and on the soul of every one is left living in the world.

[*She pauses, and the keen rises a little more loudly from the women, then sinks away.*]

(*Continuing*) Michael has a clean burial in the far north, by the grace of Almighty God. Bartley will have a fine coffin out of the white boards, and a deep grave surely. What more can we want than that? No man at all can be living forever, and we must be satisfied.

[*She kneels down again and the curtain falls slowly.*]

Reginald Rose
(1920–   )

"My main purpose has always been to project my own view of good and evil," says Reginald Rose, "and this is the essence of controversy." For the last half century, Rose, a native New Yorker, has been projecting that view onto screens large and small. He has written dozens of scripts for television and movies, as well as several stage plays. His favorite topic is injustice, and he often writes about controversial social issues. In fact, Rose's first version of *Thunder on Sycamore Street* was about an African American man moving into a white neighborhood. Sponsors, afraid of offending some audiences, pressured CBS-TV to have Rose rewrite it. The drama aired in 1953 with a white ex-convict as the central character.

Rose is most famous for his 1954 teleplay *Twelve Angry Men*, which he later rewrote as a feature film (released in 1957, starring Henry Fonda, with whom Rose co-produced it) and then, in 1964, as a stage play. *Twelve Angry Men* is the story of the members of a jury trying to decide the case of a young man accused of killing his father. At first all the jury members except one are convinced of the young man's guilt. But as the lone holdout forces the other jurors to reexamine the evidence—and their own prejudices—the jurors begin to question their beliefs. Nothing "happens" in *Twelve Angry Men*—the action consists entirely of a group of people arguing in a room—and yet the drama is gripping and suspenseful. Rose won one of his three Emmy Awards for the original teleplay, and the movie was nominated for two Academy Awards.

Rose also created a popular television series, called *The Defenders*, which ran throughout the early 1960s. The show was about a father-and-son team of criminal defense lawyers. (The son was played by Robert Reed, who later achieved fame as the father on *The Brady Bunch*. The father was played by E. G.

Marshall, who starred in the 1999 update of *The Defenders*—now a grandfather-son-granddaughter lawyer team—on cable-TV-station Showtime.) *The Defenders* was one of the first legal dramas on TV and was known, like much of Rose's other writing, for its gritty realism. In its treatment of controversial subjects, such as civil disobedience, abortion, and euthanasia, it laid the groundwork for today's realistic legal dramas—sometimes the show's stars even lost a case.

Thunder on Sycamore Street
Reginald Rose

Characters

Frank Morrison
Clarice Morrison
Roger Morrison
Christopher Morrison
Arthur Hayes
Phyllis Hayes
Mr. Harkness
Joseph Blake
Anna Blake
Judy Blake
Mrs. Blake
Charlie Denton
Mrs. Carson

Act One

*Fade in on a long shot of Sycamore Street in the pleasant and tidy
village of Eastmont. It is 6:40 P.M. and just getting dark. We see three
houses, modest but attractive, side by side, each an exact replica of
the other. Each has a tiny front lawn and a tree or two in front of it.
Each has been lived in and cared for by people who take pride in their
own hard-won respectability. The street is quiet. Walking toward the
houses now we see* ARTHUR HAYES, *a quiet, bespectacled man between
thirty-five and thirty-eight years of age. He lives in the second of the
three houses. He walks slowly, carrying a newspaper under his arm
and smoking a pipe. He stops in front of his house and, almost in a*

daze, knocks the dottle out of his pipe against his heel. As he is doing this, we see FRANK MORRISON *enter, also carrying a newspaper. He is a heavy man, forceful and aggressive, with a loud voice and a hearty laugh. He is about forty years of age.* FRANK MORRISON *lives right next door to* ARTHUR, *in the first of the three houses. He sees* ARTHUR *and waves.*

Frank (*jovially*). Hey, Artie. How ya doin'?

[ARTHUR *is preoccupied. He doesn't register at first. He looks blankly at* FRANK.]

(*Laughing*) Hey . . . wake up, boy. It's almost time for supper.

[ARTHUR *snaps out of it and forces a smile.*]

Arthur (*quietly*). Oh . . . hello, Frank. Sorry, I didn't see you.
Frank. Didn't see me? Hey, wait till I tell Clarice. That diet she's got me on must be working. You have to look twice to see me! (*Laughing hard,* FRANK *reaches for his keys.*) That's a hot one!

[ARTHUR *smiles weakly.*]

Say . . . isn't this late for you to be getting home?
Arthur. No, I don't think so. (*He looks at his watch.*) It's twenty to seven. I always get home about this time.
Frank. Yeah. Well, I wouldn't want you to be late tonight. You know what tonight is, don't you?
Arthur (*slowly*). Yes, I know what tonight is.
Frank (*a little hard*). Good.

[*We hear footsteps and see a man walk by them. He is* JOSEPH BLAKE, *a man in his late thirties, a big, powerful, but quiet man.* JOSEPH BLAKE *lives in the third house on the street. As he walks by them, they both look at him silently.* ARTHUR *turns away then, but* FRANK *continues to stare at him. Camera moves in on* FRANK *as he stares coldly at* JOSEPH BLAKE. *His face is hard, full of hatred. The footsteps recede.*]

Frank (*low*). See you later, Artie.

[FRANK *turns and fits the key into the lock. There is utter silence. He fumbles with the lock, then silently swings the door open. He walks into the small foyer. The living room ahead is brightly lighted, but we see no one.* FRANK *walks slowly, silently into the living room. As he enters it, we hear a dozen pistol shots.* FRANK *stiffens, clutches himself, and falls to the floor as if dead. Then, we hear a chorus of shrill screams and two small boys wearing cowboy hats and carrying pistols fling themselves upon* FRANK'S *body.* FRANK *doesn't move as they clamber over him. One is* ROGER, *age ten; the other is* CHRISTOPHER, *age six.* CHRISTOPHER *wears "Dr. Dentons."*]

Christopher (*screaming*). I got him! I got him first.
Roger. You did not!
Christopher. I did so! Get offa him. I got him first. (*Calling*) Hey, Mom . . .
Roger (*superior*). Boy, are you stupid! I got him three times before you even pulled the trigger.
Christopher (*squeaking*). What d'ya mean? I got him before you even——

[ROGER *tries to push* CHRISTOPHER *off* FRANK'S *still motionless body.*]

Before you even—— (CHRISTOPHER *grunts and fights back.*) Cut it out! Hey, Mom . . .

[CLARICE, FRANK'S *wife, a pleasant-looking woman in her early thirties, comes to living room door from kitchen. She wears an apron. She calls out before she sees them.*]

Clarice. Now, you boys stop that noise. (*She sees* ROGER *pushing* CHRISTOPHER.) Roger!
Christopher. Cut it out, willya. I got him——
Clarice. Roger! Stop that pushing. . . .
Christopher. I'm gonna sock you. . . .
Clarice (*angrily*). Christopher, don't you dare! Frank! Will you do something . . . please!

Roger. Go ahead. Sock me. You couldn't hurt a flea!
Christopher (*winding up*). Who says so?
Roger. Boy, you must be deaf. I said so!
Clarice. Frank!

[*As* CHRISTOPHER *swings at* ROGER, FRANK *suddenly comes to life with a tremendous roar. He rolls over, toppling both boys to the floor, and with lightning swiftness, he grabs both of their cap pistols. He stands up, grinning. They both look at him, startled.*]

Frank (*barking*). Get up! (*They both do, slowly.*) Get your hands up! (*They look at each other.*) Make it snappy if you don't want to draw lead.

[CHRISTOPHER *shrugs and raises his hands.*]

(*To* ROGER) You too, hombre!
Roger. Aaaah, Dad . . .
Frank. Last warning.
Roger (*disgusted*). Come on. . . .

[FRANK *shoots him with the cap pistol.*]

What are you so serious about? (*He walks away.*)

[FRANK *watches him, still not giving up the cowboy pose.*]

Clarice. All right. Now, that's enough gunplay. All three of you can just settle down. (*To* FRANK) Hand 'em over.

[*He grins and gives her the guns. Then he bends over and kisses her.*]

Frank. Hello, honey.

[*She kisses him dutifully, then speaks to* ROGER, *handing him the guns.*]

Clarice. Put these in your room and come back with your hands washed. We're sitting down to supper right now.
Roger (*desperately*). Right now? I gotta watch "Rangebusters."

Clarice. Not tonight. I told you we were eating early.
Roger. Ah, Mom . . . please . . .
Clarice. Absolutely not. Come on, now. Inside . . .

[ROGER *slumps off.* CLARICE *turns to* CHRISTOPHER *as* FRANK *begins to take off his coat.*]

And you're going to bed, mister.
Christopher. No! I can't go to bed!
Clarice. Christopher!
Christopher (*backing away*). I'm not tired yet. Honest!

[FRANK *is hanging his coat up in the foyer.* CLARICE *advances toward* CHRIS, *who looks for means of escape.*]

Clarice. I'm not going to argue with you.
Christopher. Mom, fifteen minutes. Come on. Please . . .
Clarice. I'm going to start counting. One, two——
Christopher (*fast*). Three, four, five, six, seven, eight, nine, ten.

[*He runs away from her but right into the arms of* FRANK, *who picks him up.*]

Frank. Trapped! Let's go, pal.
Christopher. Aaah . . .

[FRANK *carries him past* CLARICE, *who kisses him on the way by. As they reach the door that leads into bedroom,* ROGER *comes out.* CHRISTOPHER, *in his father's arms, raps* ROGER *on the head with his knuckle.*]

Roger. Hey!
Christopher (*grinning*). Good night, Rog.
Roger. Stupid!
Frank. All right, now. That's enough out of both of you. I don't want to hear another peep.

[FRANK *takes* CHRISTOPHER *into bedroom. Camera follows* ROGER *over to a dining table set at one end of living room near a picture window. This would probably be an L-shaped living room/dining room setup*

*and would be exactly the same in all three houses. The only differ-
ence in the three interior sets will be the way in which they are dec-
orated. There are dishes on the table, glassware, etc.* ROGER *slumps
into his chair and takes a piece of bread. He munches on it as* CLARICE
*comes in from kitchen carrying a steaming bowl of stew. She sets it
down and sits down.*]

Clarice (*calling*). Frank!
Frank (*off*). Okay. I'll be right there.
Roger. Hey, Mom, what are we eating so early for?
Clarice (*serving*). Don't say "Hey, Mom."
Roger. Well, what are we eating so early for?
Clarice. Because we feel like eating early. (*Calling*) Frank!

[FRANK *walks in, loosening his tie.*]

Frank. What's for supper?
Clarice. Beef stew.
Roger. Look, if I could see the first five minutes of "Range-
busters"——

[CLARICE *ladles out the stew as* FRANK *sits at the table.*]

Clarice. Roger, I'm not going to tell you again.
Roger (*anguished*). But, Mom, you don't know what's happen-
ing. There's this sneaky guy——
Frank. Come on, boy, dig into your dinner.

[ROGER *makes a face and gives up the battle.*]

(*To* CLARICE) What time is the sitter coming?
Clarice. Ten after seven. Do you know that's the third time
today you've asked me.
Frank. Just want to be sure.
Clarice. I don't see why they have to make it so early anyway.

[FRANK *has a mouthful of food, so he shrugs.*]

Roger. Make what so early, Dad?
Clarice. Nothing. Eat your dinner.
Frank. Good stew.
Clarice. There's plenty more.
Frank (*chewing*). Mmmm. Hmmmm. Do anything special today, Rog?
Roger. Nope. Just kinda hung around.
Frank. Well, I don't know why you don't get out and do something. A boy your age . . .
Roger. Some of the kids dumped garbage on the Blakes' lawn again.
Frank (*casually*). That so? What about you?
Roger. Ah, what fun is that after you do it a couple of times?
Frank (*chewing*). Mmmm. Hey, how about eating your stew.
Roger. I'm not hungry.
Clarice. Frank, I wish you'd do something about that boy's eating. He's beginning to look like a scarecrow.
Frank. He'll be all right. What time is it?
Clarice (*looking at watch*). Five of seven.
Frank. We'd better snap it up.
Clarice. Plenty of time. I'm leaving the dishes till later.
Frank. Y'know, Clarry, this really ought to be something tonight.

[ROGER *starts to get up, but stops.*]

Roger. What ought to be something?
Clarice. You just sit down and pay attention to your dinner. There's a glass of milk to be finished before you get up.
Roger (*grudgingly*). OK. (*He sips the milk for a moment.*) Where you going tonight, Dad?
Frank. We're going for a little walk.
Roger. Well, what d'ya have to go out so early for?
Frank. Just like that.

Roger (*aggressively*). Well, what the heck is the big secret, that's what I'd like to know. Everybody's acting so mysterious.

Frank (*sharply*). That's enough. Now I don't want to hear any more questions out of you. Your mother and I have some business to attend to, and that's it. You mind yours.

[ROGER, *stunned, looks at his father, then down at his plate. There is an awkward silence.* FRANK *eats stolidly. They watch him.*]

(*To* CLARICE) Where's that sitter?

Clarice. It's not time yet. Take it easy, Frank.

[FRANK *gets up from the table, goes over to a box of cigars on top of the TV set, and lights one.* CLARICE *and* ROGER *watch him silently.*]

Aren't you going to have some dessert, Frank? There's some cherry pie left.

Frank. I'll have it later. (*He puffs on the cigar.*)

Roger (*low*). I'm sorry, Dad.

Frank (*turning*). Well, it's about time you learned some respect, d'you hear me? If I want you to know something I'll tell it to you.

Roger (*softly*). OK . . .

Clarice (*quickly*). Have some pie, honey. I heated it special.

[FRANK *goes to the table and sits down. He puts the cigar down and* CLARICE *begins to cut him some pie.*]

How late do you think we'll be, Frank?

Frank. I don't know.

Clarice. Do you think I ought to pack a thermos of hot coffee? It's going to be chilly.

Frank. Might not be a bad idea. (FRANK *now begins to show the first signs of being excited about the evening. He speaks, almost to himself.*) Boy, I can't wait till I see his face. The nerve of him. The absolute nerve. (*Grinning*) What d'you think he'll do when we all——

Clarice (*looking at* ROGER). Frank . . .

Frank (*as* ROGER *stares*). Oh. Yeah, go ahead, Rog. You can turn on your program.

Roger. Gee thanks, Dad. (*He jumps up, goes to the TV set, and turns it on.*)

[FRANK *and* CLARICE *watch him get settled in front of TV set. We hear dialogue from set faintly.* ROGER *watches in background, enraptured.*]

Frank (*quietly*). What are they saying on the block?
Clarice. I didn't speak to anyone. I was ironing all day.
Frank. Charlie Denton called me at the office. I was right in the middle of taking an order from Martin Brothers for three A-81 tractors.
Clarice. Three? Frank, that's *wonderful!*
Frank. Not bad. Anyway, I made Mr. Martin wait while I spoke to Charlie. Charlie says it's gonna be one hundred percent. Every family on the block. He just called to tell me that.
Clarice. Well, that's good. Everyone should be in on this.
Frank (*eating*). Clarry, I'm telling you this is going to be a job well done. It's how you have to do these things. Everybody getting together first . . . and boom, it's over. I can't wait till it's started. It's been long enough.
Clarice. I saw her out the window today, hanging clothes in her yard like nothing was wrong. She didn't even look this way.
Frank. What time is it?
Clarice. Now you just asked me two minutes ago. It's about three minutes to seven. What's the matter with you? You'll be getting yourself an ulcer over this thing. Relax, Frank. Here, have some more pie.
Frank. No. No more.

[*He gets up and walks around nervously, slapping his fist into his palm.* ROGER *is looking at him now. He is tense, excited, completely caught up in the impending event.*]

This is something big, you know that, Clarry? We're getting action without pussyfooting for once. That's it. That's the big part. There's too much pussyfooting going on all the time. Can't

hurt anyone's feelings. Every time you turn around, you're hurting some idiot's feelings. Well that's tough, I say. . . .
Clarice (*indicating* ROGER). Frank . . .
Frank. He can hear! He's old enough. You want something bad, you gotta go out and get it! That's how this world is. Boy, I like this, Clarry. You know what it makes me feel like? It makes me feel like a man! (*He stalks up and down the room for a few moments as they watch him. Then he goes to the window and stands there looking out.*)
Clarice (*quietly*). I think I'll just stack the dishes. (*She starts to do it.*)

[*The doorbell rings.* ROGER *jumps up.*]

Roger. I'll get it. (*He goes to the door and opens it.*)

[ARTHUR HAYES *stands there a bit apologetically. He wears no overcoat, having just come from next door. He looks extremely upset.*]

Arthur. Rog, is your dad in?
Roger. Sure. Come on in, Mr. Hayes.

[ARTHUR *walks in slowly.* FRANK *turns around, still excited. He goes over to* ARTHUR.]

Frank (*loud*). Hey, Artie. Come on in.
Arthur. Hello, Frank. . . .
Frank (*laughing*). What can I do for you?

[ARTHUR *looks hesitatingly at* ROGER.]

Oh, sure. Rog, go help your mother.
Roger (*annoyed*). OK. . . . (*He walks off to dining table.*)
Frank (*chuckling*). That's some kid, isn't he, Artie? How old is yours now?
Arthur. Twenty-one months.

Frank. Yeah. Well, that's still nothing but a crying machine. Wait a couple years. He'll kill you.

Arthur. I guess so.

Frank. And how! Sit down for a minute, Artie. What's on your mind?

Arthur (*sitting. Hesitantly*). Well, I don't know . . . I just . . . well . . . I just wanted . . . to talk.

Frank. No kidding. Say, y'know you look a little green around the gills? What's the matter?

[ARTHUR HAYES *takes off his eyeglasses and begins to polish them, a nervous habit in which he indulges when upset.*]

Arthur. Nothing. I've had an upset stomach for a couple of days. Maybe that's it.

Frank (*nodding*). Yeah, that'll get you down all right. Probably a virus.

[ARTHUR *nods and they look at each other awkwardly for a moment.*]

Well, what did you want to talk to me about?

[ARTHUR *looks at the floor, trying to frame his answer carefully, afraid to offend. Finally he blurts it out.*]

Arthur. What do you think about this thing tonight?

Frank (*surprised*). What do you mean what do I think about it?

Arthur. Well, I've been kind of going over it all day, Frank. I talked with Phyllis before.

Frank (*a little hard*). And . . .

Arthur. Well, it was just talk. We were just talking it over to get clear on it, you know.

Frank. Go ahead.

Arthur. And . . . well, look, Frank, it's a pretty hard thing. Supposing it were you?

Frank. It's not.

Arthur. Well, I know that, but supposing it were?

[FRANK *stands up and goes over to* ARTHUR.]

Frank. Your glasses are clean. You wear 'em out, you have to buy a new pair.

[ARTHUR *looks down at his glasses then puts them on nervously.*]

Now, what about it, Artie? What if I was the guy?
Arthur. Well, you know . . . how would you feel?
Frank. How would I feel, huh? Now, that's a good question, Artie. I'll answer it for you. It doesn't make any difference how I'd feel. Now let me ask you a question. Is he a lifelong buddy of yours?
Arthur. Well, now, you know he's not, Frank.
Frank. Do you know him to say hello to?
Arthur. That's not the idea. He's——
Frank. Artie . . . you don't even know the guy. What are you getting yourself all hot and bothered about? We all agreed, didn't we?
Arthur. Yes . . . everybody agreed.
Frank. You. Me. The Dentons. The McAllisters. The Fredericks. The Schofields. Every family on Sycamore Street for that matter. We all agreed. That's how it is. The majority. Right?
Arthur. Well . . . I think we all ought to talk it over, maybe. Let it wait a few days. (*He takes off his glasses again and begins to wipe them.*)
Frank. Artie . . . we talked it over. (FRANK *takes the handkerchief out of* ARTHUR's *hand and tucks it into his pocket.*) In about ten minutes we're starting. We expect to have a solid front, you know what I mean? Everybody. You included. You're my next door neighbor, boy. I don't want to hear people saying Artie Hayes wasn't there.
Arthur (*hesitantly*). Well, I don't know, Frank. I thought——

[*The phone rings.* FRANK *goes toward it.*]

Frank. Go home, Artie. Don't worry about it. I'll see you in a few minutes.

[FRANK *goes to the phone and picks it up.* ARTHUR *stares at him.*]

Hello . . .

[ARTHUR *turns away and walks slowly to door.*]

Speaking.

[ARTHUR *goes out, dazed and frightened.* CLARICE *comes into living room and stands waiting as* FRANK *listens to phone.*]

(*Angry*) What do you mean you can't get here? (*Pause*) Well, this is a great time to call! (*Pause*) I know. Yeah. (*He slams the phone down. To* CLARICE.) Our sitter can't get here. How d'you like that?
Clarice. What's wrong with her?
Frank. I don't know. She's got a cold, or something. Nice dependable girl you pick.
Clarice (*snapping*). Well, I didn't exactly arrange for her to get a cold, you know.
Frank. Look, Clarry, we're going to this thing no matter what.
Clarice. Well, I'm not leaving Chris with Roger. They'll claw each other to pieces.
Frank. Then we'll take them with us.
Clarice. You wouldn't . . .
Frank. Who wouldn't? We're doing it for them as much as anyone else, aren't we? Well, they might as well see it.
Clarice. Maybe I'd better stay home with them.
Frank. No, sir. You've been in on this from the beginning. You're going. Come on, get Chris dressed. We haven't got much time.
Clarice. Well . . . whatever you think Frank. . . .

Frank. I'm telling you it's all right. Won't hurt 'em a bit. (*To* ROGER) What d'you say, son? Want to come along?
Roger (*eagerly*). Oh, boy! Really?

[FRANK *nods and grins.* ROGER *leaps happily.*]

Gee, Dad, you're the greatest guy in all the whole world. (*He runs over and hugs* FRANK.)
Frank (*grinning*). Go on, Clarry. Make it snappy.

[CLARICE *goes into the bedroom. Doorbell rings.*]

Roger. I'll get it, Dad. (*He runs to the door and opens it.*)

[CHARLIE DENTON, *forty years old and eager as a child, stands there. He comes in fast, excited.*]

Charlie. Hiya, Rog. Frank, you all set?
Frank. Hello, Charlie. Another minute or two. How's it look?
Charlie. Great. I'm checking house to house. Everybody's ready.
Frank. Good. Any changes?
Charlie. Nope. It's gonna be fast and quiet. What time you got?
Frank (*calling*). Clarry, what time is it?
Clarice (*calling*). Twelve after.
Charlie (*looking at watch*). Make it thirteen. At fifteen we go.
Frank. Right. Hey listen, you better look in on Artie Hayes next door. He's been acting a little peculiar.
Charlie. I spoke to him a little while ago on the street. I think he was coming over to see you. Don't worry about a thing. I'll be watching him. See you, Frank. Let's make this good.
Frank. You bet we will. It looks like a beaut. Take off.

[CHARLIE *goes out fast.*]

Get on your coat, Rog. (*Calling*) Clarry!

[ROGER *goes to closet and begins to get his coat.* FRANK *stalks nervously up and down.*]

Clarice (*calling*). In a minute . . .

[FRANK *goes to the window and looks out. He watches and waits. We can see the excitement building within him.* ROGER, *hat and coat on, joins him at window.* FRANK *puts his arm on* ROGER'S *shoulder and talks, half to himself.*]

Frank (*low*). How do you like that Artie Hayes? Maybe we ought to think it over! I could've belted him one. How do you like that guy!
Roger. What do you mean, Dad?
Frank (*calling*). Clarry!
Clarice (*calling*). Here I am. Come on, Chris.

[CLARICE *walks into living room followed by a very sleepy* CHRISTOPHER. *He is in his hat and coat. He wanders over to* FRANK.]

Frank. What time is it?
Clarice. Almost fourteen after.
Frank. Almost fifteen. Put on your coat.

[CLARICE *goes to the closet and does so.* FRANK *follows her and gets his. He puts it on.* CLARICE *picks up a large thermos from the foyer table.*]

Clarice (*low*). Frank . . . I'm busting with excitement.
Frank (*low*). Yeah. So'm I, honey. (*Louder*) Come over here, boys.

[*The two boys walk over to them.*]

Stand here.

[*They wait now behind the closed front door, all four of them tense, quiet, hardly able to stand the suspense. They wait for several sec-*

onds, and then, in the street, we begin to hear the heavy tread of marching feet.]

Christopher. Hey, Daddy, . . . where we going?
Frank. Ssh. Be quiet, son.

[*He bends over and picks* CHRISTOPHER *up. The sound of marching feet grows louder and stronger. They wait till it reaches a crescendo.* FRANK *speaks quietly now.*]

Let's go.

[*He opens the front door and they walk into a mob of grimly advancing men and women. They join the mob and walk with them quietly, and the only sound we hear is the frightening noise of the tramping feet. Fade out.*]

Act Two

Fade in on long shot of Sycamore Street. It is once again 6:40 P.M., the same night. We have gone backward in time, and we now duplicate exactly the scene which opened Act One. ARTHUR HAYES *walks on, stops in front of his house, knocks his pipe against his heel.* FRANK MORRISON *enters. Each of the movements they make, the attitudes they strike, and the inflections they use must be exact imitations of the Act One business. The audience must feel that this scene is a clip of film which we are rerunning.*

Frank (*jovially*). Hey, Artie. How ya doin'?

[ARTHUR *is preoccupied. He doesn't register at first. He looks blankly at* FRANK.]

(*Laughing*) Hey . . . wake up, boy. It's almost time for supper.

[ARTHUR *snaps out of it and forces a smile.*]

Arthur (*quietly*). Oh . . . hello, Frank. Sorry. I didn't see you.
Frank. Didn't see me? Hey, wait till I tell Clarice. That diet she's got me on must be working. You have to look twice to see me! (*Laughing hard,* FRANK *reaches for his keys.*) That's a hot one!

[ARTHUR *smiles weakly.*]

Say . . . isn't this late for you to be getting home?
Arthur. No, I don't think so. (*He looks at his watch.*) It's twenty to seven. I always get home about this time.
Frank. Yeah. Well, I wouldn't want you to be late tonight. You know what tonight is, don't you?
Arthur (*slowly*). Yes, I know what tonight is.
Frank (*a little hard*). Good.

[*We hear footsteps and see a man walk by them. He is* JOSEPH BLAKE, *a man in his late thirties, a big, powerful, but quiet man.* JOSEPH BLAKE *lives in the third house on the street. As he walks by them they both look at him silently. And now, for the first time, this scene moves in a different direction than did the scene at the beginning of Act One. Instead of coming in close on* FRANK, *the camera comes in close on* ARTHUR HAYES *as he stands nervously in front of his door, afraid to look at either* JOSEPH BLAKE *or* FRANK MORRISON. *We hear* JOSEPH's *footsteps fade out.* ARTHUR *reaches for his keys.*]

(*Low, off*) See you later, Artie.

[ARTHUR *winces at this. We hear* FRANK's *door opening and closing softly.* ARTHUR *turns now and looks off at* JOSEPH BLAKE's *house for a moment. Then he turns and opens his door. As he enters his foyer we hear dance music playing softly. The living room is lighted and looking in from the foyer, we can see* MR. HARKNESS, ARTHUR's *father-in-law, seated in an armchair reading the newspaper. He is perhaps sixty-five years old and usually does nothing more than sit reading the newspapers. He looks up as* ARTHUR *comes in.*]

Mr. Harkness. Hello, Arthur. (*Calling off*) Here he is, Phyllis. (*To* ARTHUR) Little bit late, aren't you?

[ARTHUR *is hanging up his coat. He is obviously worried. His face shows concern. His entire manner is subdued. He speaks quietly, even for* ARTHUR.]

Arthur. No. Usual time.

[MR. HARKNESS *takes out a pocket watch, looks at it, shakes it.*]

Mr. Harkness. Mmm. Must be fast.

[*He goes back to his newspaper.* ARTHUR *walks into the living room tiredly.*]

Arthur (*not caring*). How's your cough?
Mr. Harkness (*reading*). Still got it. I guess I must've swigged enough cough syrup to float a rowboat today. Waste of time and money!

[PHYLLIS *enters from kitchen as* ARTHUR *goes over to phonograph from which the dance music is blasting. He is just ready to turn it off as she enters.*]

Cough'll go away by itself like it always does.
Phyllis (*brightly*). Hello, darling. Ah . . . don't turn it off.

[*He turns as she walks over to him. She kisses him possessively and leads him away from the phonograph. The music continues.*]

How did it go today, dear?
Arthur. All right. Nothing special.
Phyllis. What about the Franklin closing?
Arthur. It's called off till tomorrow.
Phyllis. How come?
Arthur. I didn't ask them.

Phyllis. Well, you'd think they'd at least give you a reason. You should've asked. I don't like it when people push you around like that.

[ARTHUR *goes over to a chair without answering. A pipe is on an end table next to the chair. He begins to fill it.* PHYLLIS *goes to a small bar on which is a cocktail shaker and one glass. She picks up the shaker.*]

Arthur. What's that?
Phyllis. I made you a drink.
Arthur. No. No thanks. I don't want a drink now.
Phyllis. Oh, Artie! I made it specially for you. You look tired. Come on, it'll do you good. (*She begins to pour the drink.*) Sit down, dear. I'll bring it over to you.

[ARTHUR *sits down.* PHYLLIS *finishes pouring the drink and brings it to him. He takes it. She waits, smiling, for him to drink it.*]

Arthur. How come you made me a drink tonight?
Phyllis. Just for luck. Taste it.

[*She sits on the arm of the chair. He tastes it slowly. She puts her arm around him.*]

Good?
Arthur (*slowly*). It's good.
Phyllis. I thought you'd like it.
Arthur. Where's Billy?
Phyllis. Asleep.
Arthur. Isn't it kind of early?
Phyllis. He didn't get much of a nap today. The poor baby couldn't keep his eyes open. Artie, he's getting to be such a devil. You should've seen him this afternoon. He got into my bag and took my lipstick. If I only could've taken a picture of his face. He walked into the kitchen and I swear I almost screamed. You never saw anything so red in your life. Drink your drink, darling. It took me ten minutes to scrub it off.

[*Obediently,* ARTHUR *sips his drink.*]

Arthur (*mildly*). I'd like to have seen him before he went to bed.
Phyllis. Now, you know I had to get finished early tonight, Artie. (*She gets up and goes toward the kitchen.*) We're eating in a few minutes. I'm just making melted cheese sandwiches. We can have a snack later if you're hungry.
Arthur. Later?
Phyllis (*looking at him oddly*). Yes, later. When we get back.

[ARTHUR *puts his drink down. All of his movements are slow, almost mechanical, as if he has that day aged twenty years.* PHYLLIS *goes into the kitchen. He takes off his glasses and begins polishing them.*]

Mr. Harkness. Melted cheese sandwiches.
Arthur (*not hearing*). What?
Mr. Harkness. I said melted cheese sandwiches. That gluey cheese. Do you like it?
Arthur. No.
Mr. Harkness. Me neither. Never did. (*He goes back to his paper.*)

[ARTHUR *gets up and goes to phonograph. He stands over it, listening.* PHYLLIS *comes in carrying a tray on which are three glasses of tomato juice. She gives it to* ARTHUR.]

Phyllis. Put these on the table like a good boy.

[*He takes it and looks at her strangely.*]

What's the matter with you, Artie? You've hardly said a word since you got home . . . and you keep looking at me. Are you sick, or something?
Arthur. No. I'm not sick.
Phyllis. Here, let me feel your head. (*She does so.*) No, you feel all right. What is it?
Arthur. Nothing. I'm just tired, I guess.
Phyllis. Well, I hope you perk up a little. (*She goes off into kitchen.*)

[ARTHUR *goes slowly to dining table, which is set in the same spot as the Morrison dining table. He puts the glasses on it and sets the tray on the end table. He takes a sip of his drink.* PHYLLIS *comes in from the kitchen carrying a platter of melted cheese sandwiches. She goes to the table, puts it down.*]

Dinner. Come on, Dad, while they're hot. Artie . . .
Arthur. You go ahead. I'm not hungry.
Phyllis. Oh, now, let's not start that. You have to eat. Try one. They're nice and runny.
Arthur. Really, I'm not hungry.
Phyllis. Well, you can at least sit with us. I haven't seen you since half-past eight this morning.

[ARTHUR *goes slowly over to the table and sits down.* MR. HARKNESS *ambles over.*]

Mr. Harkness. Well, I'm good and hungry. Tell you that. Got any pickles?
Phyllis. No pickles. You know they give you heartburn.
Mr. Harkness. Haven't had heartburn in a long time. Wouldn't mind a slight case if it came from pickles.

[*They are all seated now,* PHYLLIS *facing the window.* ARTHUR *sits quietly.* MR. HARKNESS *busies himself drinking water while* PHYLLIS *serves the sandwiches, potato salad, etc.*]

Phyllis. Artie . . . potato salad?
Arthur. No. Look, Phyllis . . .
Phyllis. Just a little.

[*She puts a spoonful on a heavily loaded plate and passes it to him. He takes it. Now she serves her father.*]

Phyllis. Potato salad, Dad?
Mr. Harkness. I'll help myself.

[*She puts the bowl down and helps herself, as does* MR. HARKNESS.]

Phyllis (*brightly*). What happened at the office, dear? Anything new?

Arthur. No. It was quiet.

Phyllis. Did you hear about the Walkers wanting to sell their house?

Arthur. No.

Phyllis. You know, for a real-estate man you hear less about real estate than anyone I ever saw. I spoke to Margie Walker this morning. I just got to her in time. You're going to handle the sale. She told me she hadn't even thought of you till I called. Why is that, dear?

Arthur. I don't know why it is.

Phyllis. Well, anyway, she's expecting you to call her tomorrow. It ought to be a very nice sale for you, dear.

[ARTHUR *nods and looks down at his plate. There is silence for a moment.*]

Mr. Harkness (*chewing*). This stuff gets under my teeth.

Phyllis. Dad!

Mr. Harkness. Well, I can't help it, can I?

[*They eat for a moment and then* PHYLLIS, *looking out the window, sees movement in the house next door, the Blake house. She can no longer hold back the topic she's been trying not to discuss in front of* ARTHUR.]

Phyllis. Look at them. Every shade in the house is down. (*She looks at her watch.*) There isn't much more time. I wonder if they know. Do you think they do, Artie?

Arthur (*tired*). I don't know.

Phyllis. They must. You can't keep a thing like this secret. I wonder how they feel. (*She looks at* ARTHUR.) Artie, aren't you going to eat your dinner?

Arthur (*slowly*). How can you talk about them and my dinner in the same breath?

Phyllis. For heaven's sakes . . . I don't know what's the matter with you tonight.

Arthur (*quietly*). You don't, do you?

[*He gets up from the table and walks over to the phonograph. He stands there holding it with both hands, listening to the slick dance music. Then, abruptly, he turns it off.* PHYLLIS *looks as if she is about to protest, but then she decides not to.*]

Mr. Harkness. What d'you suppose is gonna happen over there? Boy, wouldn't I like to go along tonight.
Phyllis (*looking at* ARTHUR). Dad, will you please stop?
Mr. Harkness. Well, I would! How do you think it feels to be sixty-two years old and baby-sitting when there's real action going on right under your nose? Something a man wants to get into.
Arthur (*turning*). Be quiet!
Mr. Harkness. Now listen here——
Arthur. I said be quiet! (*He takes off his glasses and walks over to the table.*)
Phyllis. Artie, stop it! There's no need for you to raise your voice like that.

[ARTHUR *speaks more quietly now, feeling perhaps that he has gone too far.*]

Arthur. Then tell your father to keep his ideas to himself!
Mr. Harkness (*angrily*). Wait a minute!

[PHYLLIS, *in the ensuing argument, is quiet, calm, convincing, never losing her temper, always trying to soothe* ARTHUR, *to sweeten the ugly things she says by saying them gently.*]

Phyllis. Dad, be quiet. Listen, Artie, I know you're tired, darling, but there's something we might as well face. In about fifteen or twenty minutes you and I and a group of our friends and neighbors are going to be marching on that house next door. Maybe it's not such a pleasant thing to look forward to, but something has to be done. You know that, Artie. You agreed to it with all the others.
Arthur. I didn't agree to anything. You agreed for the Hayes household. Remember?

Phyllis. All right, I agreed. I didn't hear you disagreeing. Oh, what's the difference, darling? You've been acting like there's a ten-ton weight on your back ever since you heard about it. And there's no point to it. It's all decided.

Arthur. All decided. What right have we got to decide?

Phyllis. It's not a question of right, Artie. Don't you see? It's something we have to do, right or wrong. Do you want them to live next door to you? Do you really want them?

Arthur. I always thought a man was supposed to be able to live anywhere he chooses no matter what anyone else wants.

Phyllis. But, dear, this isn't anywhere. This is Sycamore Street. It's not some back alley in a slum! This is a respectable neighborhood. Artie, let's be realistic. That's one of the few things we can really say we have. We're respectable. Do you remember how hard we worked to get that way?

Arthur. Respectable! Phyllis, for heaven's sakes. We're talking about throwing a man out of his own home. What is the man? He's not a monster. He's a quiet guy who minds his own business. How does that destroy our respectability?

Phyllis (*hard*). He got out of prison two months ago. He's a common hoodlum.

Arthur. We don't know for sure.

Phyllis. We know. Charlie Denton doesn't lie. He saw the man's picture in the Rockville papers just fifty miles from here the day he got out. Tell me, what does he do for a living? Where did he get the money to buy that house?

Arthur. I don't think that's any of your business.

Phyllis. But, Artie, the man was in jail for four years. That's our business! How do you know what he did? How do you know he won't do it again?

Arthur. We have police.

Phyllis. Police! Will the police stop his child from playing with Billy? What kind of a child must that be? Think about it. Her father is an ex-convict. That's a lovely thing to tell our friends. Why yes . . . you know Billy's little friend Judy. Of course you do. Her father spent a great deal of time in prison. Charming people. It's beautiful for the neighborhood, isn't it, Artie? It makes real-estate prices just skyrocket up. Tell me, who do you think'll be moving in next . . . and where'll we go?

[ARTHUR *doesn't answer. He sits down in a chair, troubled, trying to find an argument.* PHYLLIS *watches him closely.*]

Mr. Harkness. Listen, Artie——

[*But* PHYLLIS *puts her hand on his arm to shut him up.* ARTHUR *is thinking and she wants to see if her argument has worked.*]

Arthur. Look, Phyllis, this is a mob we're getting together. We're going to order this man out of his house . . . or we're going to throw him out. What right have we got to do it? Maybe most of us'd rather not have him as a neighbor, but, Phyllis, the man is a human being, not an old dog. This is an ugly thing we're doing. . . .
Phyllis. We've got to do something to keep our homes decent. There's no other way. Somebody's always got to lose, Artie. Why should it be all of us when there's only one of him?
Arthur. I . . . I don't know.

[ARTHUR *suddenly gets up and goes toward the front door as if going out. He buttons his jacket.* PHYLLIS *gets up, concerned.*]

Phyllis. Where are you going?
Arthur. I'm going to talk to Frank Morrison.
Phyllis. All right. Maybe Frank'll make sense to you. (*Calling*) Wear your coat.

[*But* ARTHUR *has opened the door and intends to go out without it.* PHYLLIS *looks at her watch.*]

Arthur, it's freezing out!

[*He is outside the door now.*]

You'll catch cold.

[*The door closes. She stands watching after him, obviously upset. Her father resumes his eating. She looks at the door for a long time. Then, without looking around*]

Dad . . .
Mr. Harkness. Mmmm?
Phyllis. What do you think he'll do?
Mr. Harkness. Well . . . I don't know. You got any more of these cheese businesses? I'm hungry.
Phyllis. No. (*She goes to the window and looks out.*)
Mr. Harkness. Why don't you sit down, Phyl? He'll be all right.
Phyllis. What do you mean, all right? Look at him. He's standing in front of Frank's house afraid to ring the bell.
Mr. Harkness. He'll calm down. Come away from that window and sit down. Have some coffee.

[*She moves away from window and sits at table.*]

Phyllis. I've never seen him like this before.
Mr. Harkness. Well, what are you worried about? Tell you what. I'll go along with you. Boy, wouldn't I like to be in on a thing like this once. Let Artie stay home and mind the baby if that's how he feels.

[PHYLLIS *turns to her father violently, and for the first time we see how much* ARTHUR's *decision means to her.*]

Phyllis (*fiercely*). He's got to go! Don't you understand?
Mr. Harkness. What the dickens is eating you? No, I don't understand.

[PHYLLIS *gets up and goes to the window. She looks out tensely.*]

Would you mind telling me what you're talking about?
Phyllis (*startled*). Oh no!

[*She turns and runs to the front door. She starts to open it and run out. As she gets it half open, we hear a low voice calling.* CHARLIE DENTON's *voice.*]

Charlie (*low*). Artie! Hey, Artie!

[*She closes the door silently and stands against it, frightened. Cut to street in front of* FRANK's *house.* ARTHUR *stands there, having just been hailed by* CHARLIE. *He turns, and then we see* CHARLIE *hurrying down the street toward him.* CHARLIE *gets to him, takes him by the arm.*]

(*Low*) What are you doing out here now?
Arthur (*guiltily*). Nothing. I was . . . well, I was getting some air, that's all.
Charlie. Look, boy, this thing has got to be timed on the button. Everybody's supposed to be in his house right now. Nobody's supposed to be wandering around the streets. What time've you got?
Arthur (*with an effort*). Listen, Charlie, I want to talk to you about tonight.
Charlie. I haven't got time to talk.
Arthur. Please. It's important.
Charlie (*tough*). What the heck's the matter with you.
Arthur. Nothing. Nothing, Charlie . . .
Charlie. What time've you got? (*He grabs* ARTHUR's *wrist and holds it up to the light. He holds his own wrist next to it and compares the watches.*) You're three minutes *slow.*
Arthur. I know. This watch . . . it runs slow, Charlie. . . .
Charlie. Well, fix it, will ya? The timing's the most important part.
Arthur. I will. Look, about this thing tonight . . .
Charlie. Listen, if you're gonna start in with me about the plan, take it up with the committee, will ya, please? All of a sudden everybody's an expert on how to run the show. If you want the organizing job, I'll be glad to give it to you.
Arthur. No, it's not that. It's organized very well. There's something else.

Charlie. Are you gonna fix that watch?

Arthur. I will. I've been meaning to set it all day. Listen . . . these people . . . the Blakes. They've got a kid. . . .

Charlie. So has my mother. Here, gimme this. (*He grabs* ARTHUR's *wrist and sets his watch.*) There. At seven-fifteen on the nose we go. Now get back into your house. (*He walks off fast.*)

Arthur. Charlie . . .

[*But* CHARLIE *keeps going.* ARTHUR *watches him. Then he goes up to* FRANK MORRISON's *front door and rings the bell. From inside we hear* ROGER *calling.*]

Roger (*off*). I'll get it.

[ROGER *opens the front door, and now again,* ROGER's *and* ARTHUR's *movements must be exactly as they were in the first act, except that now the camera catches them from outside the house.*]

Arthur. Rog, is your Dad in?

Roger. Sure. Come on in, Mr. Hayes.

[ARTHUR *walks in slowly. The door closes.*]

[*Fade out.*]

[*Fade in on the living room of* ARTHUR's *house.* PHYLLIS *sits tensely waiting for him. The dining table is cleared.* MR. HARKNESS *is back in his easy chair reading the papers. We hear a key in the lock, the door opens, and* ARTHUR *enters. He walks slowly, despising himself for not having been stronger with* FRANK *or* CHARLIE. PHYLLIS *gets up as he comes in. He doesn't look at her but walks over to the window and stands there. She comes up behind him. He doesn't turn around.*]

Phyllis. Artie . . . Artie, are you all right?

[*He turns around slowly, speaks heavily.*]

Arthur. Yeah, I'm fine.

Phyllis. What happened? What'd you say to them?

Arthur. I said nothing.

Phyllis (*hopefully*). Well, what do you mean you said nothing. Didn't you talk about it?

Arthur. No, I didn't talk about it. I didn't talk about anything. Will you leave me alone?

[*She backs away, alarmed. Then she looks at her watch.*]

Phyllis (*softly*). We only have a couple of minutes, dear.

Arthur. I'm not going out there.

Phyllis. I'd better get our coats.

Arthur. Did you hear what I just said?

Phyllis. We'll have to bundle up. It's only about twenty degrees out. Did you know that?

Arthur. I said I'm not going.

[PHYLLIS *backs away from him. He turns to the window. We can see that she is hugely upset, almost desperate. She looks at him fiercely.* MR. HARKNESS *gets up quietly with his paper and goes into the next room. We hear the door close.* ARTHUR *doesn't move.*]

Phyllis (*strongly*). I want to tell you something. I'm going to get our coats now, and we're going to put them on, and we're going to stand in the doorway of our house until it's seven-fifteen.

Arthur (*turning*). Stop it.

Phyllis. And then we're going to walk out into the gutter, you and me, the Hayes family, and we're going to be just like everybody else on Sycamore Street!

Arthur (*shouting*). Phyllis! I've told you . . . I'm not going to be a part of this thing!

[PHYLLIS *studies him for a long moment.*]

Phyllis. Listen to me, Artie. Listen to me good. I didn't think you needed to hear this before. But you're going to hear it now.

We're going out there. Do you want to know why? Because we're not going to be next!

Arthur. You're out of your mind!

Phyllis (*roaring*). Sure I am! I'm out of my mind all right. I'm crazy with fear because I don't want to be different. I don't want my neighbors looking at us and wondering why we're not like them.

Arthur (*amazed*). Phyllis . . . you're making this up! They won't think that.

Phyllis. They will think that! We'll be the only ones, the odd ones, who wanted to let an ex-convict live with us. They'll look the other way when we walk the streets. They'll become cold and nasty . . . and all of a sudden we won't have any neighbors. (*Pointing at the Blake house*) We'll be like them!

[ARTHUR *stands looking at her, and it begins to sink in. She knows it and goes after him.*]

We can't be different! We can't afford it! We live on the good will of these people. Your business is in this town. Your neighbors buy us the bread we eat! Do you want them to stop?

Arthur. I don't know . . . Phyllis . . . I don't know what to think . . . I . . . can't throw a stone at this man.

Phyllis (*strong*). You can! You've got to, or we're finished here.

[*He stares at her, not knowing what to say next. She has almost won and knows it. She looks at her watch.*]

Now just . . . wait . . . just stand there. . . . (*She runs to the closet and takes out their overcoats. She throws hers on and brings his to him, holds it for him.*) Put it on!

Arthur. I . . . can't. They're people. It's their home.

Phyllis (*shouting*). We're people too! I don't care what happens to them. I care what happens to us. We belong here. We've got to live here. Artie, for the love of God, we don't even know them. What's the difference what happens to them? What about us?

[*He has no answer. She begins to put his coat on. He stands there, beaten, wrecked, moving his arms automatically, no longer knowing the woman who is putting on his coat. She talks as she helps him.*]

There. It won't be long. I promise you. It won't be long. That's my Artie. That's my darling. Let's button up, dear. It's cold. We'll be back in an hour, and it'll be over. There. Now put on your gloves, darling.

[*She takes him by the arm and he stands there letting her do as she will. He puts on his gloves without knowing he is doing it, and they wait together, there in the doorway. She looks at him, trying to read him, as we begin to hear the cold and chilling sound of the tramping feet.* MR. HARKNESS *comes out of the bedroom and stands there look- ing at them.* PHYLLIS *looks at her watch. The tramping grows louder. They wait in silence. Then she opens the door. We see the crowd, grimly marching, and the* MORRISONS *are at the head of it. No one looks at the* HAYESES. *The dull thud of the tramping feet is sickening to hear.* ARTHUR *closes his eyes. Slowly now* PHYLLIS *pushes him for- ward. He steps out of the house and moves ahead to join the others, as if in a dream.* PHYLLIS *follows, catches up, and takes his arm as they join the marching mob. Fade out.*]

Act Three

Fade in on a long shot of Sycamore Street. It is once again 6:40 P.M., same night. We have gone backward in time, and again we duplicate the scene which opened Acts One and Two. ARTHUR HAYES *walks on, stops in front of his house, knocks his pipe against his heel.* FRANK MORRISON *enters. Again, each of the movements must be exact imi- tations of the movements in Acts One and Two. It is as if we are starting the play again.*

Frank (*jovially*). Hey, Artie. How ya doin'?

[ARTHUR *is preoccupied. He doesn't register at first. He looks blankly at* FRANK.]

(*Laughing*) Hey ... wake up, boy. It's almost time for supper.

[ARTHUR *snaps out of it and forces a smile.*]

Arthur (*quietly*). Oh ... hello, Frank. Sorry. I didn't see you.
Frank. Didn't see me? Hey, wait till I tell Clarice. That diet she's got me on must be working. You have to look twice to see me! (*Laughing hard,* FRANK *reaches for his keys.*) That's a hot one!

[ARTHUR *smiles weakly.*]

Say ... isn't this late for you to be getting home?
Arthur. No, I don't think so. (*He looks at his watch.*) It's twenty-to seven. I always get home about this time.
Frank. Yeah. Well, I wouldn't want you to be late tonight. You know what tonight is, don't you?
Arthur (*slowly*). Yes, I know what tonight is.
Frank (*a little hard*). Good.

[*We hear footsteps and see a man walk by them. He is* JOSEPH BLAKE. *They both look at him silently. Camera now follows him as he walks silently toward his house, the third of the three houses we see. As he walks, we hear faintly in background*]

Frank (*off*). See you later, Artie.

[*We hear* FRANK's *door open and close. Then we hear* ARTHUR's *door open, and, for an instant, we hear the same dance music coming from* ARTHUR's *house that we heard in Act Two. Then* ARTHUR's *door closes. By this time* JOSEPH BLAKE *is in front of his door. He looks off silently at the other two houses. Then he opens his front door and enters his house. As he closes the door we hear running feet, and then we see* JUDY, JOE's *six-year-old daughter, in a bathrobe and slippers, running at him.*]

Judy (*calling*). Daddy, Daddy, Daddy, Daddy. (*She runs into his arms.*)

[*He lifts her up and hugs her.*]

Joe. Mmm. You smell sweet.
Judy (*excited*). I had a hairwash with Mommy's special shampoo. It smells like gar . . . gar . . .
Joe. Gardenias. Did anyone ever tell you you smelled like gardenias even without Mommy's shampoo?
Judy (*grinning*). You're silly.

[*He tickles her and she giggles.*]

Anna (*calling*). Judy!
Judy (*importantly*). We've got company.
Joe. Oh? Who is it, darling?
Anna (*calling*). Judy!
Judy. A lady.

[JOE *puts her down. She runs inside.* JOE *takes off his coat, puts it into the closet, and walks into the living room.* JOE's *wife,* ANNA, *stands near a chair.* ANNA, *in her early thirties, is a quiet, small woman who has obviously been through a great deal of suffering in the past five years. She looks extremely nervous and upset now. Seated at the far end of the room in a rocking chair is* JOE's *mother,* MRS. BLAKE. *She is quite old, quite spry for her years, and inclined to be snappish. Also seated in the room is a middle-aged woman, a neighborhood busybody named* MRS. CARSON. *She wears an odd, old-fashioned hat and sits stiffly, not at home, quite uncomfortable, but determined to do what she has come to do. The living room again is an exact duplicate of the Morrison and Hayes living rooms. It is furnished sparsely and not well. It is obvious that the Blakes have not been living there long. As* JOE *gets into the room,* ANNA *comes toward him.*]

Anna. Joe, this is Mrs. Carson.

Joe (*politely*). Mrs. Carson.

[*He turns to her for a moment. She nods curtly. Then he turns back to* ANNA *and kisses her gently.*]

Hello, darling.
Anna. Joe . . .

[*But he walks away from her and goes to his mother. He bends over and kisses her on the forehead.*]

Mrs. Blake. Your face is cold.
Joe (*smiling*). It's freezing out. How do you feel?
Mrs. Blake. Just fine, Joe.

[*He pats her cheek and turns to find* JUDY *behind him, holding a piece of drawing paper and a crayon. On the paper is a childish scribble that looks vaguely like a boat.* ANNA, *a tortured expression on her face, wants to say something, but* JOE *looks at the drawing, grinning.*]

Judy. Daddy . . .
Joe. The *Queen Mary!* Now that is what I call beautiful.
Judy. It is not! It's just s'posed to be a sailboat. How do you draw a sail?
Anna (*shakily*). Joe . . . Mrs. Carson . . .
Joe. Well, let's see. . . . (*He takes the crayon and paper and studies it.*) I suppose you think it's easy to draw a sail.
Judy (*serious*). No. I don't.
Anna (*sharply*). Joe. (*She comes over and snatches the paper away from him.*)

[*He looks at her.*]

Judy, go into your room.
Joe. Wait a minute, Anna. Take it easy.
Anna (*near tears*). Judy, did you hear me?
Joe. Darling, what's the matter with you?
Anna. Joe . . .

Judy. Mommy, do I have to?

Joe (*gently*). Maybe you'd better go inside for a few minutes, baby.

[JUDY *unhappily goes into her room.* ANNA *waits till we hear the door close.* JOE *puts his arms around her.*]

Tell me. What's wrong, Anna?

Anna (*almost sobbing*). Joe! I don't understand it! Mrs. Carson says . . . She . . .

Joe (*gently*). Mrs. Carson says what?

Anna (*breaking down*). She says . . . Joe . . . they're going to throw us out of our house. Tonight! Right now! What are we going to do?

Joe (*softly*). Well, I don't know. Who's going to throw us out of our house?

[*But* ANNA *can't answer.* JOE *grips her tightly, then releases her and walks to* MRS. CARSON, *who sits stolidly, waiting.*]

Who's going to throw us out, Mrs. Carson? Do you know?

Mrs. Carson. Well, like I told Mrs. Blake there, I suppose it's none of my business, but I'm just not the kind that thinks a thing like this ought to happen to people without them getting at least a . . . well, a warning. Know what I mean?

Joe. No, I don't know what you mean, Mrs. Carson. Did someone send you here?

Mrs. Carson (*indignantly*). Well, I should say not! If my husband knew I was here he'd drag me out by the hair. No, I sneaked in here, if you please, Mr. Blake. I felt it was my Christian duty. A man ought to have the right to run away, I say.

Joe. What do you mean, "run away," Mrs. Carson?

Mrs. Carson. Well, you know what I mean.

Joe. Who's going to throw us out?

Mrs. Carson. Well, everybody. The people on Sycamore Street. You know. They don't feel you ought to live here, because . . . Now I don't suppose I have to go into that.

Joe (*understanding*). I see.

Anna (*breaking in*). Joe, I've been waiting and waiting for you to come home. I've been sitting here . . . and waiting. Listen . . .

Joe (*quietly*). Hold it, Anna. (*To* MRS. CARSON) What time are they coming, Mrs. Carson?

Mrs. Carson. Quarter after seven. That's the plan. (*She looks at her watch and gets up.*) It's near seven now. They're very angry people, Mr. Blake. I don't think it'd be right for anyone to get hurt. That's why I'm here. If you take my advice, you'll just put some stuff together in a hurry and get out. I don't think there's any point in your calling the police either. There's only two of 'em in Eastmont and I don't think they'd do much good against a crowd like this.

Joe. Thank you, Mrs. Carson.

Mrs. Carson. Oh, don't thank me. It's like I said. I don't know you people, but there's no need for anyone getting hurt long as you move out like everybody wants. No sir. I don't want no part nor parcel to any violence where it's not necessary. Know what I mean?

Joe. Yes, I know what you mean.

Mrs. Carson. I don't know why a thing like this has to start up, anyway. It's none of my business, but a man like you ought to know better than to come pushing in here . . . a fine old neighborhood like this! After all, right is right.

Joe (*controlled*). Get out, Mrs. Carson.

Mrs. Carson. What? Well, I never! You don't seem to know what I've done for you, Mr. Blake.

Anna. Joe . . .

Joe. Get out of this house.

[*He goes to a chair in which lies* MRS. CARSON'*s coat. He picks it up and thrusts it at her. She takes it, indignant and a bit frightened.* JOE *turns from her. She begins to put her coat on.*]

Mrs. Carson. Well, I should think you'd at least have the decency to thank me. I might've expected this though. People like you!

Anna. Mrs. Carson, please . . .

Joe. Anna, stop it! (*He strides to the door and holds it open.*)

[MRS. CARSON *walks out.*]

Mrs. Carson. I think maybe you'll be getting what you deserve, Mr. Blake. Good night. (*She goes out.*)

[JOE *slams the door.*]

Anna. It's true. I can't believe it! Joe! Did you hear what she said? (*She goes to* JOE, *who still stands at the door, shocked.*) Well, what are you standing there for?
Joe (*amazed*). I don't know.
Anna. Joe, I'm scared. I'm so scared, I'm sick to my stomach. What are we going to do?

[JOE *puts his arms around her as she begins to sob. He holds her close till she quiets down. Then he walks her slowly over to his mother.*]

Joe (*to his mother*). Will you read to Judy for a few minutes, Mother? It's time for her story.

[MRS. BLAKE *starts to get up.*]

Winnie the Pooh. She'll tell you what page.

[MRS. BLAKE *nods and gets up and goes into* JUDY's *room.*]

Anna. What are you doing, Joe? We've only got fifteen minutes. . . . Don't you understand?
Joe (*quietly*). What do you want me to do? I can't stop them from coming here.

[*She goes to him and looks up at him, pleading now.*]

Anna (*whispering*). Joe. Let's get out. We've got time. We can throw some things into the car. . . .

Joe. Isn't it a remarkable thing? A quiet street like this and people with thunder in their hearts.

Anna. Listen to me, Joe—please. We can get most of our clothes in the car. We can stop at a motel. I don't care where we go. Anywhere. Joe, you're not listening. (*Loud*) What's the matter with you?

Joe. We're staying.

Anna (*frightened*). No!

Joe. Anna, this is our home and we're staying in it. No one can make us get out of our home. No one. That's a guarantee I happen to have since I'm born.

Anna (*sobbing*). Joe, you can't! Do you know what a mob is like? Do you know what they're capable of doing?

Joe. It's something I've never thought of before . . . a mob. I guess they're capable of doing ugly things.

Anna. Joe, you're talking and talking and the clock is ticking so fast. Please . . . please . . . Joe. We can run. We can go somewhere else to live. It's not so hard.

Joe. It's very hard, Anna, when it's not your own choice.

Anna (*sobbing*). What are you talking about? What else've we got to do? Stand here and fight them? We're not an army. We're one man and one woman and an old lady and a baby.

Joe. And the floor we stand on belongs to us. Not to anyone else.

Anna. They don't care about things like that. Joe, listen to me, please. You're not making sense. Listen . . . Judy's inside. She's six years old now and she's only really known you for a few weeks. We waited four years for you, and she didn't remember you when you picked her up and kissed her hello, but, Joe, she was so happy. What are you gonna tell her when they set fire to her new house?

Joe. I'm gonna tell her that her father fought like a tiger to stop them.

Anna (*crying*). Oh, no! No! No! What good will that do? Joe . . . please . . . please . . .

Joe (*thundering*). Stop it!

[ANNA *turns away from him and covers her face. After a long pause, quietly*]

It's this way, Anna. We have a few things we own. We have this house we've just bought with money left from before . . . money you could have used many times. We have a mortgage and a very old car and a few pieces of furniture. We have my job.
Anna (*bitterly*). Selling pots and pans at kitchen doors.
Joe (*patiently*). We have my job. And we have each other and that's what we have. Except there's one more thing. We have the right to live where we please and how we please. We're keeping all of those things, Anna. They belong to us.

[*He comes up behind her and puts his hands on her shoulders. She sinks down in a chair, turned away from him, and sobs. He stands over her. She continues to sob. He holds her and tries to quiet her. The bedroom door opens and* JUDY *bounces into the room.* JOE *gets up and goes to her as* ANNA *tries to dry her tears.*]

Judy. Grandma says I'm supposed to go to bed now. Do I have to, Daddy?
Joe (*smiling*). It's time, honey.
Judy (*disappointed*). Gee whiz. Some night, I'm gonna stay up until four o'clock in the morning!
Joe. Some night, you can. (*He kisses her.*) Good night, baby. Give Mommy a kiss.

[JUDY *goes to* ANNA *and speaks as she is kissing her.*]

Judy. Really? I really can stay up till four o'clock?
Joe. Really.
Judy. Night, Mommy.
Anna. Good night, darling.

[JUDY *runs off gleefully to the bedroom.*]

Judy. Oh boy! (*Calling*) Grandma . . .

[*The door closes.* ANNA *gets up and goes to window. She is still terrified, but a bit calmer now. She looks out and then turns to* JOE. *He watches her.*]

Anna. What've we done to hurt them? What've we done? I don't understand.

Joe (*softly*). Well, I guess maybe they think we've destroyed the dignity of their neighborhood, darling. That's why they've thrown garbage on our lawn.

Anna. Dignity! Throwing garbage. Getting together a mob. Those are dignified things to do. Joe, how can you want to stay? How can you want to live on the same street with them? Don't you see what they are?

Joe. They're people, Anna. And I guess they're afraid, just like we are. That's why they've become a mob. It's why people always do.

[*The bedroom door opens and* JOE's *mother enters. She goes to her rocker and sits in it and begins to rock.*]

Anna. What are they afraid of?

Joe. Living next door to someone they think is beneath them. An ex-convict. Me.

[ANNA *runs to* JOE *and grips him excitedly.*]

Anna. What do they think you did? They must think you're a thief or a murderer.

Joe. Maybe they do.

Anna. Well, they can't. You'll tell them. You'll tell them, Joe.

Joe. Anna, listen . . .

Anna. It could've happened to any one of them. Tell them you're not a common criminal. You were in an accident, and that's all it was. An accident. Joe, they'll listen. I know they will.

Joe. No, Anna . . .

Anna (*eagerly*). All you have to do is tell them and they'll go away. It's not like you committed a crime or anything. You were speeding. Everybody speeds. You hit an old man, and he died. He walked right in front——

Joe. They're not asking what I did, Anna.

Anna (*pleading*). Joe, please. Look at me. I'm so frightened. . . . You have to tell them.

Joe. Anna, we have our freedom. If we beg for it, then it's gone. Don't you see that?

Anna (*shouting*). No!

[*He comes to her and grips her, and speaks to her with his face inches from hers.*]

Joe. How can I tell it to you? Listen, Anna, we're only little people, but we have certain rights. Judy's gonna learn about them in school in a couple of years . . . and they'll tell her that no one can take them away from her. She's got to be able to believe that. They include the right to be different. Well, a group of our neighbors have decided that we have to get out of here because they think we're different. They think we're not nice. (*Strongly*) Do we have to smile in their faces and tell them we are nice? We don't have to win the right to be free! It's the same as running away, Anna. It's staying on their terms, and if we can't stay here on our terms, then there are no more places to stay anywhere. For you—for me—for Judy—for anyone, Anna.

[*She sees it now and she almost smiles, but the tears are running down her cheeks and it's difficult to smile. JOE kisses her forehead.*]

(*Quietly*) Now we'll wait for them.

[ANNA *goes slowly to a chair and sits in it.* MRS. BLAKE *rocks rhythmically on her rocking chair.* JOE *stands firm at one side of the room and they wait in silence. Suddenly the ticking of the clock on the mantelpiece thunders in our ears, and the monotonous beat of it is all we hear. They wait.* ANNA *looks at* JOE *and then speaks softly.*]

Anna. Joe. My hands are shaking. I don't want them to shake.

[JOE *walks over to her, stands over her strongly, and clasps both her hands together. Then he holds them in his till they are still. The clock ticks on, and now we cut to it. It reads ten after seven. Dissolve to a duplicate of the clock which now reads quarter after seven. Cut to long shot of room as we begin to hear the tramping of the feet down*]

the street. They wait. The rocker rocks. The clock ticks. The tramp-
ing grows louder. JOE *stands in the center of the room, hard and firm.*
Then he turns to his mother and speaks gently and softly.]

Joe. Go inside, Mother.
Mrs. Blake (*slowly*). No, Joe. I'm staying here. I want to watch
you. I want to hear you. I want to be proud.

[*She continues to rock, and now the tramping noise reaches a*
crescendo and then stops. For a moment there is silence, absolute
silence, and then we hear a single angry voice.]

Charlie Denton (*shouting*). Joseph Blake! (*There is a chorus of*
shouts and a swelling of noise.) Joseph Blake . . . come out here!

[*The noise from outside grows in volume. Inside only the rocking*
chair moves.]

First Man (*shouting*). Come out of that house!

[*The noise, the yelling of the crowd, continues to grow. Inside the*
room no one gives a signal that they have heard.]

Second Man (*shouting*). We want you, Joseph Blake!
Frank Morrison (*shouting*). Come out—or we'll drag you out!

[*The yelling continues, grows louder. Still the* BLAKES *do not move.*
Then suddenly a rock smashes through the window. Glass sprays to
the floor. The pitch of the noise outside rises even more. JOE *begins*
to walk firmly to the door.]

Anna (*softly*). Joe . . .

[*But he doesn't hear her. He gets to the door and flings it open vio-*
lently and steps outside. As he does, the shouting, which has reached
its highest pitch, stops instantly, and from deafening noise we plunge
into absolute silence, broken only by the steady creaking of the rock-

ing chair inside. JOE *stands there in front of his house like a rock. Now for the first time we see the crowd. The camera plays over the silent faces watching him—the faces of the men and women and children. The* MORRISONS *are directly in front,* CHARLIE DENTON *is further back.* MRS. CARSON *is there. And far to the rear we see* ARTHUR HAYES *and* PHYLLIS. *Still the silence holds. Then, little by little, the people begin to speak. At first we only hear single voices from different parts of the crowd.*]

First Man (*shouting*). Look at him, standing there like he owns the block!

[*There is a chorus of ad-lib approvals.*]

Second Man (*shouting*). Who do you think you are busting in where decent people live?

[*Another chorus of approvals.* JOE *stands like a fierce and powerful statue.*]

First Woman (*shouting*). Why don't you go live with your own kind . . . in a gutter somewhere?

[*Another chorus of approvals. The camera moves about catching the eagerness, the mounting temper of the crowd, then the shame and anguish of* ARTHUR HAYES, *then the giant strength of* JOE.]

First Man (*shouting*). Your limousine is waiting, Mr. Blake. You're taking a one-way trip!

[*There are a few laughs at this, and now the crowd, although not moving forward, is a shouting mass again.* JOE *still waits quietly.*]

Charlie Denton (*shouting*). Well, what are we waiting for? Let's get him!

[*The intensity of the noise grows, and the mob begins to move forward. Then, with a tremendous roar,* FRANK MORRISON *stops them.*]

Frank (*roaring*). Quiet! Everybody shut up.

[*The noise dies down gradually.*]

(*To crowd*) Now, listen to me! This thing is gonna be handled the way we planned at the meeting.

[ROGER, *standing next to* FRANK, *looks at him adoringly.* CHRIS *holds* CLARICE's *hand and looks around calmly.*]

Clarice (*loud*). That's right! It's what we agreed on.
Frank (*shouting*). This man here is gonna be asked politely and quietly to pack his things and get his family out of here. We don't have to tell him why. He knows that. He's gonna be given a chance to leave right now. If he's got any brains in his head, he'll be out in one hour—and nobody'll touch him or his house. If he hasn't——

[*There is a low-throated, ominous murmur from the crowd.*]

Right! This thing is gonna be done fair and square. (*Turning to* JOE) What d'ya say, Mr. Blake?

[JOE *looks at him for a long time. The crowd waits silently.* ARTHUR HAYES *lowers his head and clenches his fists, and looks as if he wants to be sick. The crowd waits. When* JOE *speaks, it is with a controlled fury that these people have never heard before. He speaks directly to* FRANK.]

Joe. I spit on your fairness!

[*The crowd gasps.* JOE *waits, then he thunders out.*]

I own this house and God gave me the right to live in it. The man who tries to take it away from me is going to have to climb over a pile of bones to do it. You good people of Sycamore Street are going to have to kill me tonight! Are you ready, Mr. Morrison? Don't bother to be fair. You're the head man here. Be first!

[*The crowd, rocked back on its heels, doesn't know what to do. Behind* JOE, *in the house, we see framed in the doorway the rocking chair moving steadily, and* ANNA *standing next to it.* FRANK *is stunned by this outburst. He calls for action. But not with the force he displayed earlier.*]

Frank. You heard him, everybody. . . .Let's get him.
Joe. I asked for you first, Mr. Morrison!
Frank (*shouting*). Listen to me! Let's go, men!

[*But the crowd is no longer moving as a whole. Some of them are still strongly with* FRANK, *including* CHARLIE, *the* FIRST MAN, *the* SECOND MAN, *and several of the others. But others are not so sure of themselves now.*]

Charlie (*roaring*). Don't let him throw you, Frank! He asked for it. Let's give it to him!

[JOE *looks only at* FRANK. *Waits calmly for him.*]

Frank (*roaring*). Come on!

[*He takes a step forward, but the people behind him don't follow. He turns to them.*]

What's the matter with you people?
Joe. They're waiting for you, Mr. Morrison.

[FRANK *whirls and faces him, and they look long and hard at each other. Cut to* CHARLIE DENTON *at rear of crowd. He has a stone in his hand.*]

Charlie (*shouting*). Let's start it off, Frankie boy.

[*He flings the stone. We hear it hit and drop to the ground. The crowd gasps. Cut to* JOE. *There is blood running down the side of his head. He stands there firmly. Cut to* ARTHUR HAYES. *He looks up in horror, and then a transformation comes over him. He seems to grow taller and broader. His face sets strongly and he begins to stride forward, elbowing people aside.* PHYLLIS *knows. She clings to him to pull him back.*]

Phyllis (*screaming*). Artie . . . Artie . . . don't . . .

[*But he breaks loose from her and pushes forward. Whoever is in his way is knocked aside, and finally he reaches* JOE. *He looks up at* JOE. *Then he turns and stands next to him. He takes off his eyeglasses and flings them into the crowd.*]

Arthur (*strong*). Throw the next stone at me, neighbors. I live here too!

[*Now the crowd is uncertain as the two men stand together and the blood runs down* JOE's *face.* FRANK *tries to rally them. During his next lines we shoot through the open door into the living room.* MRS. BLAKE *gets up from her rocking chair and takes* ANNA's *hand. Together they walk to the front door, come outside, and stand proudly behind* JOE *and* ARTHUR.]

Frank. Listen to me! Pay attention, you people. Let's remember what we came here to do . . . and why! This man is garbage! He's cluttering up our street. He's wrecking our neighborhood. We don't want him here. We agreed, every last man and woman of us . . . we agreed to throw him out! Are we gonna let him stop us? If we do—you know what'll happen.

[MRS. BLAKE *and* ANNA *are out of the house now. They wait, along with* JOE *and* ARTHUR. *The crowd listens.* FRANK *shouts on, running from person to person, as the crowd begins ashamedly to drift away.* CHRISTOPHER *clings to* FRANK's *jacket, and begins to sob.*]

Frank. You know what Sycamore Street'll be like. I don't have to tell you. How do we know who we'll be rubbing elbows with next? Listen, where are you going? We're all together in this! What about our kids? Listen to me, people. Our kids'll be playing and going to school with his. How do you like that, neighbors? Makes you a little sick, doesn't it? Come back here! I'm telling you we've got to do this! Come back here!

[*But the crowd continues to drift away. Finally only the* MORRISONS *and* PHYLLIS HAYES *are left in the street.* JOE *and his family, and* ARTHUR, *watch them proudly.* ROGER *looks at his bewildered father and then he turns away, takes* CLARICE's *hand, and his father is no longer the greatest guy in the world.* FRANK *looks down at the sobbing* CHRISTOPHER, *and picks him up and walks slowly off.* CLARICE *and* ROGER *follow. The* BLAKES *turn and go into their house, leaving* ARTHUR *on the porch. And standing alone, starkly in the middle of the street, is* PHYLLIS. ARTHUR *looks at her as she stands, heartbreakingly alone, for a long time.*]

Arthur (*sadly*). Well, what are you standing there for? My neighbor's head is bleeding!

[*And then, slowly, knowing that* ARTHUR *is no longer a grown-up child,* PHYLLIS *moves forward into* JOSEPH BLAKE's *house.*]

FADE OUT

Twelve Angry Men
Reginald Rose

Characters

Foreman, a small, petty man who is impressed with the authority he has and handles himself quite formally. Not overly bright, but dogged.

Juror No. 2, a meek, hesitant man who finds it difficult to maintain any opinions of his own. Easily swayed and usually adopts the opinion of the last person to whom he has spoken.

Juror No. 3, a very strong, very forceful, extremely opinionated man within whom can be detected a streak of sadism. A humorless man who is intolerant of opinions other than his own and accustomed to forcing his wishes and views upon others.

Juror No. 4, seems to be a man of wealth and position. A practiced speaker who presents himself well at all times. Seems to feel a little bit above the rest of the jurors. His only concern is with the facts in this case, and he is appalled at the behavior of the others.

Juror No. 5, a naive, very frightened young man who takes his obligations in this case very seriously, but who finds it difficult to speak up when his elders have the floor.

Juror No. 6, an honest but dull-witted man who comes upon his decisions slowly and carefully. A man who finds it difficult to create positive opinions, but who must listen to and digest and accept those opinions offered by others which appeal to him most.

Juror No. 7, a loud, flashy, gladhanded salesman type who has more important things to do than to sit on a jury. He is quick to show temper, quick to form opinions on things about which he knows nothing. Is a bully and, of course, a coward.

Juror No. 8, a quiet, thoughtful, gentle man. A man who sees all sides of every question and constantly seeks the truth. A man of strength tempered with compassion. Above all, a man who wants justice to be done and will fight to see that it is.

Juror No. 9, a mild, gentle old man, long since defeated by life and now merely waiting to die. A man who recognizes himself for what he is and mourns the days when it would have been possible to be courageous without shielding himself behind his many years.

Juror No. 10, an angry, bitter man. A man who antagonizes almost at sight. A bigot who places no values on any human life save his own. A man who has been nowhere and is going nowhere and knows it deep within him.

Juror No. 11, a refugee from Europe who has come to this country in 1941. A man who speaks with an accent and who is ashamed, humble, almost subservient to the people around him, but who will honestly seek justice because he has suffered through so much injustice.

Juror No. 12, a slick, bright advertising man who thinks of human beings in terms of percentages, graphs, and polls and has no real understanding of people. A superficial snob, but trying to be a good fellow.

Act One

Fade in on a jury box. Twelve men are seated in it, listening intently to the voice of the judge as he charges them. We do not see the judge. He speaks in slow, measured tones and his voice is grave. The camera drifts over the faces of the jurymen as the judge speaks and we see that most of their heads are turned to camera's left. NO. 7 *looks down at his hands.* NO. 3 *looks off in another direction, the direction in which the defendant would be sitting.* NO. 10 *keeps moving his head back and forth nervously. The judge drones on.*

Judge. Murder in the first degree—premeditated homicide— is the most serious charge tried in our criminal courts. You've heard a long and complex case, gentlemen, and it is now your duty to sit down to try and separate the facts from the fancy. One man is dead. The life of another is at stake. If there is a reasonable doubt in your minds as to the guilt of the accused . . . then you must declare him not guilty. If, however, there is no reasonable doubt, then he must be found guilty. Whichever way you decide, the verdict must be unanimous. I urge you to deliberate honestly and thoughtfully. You are faced with a grave responsibility. Thank you, gentlemen.

[*There is a long pause.*]

Clerk (*droning*). The jury will retire.

[*And now, slowly, almost hesitantly, the members of the jury begin to rise. Awkwardly, they file out of the jury box and off-camera to the left. Camera holds on jury box, then fades out.*

Fade in on a large, bare, unpleasant-looking room. This is the jury room in the county criminal court of a large Eastern city. It is about 4:00 P.M. The room is furnished with a long conference table and a dozen chairs. The walls are bare, drab, and badly in need of a fresh coat of paint. Along one wall is a row of windows which look out on the skyline of the city's financial district. High on another wall is an electric clock. A washroom opens off the jury room. In one corner of the room is a water fountain. On the table are pads, pencils, ashtrays. One of the windows is open. Papers blow across the table and onto the floor as the door opens. Lettered on the outside of the door are the words "Jury Room." A uniformed guard holds the door open. Slowly, almost self-consciously, the twelve jurors file in. The guard counts them as they enter the door, his lips moving, but no sound coming forth. Four or five of the jurors light cigarettes as they enter the room. JUROR NO. 5 lights his pipe, which he smokes constantly throughout the play. JURORS NO. 2 and 12 go to the water fountain. NO. 9 goes into the washroom, the door of which is lettered "Men." Several of the jurors take seats at the table. Others stand awkwardly around the room. Several look out the windows. These are men who are ill at ease, who do not really know each other to talk to, and who wish they were anywhere but here. NO. 7, standing at a window, takes out a pack of gum, takes a piece, and offers it around. There are no takers. He mops his brow.]

No. 7 (*to* NO. 6). Y'know something? It's hot. (NO. 6 *nods.*) You'd think they'd at least air-condition the place. I almost dropped dead in court.

[NO. 7 *opens the window a bit wider. The guard looks them over and checks his count. Then, satisfied, he makes ready to leave.*]

Guard. OK, gentlemen. Everybody's here. If there's anything you want, I'm right outside. Just knock.

[*He exits, closing the door. Silently they all look at the door. We hear the lock clicking.*]

No. 5. I never knew they locked the door.
No. 10 (*blowing nose*). Sure, they lock the door. What did you think?
No. 5. I don't know. It just never occurred to me.

[*Some of the jurors are taking off their jackets. Others are sitting down at the table. They still are reluctant to talk to each other.* FOREMAN *is at head of table, tearing slips of paper for ballots. Now we get a close shot of* NO. 8. *He looks out the window. We hear* NO. 3 *talking to* NO. 2.]

No. 3. Six days. They should have finished it in two. Talk, talk, talk. Did you ever hear so much talk about nothing?
No. 2 (*nervously laughing*). Well . . . I guess . . . they're entitled.
No. 3. Everybody gets a fair trial. (*He shakes his head.*) That's the system. Well, I suppose you can't say anything against it.

[NO. 2 *looks at him nervously, nods, and goes over to water cooler. Cut to shot of* NO. 8 *staring out window. Cut to table.* NO. 7 *stands at the table, putting out a cigarette.*]

No. 7 (*to* NO. 10). How did you like that business about the knife? Did you ever hear a phonier story?
No. 10 (*wisely*). Well, look, you've gotta expect that. You know what you're dealing with.

No. 7. Yeah, I suppose. What's the matter, you got a cold?
No. 10 (*blowing*). A lulu. These hot-weather colds can kill you.

[NO. 7 *nods sympathetically.*]

Foreman (*briskly*). All right, gentlemen. Let's take seats.
No. 7. Right. This better be fast. I've got tickets to *The Seven Year Itch* tonight. I must be the only guy in the whole world who hasn't seen it yet. (*He laughs and sits down.*) OK, your honor, start the show.

[*They all begin to sit down. The* FOREMAN *is seated at the head of the table.* NO. 8 *continues to look out the window.*]

Foreman (*to* NO. 8). How about sitting down?

[NO. 8 *doesn't hear him.*]

The gentleman at the window.

[NO. 8 *turns, startled.*]

How about sitting down?
No. 8. Oh. I'm sorry. (*He heads for a seat.*)
No. 10. (*to* NO. 6). It's tough to figure, isn't it? A kid kills his father. Bing! Just like that. Well, it's the element. They let the kids run wild. Maybe it serves 'em right.
Foreman. Is everybody here?
No. 12. The old man's inside.

[*The* FOREMAN *turns to the washroom just as the door opens.* NO. 9 *comes out, embarrassed.*]

Foreman. We'd like to get started.
No. 9. Forgive me, gentlemen. I didn't mean to keep you waiting.
Foreman. It's all right. Find a seat.

[NO. 9 *heads for a seat and sits down. They look at the* FOREMAN *expectantly.*]

Foreman. All right. Now, you gentlemen can handle this any way you want to. I mean, I'm not going to make any rules. If we want to discuss it first and then vote, that's one way. Or we can vote right now to see how we stand.

No. 7. Let's vote now. Who knows, maybe we can all go home.

No. 10. Yeah. Let's see who's where.

No. 3. Right. Let's vote now.

Foreman. Anybody doesn't want to vote? (*He looks around the table. There is no answer.*) OK, all those voting guilty raise your hands.

[*Seven or eight hands go up immediately. Several others go up more slowly. Everyone looks around the table. There are two hands not raised,* NO. 9's *and* NO. 8's. NO. 9's *hand goes up slowly now as the* FOREMAN *counts.*]

Foreman. ... Nine ... ten ... eleven ... That's eleven for guilty. OK. Not guilty?

[NO. 8's *hand is raised.*]

One. Right. OK. Eleven to one, guilty. Now we know where we are.

No. 3. Somebody's in left field. (*To* NO. 8) You think he's not guilty?

No. 8 (*quietly*). I don't know.

No. 3. I never saw a guiltier man in my life. You sat right in court and heard the same thing I did. The man's a dangerous killer. You could see it.

No. 8. He's nineteen years old.

No. 3. That's old enough. He knifed his own father. Four inches into the chest. An innocent little nineteen-year-old kid. They proved it a dozen different ways. Do you want me to list them?

No. 8. No.

No. 10 (*to* NO. 8). Well, do you believe his story?

No. 8. I don't know whether I believe it or not. Maybe I don't.

No. 7. So what'd you vote not guilty for?

No. 8. There were eleven votes for guilty. It's not so easy for me to raise my hand and send a boy off to die without talking about it first.

No. 7. Who says it's easy for me?

No. 8. No one.

No. 7. What, just because I voted fast? I think the guy's guilty. You couldn't change my mind if you talked for a hundred years.

No. 8. I don't want to change your mind. I just want to talk for a while. Look, this boy's been kicked around all his life. You know, living in a slum, his mother dead since he was nine. That's not a very good head start. He's a tough, angry kid. You know why slum kids get that way? Because we knock 'em on the head once a day, every day. I think maybe we owe him a few words. That's all.

[*He looks around the table. Some of them look back coldly. Some cannot look at him. Only* NO. 9 *nods slowly.* NO. 12 *doodles steadily.* NO. 4 *begins to comb his hair.*]

No. 10. I don't mind telling you this, mister. We don't owe him a thing. He got a fair trial, didn't he? You know what that trial cost? He's lucky he got it. Look, we're all grown-ups here. You're not going to tell us that we're supposed to believe him, knowing what he is. I've lived among 'em all my life. You can't believe a word they say. You know that.

No. 9 (*to* NO. 10 *very slowly*). I don't know that. What a terrible thing for a man to believe! Since when is dishonesty a group characteristic? You have no monopoly on the truth——

No. 3 (*interrupting*). All right. It's not Sunday. We don't need a sermon.

No. 9. What this man says is very dangerous. . . .

[NO. 8 *puts his hand on* NO. 9*'s arms and stops him. Somehow his touch and his gentle expression calm the old man. He draws a deep breath and relaxes.*]

No. 4. I don't see any need for arguing like this. I think we ought to be able to behave like gentlemen.

No. 7. Right!

No. 4. If we're going to discuss this case, let's discuss the facts.

Foreman. I think that's a good point. We have a job to do. Let's do it.

No. 11 (*with accent*). If you gentlemen don't mind, I'm going to close the window. (*He gets up and does so. Apologetically*) It was blowing on my neck.

[NO. 10 *blows his nose fiercely.*]

No. 12. I may have an idea here. I'm just thinking out loud now, but it seems to me that it's up to us to convince this gentleman (*indicating* NO. 8) that we're right and he's wrong. Maybe if we each took a minute or two, you know, if we sort of try it on for size . . .

Foreman. That sounds fair enough. Supposing we go once around the table.

No. 7. OK, let's start it off.

Foreman. Right. (*To* NO. 2) I guess you're first.

No. 2 (*timidly*). Oh. Well . . . (*long pause*) I just think he's guilty. I thought it was obvious. I mean nobody proved otherwise.

No. 8 (*quietly*). Nobody has to prove otherwise. The burden of proof is on the prosecution. The defendant doesn't have to open his mouth. That's in the Constitution. The Fifth Amendment. You've heard of it.

No. 2 (*flustered*). Well, sure, I've heard of it. I know what it is. I . . . what I meant . . . well, anyway, I think he was guilty.

No. 3. OK, let's get to the facts. Number one, let's take the old man who lived on the second floor right underneath the room where the murder took place. At ten minutes after twelve on the night of the killing he heard loud noises in the upstairs apartment. He said it sounded like a fight. Then he heard the kid say to his father, "I'm gonna kill you." A second later he heard a body falling, and he ran to the door of his apartment, looked out, and saw the kid running down the stairs and out of the house. Then he called the police. They found the father with a knife in his chest.

Foreman. And the coroner fixed the time of death at around midnight.

No. 3. Right. Now what else do you want?

No. 4. The boy's entire story is flimsy. He claimed he was at the movies. That's a little ridiculous, isn't it? He couldn't even remember what pictures he saw.

No. 3. That's right. Did you hear that? (*To* NO. 4) You're absolutely right.

No. 10. Look, what about the woman across the street? If her testimony don't prove it, then nothing does.

No. 12. That's right. She saw the killing, didn't she?

Foreman. Let's go in order.

No. 10 (*loud*). Just a minute. Here's a woman who's lying in bed and can't sleep. It's hot, you know. (*He gets up and begins to walk around, blowing his nose and talking.*) Anyway, she looks out the window, and right across the street she sees the kid stick the knife into his father. She's known the kid all his life. His window is right opposite hers, across the el tracks, and she swore she saw him do it.

No. 8. Through the windows of a passing elevated train.

No. 10. OK. And they proved in court that you can look through the windows of a passing el train at night and see what's happening on the other side. They proved it.

No. 8. I'd like to ask you something. How come you believed her? She's one of "them" too, isn't she?

[NO. 10 *walks over to* NO. 8.]

No. 10. You're a pretty smart fellow, aren't you?

Foreman (*rising*). Now take it easy.

[NO. 3 *gets up and goes to* NO. 10.]

No. 3. Come on. Sit down. (*He leads* NO. 10 *back to his seat.*) What're you letting him get you all upset for? Relax.

[NO. 10 *and* NO. 3 *sit down.*]

Foreman. Let's calm down now. (*To* NO. 5) It's your turn.

No. 5. I'll pass it.

Foreman. That's your privilege. (*To* NO. 6) How about you?

No. 6 (*slowly*). I don't know. I started to be convinced, you know, with the testimony from those people across the hall. Didn't they say something about an argument between the father and the boy around seven o'clock that night? I mean, I can be wrong.

No. 11. I think it was eight o'clock. Not seven.

No. 8. That's right. Eight o'clock. They heard the father hit the boy twice and then saw the boy walk angrily out of the house. What does that prove?

No. 6. Well, it doesn't exactly prove anything. It's just part of the picture. I didn't say it proved anything.

Foreman. Anything else?

No. 6. No. (NO. 6 *goes to the water fountain.*)

Foreman (*to* NO. 7). All right. How about you?

No. 7. I don't know, most of it's been said already. We can talk all day about this thing, but I think we're wasting our time. Look at the kid's record. At fifteen he was in reform school. He stole a car. He's been arrested for mugging. He was picked up for knife-fighting. I think they said he stabbed somebody in the arm. This is a very fine boy.

No. 8. Ever since he was five years old his father beat him up regularly. He used his fists.

No. 7. So would I! A kid like that.

No. 3. You're right. It's the kids. The way they are—you know? They don't listen. (*Bitter*) I've got a kid. When he was eight years old he ran away from a fight. I saw him. I was so ashamed, I told him right out, "I'm gonna make a man out of you or I'm gonna bust you up into little pieces trying." When he was fifteen, he hit me in the face. He's big, you know. I haven't seen him in three years. Rotten kid! You work your heart out. . . . (*Pause*) All right. Let's get on with it. (*Looks away embarrassed.*)

No. 4. We're missing the point here. This boy—let's say he's a product of a filthy neighborhood and a broken home. We can't help that. We're not here to go into the reasons why slums are breeding grounds for criminals. They are. I know it. So do you. The children who come out of slum backgrounds are potential menaces to society.

No. 10. You said it there. I don't want any part of them, believe me.

[*There is a dead silence for a moment, and then* NO. 5 *speaks haltingly.*]

No. 5. I've lived in a slum all my life——
No. 10. Oh, now wait a second!
No. 5. I used to play in a back yard that was filled with garbage. Maybe it still smells on me.
Foreman. Now let's be reasonable. There's nothing personal——

[NO. 5 *stands up.*]

No. 5. There is something personal! (*Then he catches himself and, seeing everyone looking at him, sits down, fists clenched.*)
No. 3 (*persuasively*). Come on, now. He didn't mean you, feller. Let's not be so sensitive. . . .

[*There is a long pause.*]

No. 11. I can understand this sensitivity.
Foreman. Now let's stop the bickering. We're wasting time. (*To* NO. 8) It's your turn.
No. 8. All right. I had a peculiar feeling about this trial. Somehow I felt that the defense counsel never really conducted a thorough cross-examination. I mean, he was appointed by the court to defend the boy. He hardly seemed interested. Too many questions were left unasked.
No. 3 (*annoyed*). What about the ones that were asked? For instance, let's talk about that cute little switch-knife. You know, the one that fine, upright kid admitted buying.
No. 8. All right. Let's talk about it. Let's get it in here and look at it. I'd like to see it again, Mr. Foreman.

[*The* FOREMAN *looks at him questioningly and then gets up and goes to the door. During the following dialogue the* FOREMAN *knocks, the guard comes in, the* FOREMAN *whispers to him, the guard nods and leaves, locking the door.*]

No. 3. We all know what it looks like. I don't see why we have to look at it again. (*To* NO. 4) What do you think?
No. 4. The gentleman has a right to see exhibits in evidence.

No. 3 (*shrugging*). OK with me.

No. 4 (*to* NO. 8). This knife is a pretty strong piece of evidence, don't you agree?

No. 8. I do.

No. 4. The boy admits going out of his house at eight o'clock after being slapped by his father.

No. 8. Or punched.

No. 4. Or punched. He went to a neighborhood store and bought a switch-knife. The storekeeper was arrested the following day when he admitted selling it to the boy. It's a very unusual knife. The storekeeper identified it and said it was the only one of its kind he had in stock. Why did the boy get it? (*Sarcastically*) As a present for a friend of his, he says. Am I right so far?

No. 8. Right.

No. 3. You bet he's right. (*To all*) Now listen to this man. He knows what he's talking about.

No. 4. Next, the boy claims that on the way home the knife must have fallen through a hole in his coat pocket, that he never saw it again. Now there's a story, gentlemen. You know what actually happened. The boy took the knife home and a few hours later stabbed his father with it and even remembered to wipe off the fingerprints.

[*The door opens, and the guard walks in with an oddly designed knife with a tag on it.* NO. 4 *gets up and takes it from him. The guard exits.*]

No. 4. Everyone connected with the case identified this knife. Now are you trying to tell me that someone picked it up off the street and went up to the boy's house and stabbed his father with it just to be amusing?

No. 8. No, I'm saying that it's possible that the boy lost the knife, and that someone else stabbed his father with a similar knife. It's possible.

[NO. 4 *flips open the knife and jams it into the table.*]

No. 4. Take a look at that knife. It's a very strange knife. I've never seen one like it before in my life. Neither had the store-keeper who sold it to him.

[NO. 8 *reaches casually into his pocket and withdraws an object. No one notices this. He stands up quietly.*]

No. 4. Aren't you trying to make us accept a pretty incredible coincidence?
No. 8. I'm not trying to make anyone accept it. I'm just saying it's possible.
No. 3 (*shouting*). And I'm saying it's not possible.

[NO. 8 *swiftly flicks open the blade of a switch-knife and jams it into the table next to the first one. They are exactly alike. There are several gasps and everyone stares at the knife. There is a long silence.*]

No. 3 (*slowly amazed*). What are you trying to do?
No. 10 (*loud*). Yeah, what is this? Who do you think you are?
No. 5. Look at it! It's the same knife!
Foreman. Quiet! Let's be quiet.

[*They quiet down.*]

No. 4. Where did you get it?
No. 8. I got it last night in a little junk shop around the corner from the boy's house. It cost two dollars.
No. 3. Now listen to me! You pulled a real smart trick here, but you proved absolutely zero. Maybe there are ten knives like that, so what?
No. 8. Maybe there are.
No. 3. The boy lied and you know it.
No. 8. He may have lied. (*To* NO. 10) Do you think he lied?
No. 10 (*violently*). Now that's a stupid question. Sure he lied!
No. 8 (*to* NO. 4). Do you?
No. 4. You don't have to ask me that. You know my answer. He lied.
No. 8 (*to* NO. 5). Do you think he lied?

[NO. 5 *can't answer immediately. He looks around nervously.*]

No. 5. I . . . I don't know.
No. 7. Now wait a second. What are you, the guy's lawyer? Listen, there are still eleven of us who think he's guilty. You're

alone. What do you think you're gonna accomplish? If you want to be stubborn and hang this jury, he'll be tried again and found guilty, sure as he's born.

No. 8. You're probably right.

No. 7. So what are you gonna do about it? We can be here all night.

No. 9. It's only one night. A man may die.

[NO. 7 *glares at* NO. 9 *for a long while, but has no answer.* NO. 8 *looks closely at* NO. 9 *and we can begin to sense a rapport between them. There is a long silence. Then suddenly everyone begins to talk at once.*]

No. 3. Well, whose fault is that?

No. 6. Do you think maybe if we went over it again? What I mean is . . .

No. 10. Did anyone force him to kill his father? (*To* NO. 3) How do you like him? Like someone forced him!

No. 11. Perhaps this is not the point.

No. 5. No one forced anyone. But listen . . .

No. 12. Look, gentlemen, we can spitball all night here.

No. 2. Well, I was going to say——

No. 7. Just a minute. Some of us've got better things to do than sit around a jury room.

No. 4. I can't understand a word in here. Why do we all have to talk at once?

Foreman. He's right. I think we ought to get on with it.

[NO. 8 *has been listening to this exchange closely.*]

No. 3 (*to* NO. 8). Well, what do you say? You're the one holding up the show.

No. 8 (*standing*). I've got a proposition to make.

[*We catch a close shot of* NO. 5 *looking steadily at him as he talks.* NO. 5, *seemingly puzzled, listens closely.*]

No. 8. I want to call for a vote. I want you eleven men to vote by secret ballot. I'll abstain. If there are still eleven votes for guilty, I won't stand alone. We'll take in a guilty verdict right now.

No. 7. OK. Let's do it.

Foreman. That sounds fair. Is everyone agreed?

[*They all nod their heads.* NO. 8 *walks over to the window, looks out for a moment and then faces them.*]

Foreman. Pass these along.

[*The* FOREMAN *passes ballot slips to all of them, and now* NO. 8 *watches them tensely as they begin to write. Fade out.*]

Act Two

Fade in on same scene, no time lapse. NO. 8 *stands tensely watching as the jurors write on their ballots. He stays perfectly still as one by one they fold the ballots and pass them along to the* FOREMAN. *The foreman takes them, riffles through the folded ballots, counts eleven and now begins to open them. He reads each one out loud and lays it aside. They watch him quietly, and all we hear is his voice and the sound of* NO. 2 *sucking on a cough drop.*

Foreman. Guilty. Guilty. Guilty. Guilty. Guilty. Guilty. Guilty. Guilty. Guilty. (*He pauses at the tenth ballot and then reads it.*) Not guilty.

[NO. 3 *slams down hard on the table. The* FOREMAN *opens the last ballot.*]

Guilty.

No. 10 (*angry*). How do you like that!

No. 7. Who was it? I think we have a right to know.

No. 11. Excuse me. This was a secret ballot. We agreed on this point, no? If the gentleman wants it to remain secret——

No. 3 (*standing up angrily*). What do you mean? There are no secrets in here! I know who it was. (*He turns to* NO. 5.) What's the matter with you? You come in here and you vote guilty and then this slick preacher starts to tear your heart out with stories about a poor little kid who just couldn't help becoming a murderer. So you change your vote. If that isn't the most sickening——

[NO. 5 *stares at* NO. 3, *frightened at this outburst.*]

Foreman. Now hold it.
No. 3. Hold it? We're trying to put a guilty man into the chair where he belongs—and all of a sudden we're paying attention to fairy tales.
No. 5. Now just a minute . . .
No. 11. Please. I would like to say something here. I have always thought that a man was entitled to have unpopular opinions in this country. This is the reason I came here. I wanted to have the right to disagree. In my own country, I am ashamed to say——
No. 10. What do we have to listen to now—the whole history of your country?
No. 7. Yeah, let's stick to the subject. (*To* NO. 5) I want to ask you what made you change your vote.

[*There is a long pause as* NO. 7 *and* NO. 5 *eye each other angrily.*]

No. 9 (*quietly*). There's nothing for him to tell you. He didn't change his vote. I did. (*There is a pause.*) Maybe you'd like to know why.
No. 3. No, we wouldn't like to know why.
Foreman. The man wants to talk.
No. 9. Thank you. (*Pointing at* NO. 8) This gentleman chose to stand alone against us. That's his right. It takes a great deal of courage to stand alone even if you believe in something very strongly. He left the verdict up to us. He gambled for support and I gave it to him. I want to hear more. The vote is ten to two.
No. 10. That's fine. If the speech is over, let's go on.

[FOREMAN *gets up, goes to door, knocks, hands guard the tagged switch-knife and sits down again.*]

No. 3 (*to* NO. 5). Look, buddy, I was a little excited. Well, you know how it is. I . . . I didn't mean to get nasty. Nothing personal.

[NO. 5 *looks at him.*]

No. 7 (*to* NO. 8). Look, supposing you answer me this. If the kid didn't kill him, who did?

No. 8. As far as I know, we're supposed to decide whether or not the boy on trial is guilty. We're not concerned with anyone else's motives here.

No. 9. Guilty beyond a reasonable doubt. This is an important thing to remember.

No. 3 (*to* NO. 10). Everyone's a lawyer. (*To* NO. 9) Supposing you explain what your reasonable doubts are.

No. 9. This is not easy. So far, it's only a feeling I have. A feeling. Perhaps you don't understand.

No. 10. A feeling! What are we gonna do, spend the night talking about your feelings? What about the facts?

No. 3. You said a mouthful. (*To* NO. 9) Look, the old man heard the kid yell, "I'm gonna kill you." A second later he heard the father's body falling, and he saw the boy running out of the house fifteen seconds after that.

No. 12. That's right. And let's not forget the woman across the street. She looked into the open window and saw the boy stab his father. She saw it. Now if that's not enough for you . . .

No. 8. It's not enough for me.

No. 7. How do you like him? It's like talking into a dead phone.

No. 4. The woman saw the killing through the windows of a moving elevated train. The train had five cars, and she saw it through the windows of the last two. She remembers the most insignificant details.

[*Cut to close shot of* NO. 12 *who doodles a picture of an el train on a scrap of paper.*]

No. 3. Well, what have you got to say about that?

No. 8. I don't know. It doesn't sound right to me.

No. 3. Well, supposing you think about it. (*To* NO. 12) Lend me your pencil.

[NO. 12 *gives it to him. He draws a tic-tac-toe square on the same sheet of paper on which* NO. 12 *has drawn the train. He fills in an X, hands the pencil to* NO. 12.]

No. 3. Your turn. We might as well pass the time.

[NO. 12 *takes the pencil.* NO. 8 *stands up and snatches the paper away.* NO. 3 *leaps up.*]

No. 3. Wait a minute!
No. 8 (*hard*). This isn't a game.
No. 3 (*angry*). Who do you think you are?
No. 7 (*rising*). All right, let's take it easy.
No. 3. I've got a good mind to walk around this table and belt him one!
Foreman. Now, please. I don't want any fights in here.
No. 3. Did ya see him? The nerve! The absolute nerve!
No. 10. All right. Forget it. It don't mean anything.
No. 6. How about sitting down.
No. 3. This isn't a game. Who does he think he is?

[*He lets them sit him down.* NO. 8 *remains standing, holding the scrap of paper. He looks at it closely now and seems to be suddenly interested in it. Then he throws it back toward* NO. 3. *It lands in center of table.* NO. 3 *is angered again at this, but* NO. 4 *puts his hand on his arm.* NO. 8 *speaks now, and his voice is more intense.*]

No. 8 (*to* NO. 4). Take a look at that sketch. How long does it take an elevated train going at top speed to pass a given point?
No. 4. What has that got to do with anything?
No. 8. How long? Guess.
No. 4. I wouldn't have the slightest idea.
No. 8 (*to* NO. 5). What do you think?
No. 5. About ten or twelve seconds, maybe.
No. 8. I'd say that was a fair guess. Anyone else?
No. 11. I would think about ten seconds, perhaps.
No. 2. About ten seconds.
No. 4. All right. Say ten seconds. What are you getting at?
No. 8. This. An el train passes a given point in ten seconds. That given point is the window of the room in which the killing took place. You can almost reach out of the window of that room and touch the el. Right?

[*Several of them nod.*]

All right. Now let me ask you this. Did anyone here ever live right next to the el tracks? I have. When your window is open and the train goes by, the noise is almost unbearable. You can't hear yourself think.

No. 10. OK. You can't hear yourself think. Will you get to the point?

No. 8. The old man heard the boy say, "I'm going to kill you," and one second later he heard a body fall. One second. That's the testimony, right?

No. 2. Right.

No. 8. The woman across the street looked through the windows of the last two cars of the el and saw the body fall. Right? The *last* two cars.

No. 10. What are you giving us here?

No. 8. An el takes ten seconds to pass a given point or two seconds per car. That el had been going by the old man's window for at least six seconds, and maybe more, *before the body fell*, according to the woman. The old man would have had to hear the boy say, "I'm going to kill you," while the front of the el was roaring past his nose. It's not possible that he could have heard it.

No. 3. What d'ya mean! Sure he could have heard it.

No. 8. Could he?

No. 3. He said the boy yelled it out. That's enough for me.

No. 9. I don't think he could have heard it.

No. 2. Maybe he didn't hear it. I mean with the el noise . . .

No. 3. What are you people talking about? Are you calling the old man a liar?

No. 5. Well, it stands to reason.

No. 3. You're crazy. Why would he lie? What's he got to gain?

No. 9. Attention, maybe.

No. 3. You keep coming up with these bright sayings. Why don't you send one in to a newspaper? They pay two dollars.

[NO. 8 *looks hard at* NO. 3 *and then turns to* NO. 9.]

No. 8 (*softly*). Why might the old man have lied? You have a right to be heard.

No. 9. It's just that I looked at him for a very long time. The seam of his jacket was split under the arm. Did you notice that? He was a very old man with a torn jacket, and he carried two canes. I think I know him better than anyone here. This is a quiet, frightened, insignificant man who has been nothing all his life, who has never had recognition—his name in the newspapers. Nobody knows him after seventy-five years. That's a very sad thing. A man like this needs to be recognized. To be questioned, and listened to, and quoted just once. This is very important.

No. 12. And you're trying to tell us he lied about a thing like this just so that he could be important?

No. 9. No. He wouldn't really lie. But perhaps he'd make himself believe that he heard those words and recognized the boy's face.

No. 3 (*loud*). Well, that's the most fantastic story I've ever heard. How can you make up a thing like that? What do you know about it?

No. 9 (*low*). I speak from experience.

[*There is a long pause. Then the* FOREMAN *clears his throat.*]

Foreman (*to* NO. 8). All right. Is there anything else?

[NO. 8 *is looking at* NO. 9. NO. 2 *offers the* FOREMAN *a box of cough drops. The* FOREMAN *pushes it away.*]

No. 2 (*hesitantly*). Anybody . . . want a cough . . . drop?

Foreman (*sharply*). Come on. Let's get on with it.

No. 8. I'll take one.

[NO. 2 *almost gratefully slides him one along the table.*]

Thanks.

[NO. 2 *nods and* NO. 8 *puts the cough drop into his mouth.*]

No. 8. Now. There's something else I'd like to point out here. I think we proved that the old man couldn't have heard the boy say, "I'm going to kill you," but supposing he really did hear it? This phrase: How many times has each of you used it? Probably hundreds. "If you do that once more, Junior, I'm going to murder you." "Come on, Rocky, kill him!" We say it every day. This doesn't mean that we're going to kill someone.

No. 3. Wait a minute. The phrase was "I'm going to kill you," and the kid screamed it out at the top of his lungs. Don't try and tell me he didn't mean it. Anybody says a thing like that the way he said it—they mean it.

No. 10. And how they mean it!

No. 8. Well, let me ask you this. Do you really think the boy would shout out a thing like that so the whole neighborhood would hear it? I don't think so. He's much too bright for that.

No. 10 (*exploding*). Bright! He's a common, ignorant slob. He don't even speak good English!

No. 11 (*slowly*). He *doesn't* even speak good English.

[NO. 10 *stares angrily at* NO. 11, *and there is silence for a moment. Then* NO. 5 *looks around the table nervously.*]

No. 5. I'd like to change my vote to not guilty.

[NO. 3 *gets up and walks to the window, furious, but trying to control himself.*]

Foreman. Are you sure?

No. 5. Yes. I'm sure.

Foreman. The vote is nine to three in favor of guilty.

No. 7. Well, if that isn't the end. (*To* NO. 5) What are you basing it on? Stories this guy (*indicating* NO. 8) made up! He oughta write for *Amazing Detective Monthly.* He'd make a fortune. Listen, the kid had a lawyer, didn't he? Why didn't his lawyer bring up all these points?

No. 5. Lawyers can't think of everything.

No. 7. Oh, brother! (*To* NO. 8) You sit in here and pull stories out of thin air. Now we're supposed to believe that the old man didn't get up out of bed, run to the door, and see the kid beat it downstairs fifteen seconds after the killing. He's only saying he did to be important.

No. 5. Did the old man say he *ran* to the door?

No. 7. Ran. Walked. What's the difference? He got there.

No. 5. I don't remember what he said. But I don't see how he could run.

No. 4. He said he *went* from his bedroom to the front door. That's enough, isn't it?

No. 8. Where was his bedroom again?

No. 10. Down the hall somewhere. I thought you remembered everything. Don't you remember that?

No. 8. No. Mr. Foreman, I'd like to take a look at the diagram of the apartment.

No. 7. Why don't we have them run the trial over just so you can get everything straight?

No. 8. Mr. Foreman . . .

Foreman (*rising*). I heard you.

[*The* FOREMAN *gets up, goes to door during following dialogue. He knocks on door, guard opens it, he whispers to guard, guard nods and closes door.*]

No. 3 (*to* NO. 8). All right. What's this for? How come you're the only one in the room who wants to see exhibits all the time.

No. 5. I want to see this one, too.

No. 3. And I want to stop wasting time.

No. 4. If we're going to start wading through all that nonsense about where the body was found . . .

No. 8. We're not. We're going to find out how a man who's had two strokes in the past three years, and who walks with a pair of canes, could get to his front door in fifteen seconds.

No. 3. He said twenty seconds.

No. 2. He said fifteen.

No. 3. How does he know how long fifteen seconds is? You can't judge that kind of a thing.

No. 9. He said fifteen. He was very positive about it.

No. 3 (*angry*). He's an old man. You saw him. Half the time he was confused. How could he be positive about . . . anything?

[NO. 3 *looks around sheepishly, unable to cover up his blunder. The door opens, and the guard walks in, carrying a large pen-and-ink diagram of the apartment. It is a railroad flat. A bedroom faces the el tracks. Behind it is a series of rooms off a long hall. In the front bedroom is a diagram of the spot where the body was found. At the back of the apartment we see the entrance into the apartment hall from the building hall. We see a flight of stairs in the building hall. The diagram is clearly labeled, and included in the information on it are the dimensions of the various rooms. The guard gives the diagram to the* FOREMAN.]

Guard. This what you wanted?
Foreman. That's right. Thank you.

[*The guard nods and exits.* NO. 8 *goes to* FOREMAN *and reaches for it.*]

No. 8. May I?

[*The* FOREMAN *nods.* NO. 8 *takes the diagram and sets it up on a chair so that all can see it.* NO. 8 *looks it over. Several of the jurors get up to see it better.* NO. 3, NO. 10, *and* NO. 7, *however, barely bother to look at it.*]

No. 7 (*to* NO. 10). Do me a favor. Wake me up when this is over.
No. 8 (*ignoring him*). All right. This is the apartment in which the killing took place. The old man's apartment is directly beneath it and exactly the same. (*Pointing*) Here are the el tracks. The bedroom. Another bedroom. Living room. Bathroom. Kitchen. And this is the hall. Here's the front door to the apartment. And here are the steps. (*Pointing to front bedroom and then front door*) Now, the old man was in bed in this room. He says he got up, went out into the hall, down the hall to the front door, opened it, and looked out just in time to see the boy racing down the stairs. Am I right?
No. 3. That's the story.
No. 8. Fifteen seconds after he heard the body fall.
No. 11. Correct.
No. 8. His bed was at the window. It's (*looking closer*) twelve feet from his bed to the bedroom door. The length of the hall is forty-three feet, six inches. He had to get up out of bed, get his canes, walk twelve feet, open the bedroom door, walk forty-three

feet, and open the front door—all in fifteen seconds. Do you think this possible?

No. 10. You know it's possible.

No. 11. He can only walk very slowly. They had to help him into the witness chair.

No. 3. You make it sound like a long walk. It's not.

[NO. 8 *gets up, goes to the end of the room, and takes two chairs. He puts them together to indicate a bed.*]

No. 9. For an old man who uses canes, it's a long walk.

No. 3 (*to* NO. 8). What are you doing?

No. 8. I want to try this thing. Let's see how long it took him. I'm going to pace off twelve feet—the length of the bedroom. (*He begins to do so.*)

No. 3. You're crazy. You can't recreate a thing like that.

No. 11. Perhaps if we could see it . . . This is an important point.

No. 3 (*mad*). It's a ridiculous waste of time.

No. 6. Let him do it.

No. 8. Hand me a chair.

[*Someone pushes a chair to him.*]

All right. This is the bedroom door. Now how far would you say it is from here to the door of this room?

No. 6. I'd say it was twenty feet.

No. 2. Just about.

No. 8. Twenty feet is close enough. All right, from here to the door and back is about forty feet. It's shorter than the length of the hall, wouldn't you say that?

No. 9. A few feet, maybe.

No. 10. Look, this is absolutely insane. What makes you think you can——

No. 8. Do you mind if I try it? According to you, it'll only take fifteen seconds. We can spare that. (*He walks over to the two chairs now and lies down on them.*) Who's got a watch with a second hand?

No. 2. I have.
No. 8. When you want me to start, stamp your foot. That'll be the body falling. Time me from there. (*He lies down on the chairs.*) Let's say he keeps his canes right at his bedside. Right?
No. 2. Right!
No. 8. OK. I'm ready.

[*They all watch carefully.* NO. 2 *stares at his watch, waiting for the second hand to reach sixty. Then, as it does, he stamps his foot loudly.* NO. 8 *begins to get up. Slowly he swings his legs over the edges of the chairs, reaches for imaginary canes and struggles to his feet.* NO. 2 *stares at the watch.* NO. 8 *walks as a crippled old man would walk, toward the chair, which is serving as the bedroom door. He gets to it and pretends to open it.*]

No. 10 (*shouting*). Speed it up. He walked twice as fast as that.

[NO. 8, *not having stopped for this outburst, begins to walk the simulated forty-foot hallway.*]

No. 11. This is, I think, even more quickly than the old man walked in the courtroom.
No. 8. If you think I should go faster, I will.

[*He speeds up his pace slightly. He reaches the door and turns now, heading back, hobbling as an old man would hobble, bent over his imaginary canes. They watch him tensely. He hobbles back to the chair, which also serves as the front door. He stops there and pretends to unlock the door. Then he pretends to push it open.*]

No. 8 (*loud*). Stop.
No. 2. Right.
No. 8. What's the time?
No. 2. Fifteen . . . twenty . . . thirty . . . thirty-one seconds exactly.
No. 11. Thirty-one seconds.

[*Some of the jurors ad-lib their surprise to each other.*]

No. 8. It's my guess that the old man was trying to get to the door, heard someone racing down the stairs and *assumed* that it was the boy.

No. 6. I think that's possible.

No. 3 (*infuriated*). Assumed? Now, listen to me, you people. I've seen all kinds of dishonesty in my day . . . but this little display takes the cake. (*To* NO. 4) Tell him, will you?

[NO. 4 *sits silently.* NO. 3 *looks at him, and then he strides over to* NO. 8.]

No. 3. You come in here with your heart bleeding all over the floor about slum kids and injustice and you make up these wild stories, and you've got some softhearted old ladies listening to you. Well I'm not. I'm getting real sick of it. (*To all*) What's the matter with you people? This kid is guilty! He's got to burn! We're letting him slip through our fingers here.

No. 8 (*calmly*). Our fingers. Are you his executioner?

No. 3 (*raging*). I'm one of 'em.

No. 8. Perhaps you'd like to pull the switch.

No. 3 (*shouting*). For this kid? You bet I'd like to pull the switch!

No. 8. I'm sorry for you.

No. 3 (*shouting*). Don't start with me.

No. 8. What it must feel like to want to pull the switch!

No. 3. Shut up!

No. 8. You're a sadist.

No. 3 (*louder*). Shut up!

No. 8 (*strong*). You want to see this boy die because you personally want it—not because of the facts.

No. 3 (*shouting*). Shut up!

[*He lunges at* NO. 8, *but is caught by two of the jurors and held. He struggles as* NO. 8 *watches calmly.*]

No. 3 (*screaming*). Let me go! I'll kill him. I'll kill him!

No. 8 (*softly*). You don't really mean you'll kill me, do you?

[NO. 3 *stops struggling now and stares at* NO. 8. *All the jurors watch in silence as we fade out.*]

Act Three

Fade in on same scene. No time lapse. NO. 3 *glares angrily at* NO. 8. *He is still held by two jurors. After a long pause, he shakes himself loose and turns away. He walks to the windows. The other jurors stand around the room now, shocked by this display of anger. There is silence. Then the door opens and the guard enters. He looks around the room.*

Guard. Is there anything wrong, gentlemen? I heard some noise.
Foreman. No. There's nothing wrong. (*He points to the large diagram of the apartment.*) You can take that back. We're finished with it.

[*The guard nods and takes the diagram. He looks curiously at some of the jurors and exits. The jurors still are silent. Some of them slowly begin to sit down.* NO. 3 *still stands at the window. He turns around now. The jurors look at him.*]

No. 3 (*loud*). Well, what are you looking at?

[*They turn away. He goes back to his seat now. Silently the rest of the jurors take their seats.* NO. 12 *begins to doodle.* NO. 10 *blows his nose, but no one speaks. Then, finally——*

No. 4. I don't see why we have to behave like children here.
No. 11. Nor do I. We have a responsibility. This is a remarkable thing about democracy. That we are . . . what is the word? . . . Ah, notified! That we are notified by mail to come down to this place and decide on the guilt or innocence of a man we have not known before. We have nothing to gain or lose by our

verdict. This is one of the reasons why we are strong. We should not make it a personal thing.

[*There is a long, awkward pause.*]

No. 12. Well—we're still nowhere. Who's got an idea?
No. 6. I think maybe we should try another vote. Mr. Foreman?
Foreman. It's all right with me. Anybody doesn't want to vote? (*He looks around the table.*)
No. 7. All right, let's do it.
No. 3. I want an open ballot. Let's call out our votes. I want to know who stands where.
Foreman. That sounds fair. Anyone object?

[*No one does.*]

All right. I'll call off your jury numbers.

[*He takes a pencil and paper and makes marks now in one of two columns after each vote.*]

Foreman. I vote guilty. No. 2?
No. 2. Not guilty.
Foreman. No. 3?
No. 3. Guilty.
Foreman. No. 4?
No. 4. Guilty.
Foreman. No. 5?
No. 5. Not guilty.
Foreman. No. 6?
No. 6. Not guilty.
Foreman. No. 7?
No. 7. Guilty.
Foreman. No. 8?
No. 8. Not guilty.
Foreman. No. 9?

No. 9. Not guilty.
Foreman. No. 10?
No. 10. Guilty.
Foreman. No. 11?
No. 11. Not guilty.
Foreman. No. 12?
No. 12. Guilty.
No. 4. Six to six.
No. 10 (*mad*). I'll tell you something. The crime is being committed right in this room.
Foreman. The vote is six to six.
No. 3. I'm ready to walk into court right now and declare a hung jury. There's no point in this going on any more.
No. 7. I go for that, too. Let's take it in to the judge and let the kid take his chances with twelve other guys.
No. 5 (*to* NO. 7). You mean you still don't think there's room for reasonable doubt?
No. 7. No, I don't.
No. 11. I beg your pardon. Maybe you don't understand the term "reasonable doubt."
No. 7 (*angry*). What do you mean I don't understand it? Who do you think you are to talk to me like that? (*To all*) How do you like this guy? He comes over here running for his life, and before he can even take a big breath he's telling us how to run the show. The arrogance of him!
No. 5 (*to* NO. 7). Wait a second. Nobody around here's asking where you came from.
No. 7. I was born right here.
No. 5. Or where your father came from. . . .

[*He looks at* NO. 7, *who doesn't answer but looks away.*]

Maybe it wouldn't hurt us to take a few tips from people who come running here! Maybe they learned something we don't know. We're not so perfect!
No. 11. Please—I am used to this. It's all right. Thank you.
No. 5. It's not all right!

No. 7. OK, OK, I apologize. Is that what you want?
No. 5. That's what I want.
Foreman. All right. Let's stop the arguing. Who's got something constructive to say?
No. 2 (*hesitantly*). Well, something's been bothering me a little . . . this whole business about the stab wound and how it was made, the downward angle of it, you know?
No. 3. Don't tell me we're gonna start that. They went over it and over it in court.
No. 2. I know they did—but I don't go along with it. The boy is five feet eight inches tall. His father was six two. That's a difference of six inches. It's a very awkward thing to stab *down* into the chest of someone who's half a foot taller than you are.

[NO. 3 *jumps up, holding the knife.*]

No. 3. Look, you're not going to be satisfied till you see it again. I'm going to give you a demonstration. Somebody get up.

[*He looks around the table.* NO. 8 *stands up and walks toward him.* NO. 3 *closes the knife and puts it in his pocket. They stand face to face and look at each other for a moment.*]

No. 3. OK. (*To* NO. 2) Now watch this. I don't want to have to do it again. (*He crouches down now until he is quite a bit shorter than* NO. 8.) Is that six inches?
No. 12. That's more than six inches.
No. 3. OK, let it be more.

[*He reaches into his pocket and takes out the knife. He flicks it open, changes its position in his hand, and holds the knife aloft, ready to stab. He and* NO. 8 *look steadily into each other's eyes. Then he stabs downward, hard.*]

No. 2 (*shouting*). Look out!

[*He stops short just as the blade reaches* NO. 8*'s chest.* NO. 3 *laughs.*]

No. 6. That's not funny.

No. 5. What's the matter with you?

No. 3. Now just calm down. Nobody's hurt, are they?

No. 8 (*low*). No. Nobody's hurt.

No. 3. All right. There's your angle. Take a look at it. Down and in. That's how I'd stab a taller man in the chest, and that's how it was done. Take a look at it and tell me I'm wrong.

[NO. 2 *doesn't answer.* NO. 3 *looks at him for a moment, then jams the knife into the table and sits down. They all look at the knife.*]

No. 6. Down and in. I guess there's no argument.

[NO. 8 *picks the knife out of the table and closes it. He flicks it open and, changing its position in his hand, stabs downward with it.*]

No. 8 (*to* NO. 6). Did you ever stab a man?

No. 6. Of course not.

No. 8 (*to* NO. 3). Did you?

No. 3. All right, let's not be silly.

No. 8. Did you?

No. 3 (*loud*). No, I didn't!

No. 8. Where did you get all your information about how it's done?

No. 3. What do you mean? It's just common sense.

No. 8. Have you ever seen a man stabbed?

No. 3 (*pauses and looks around the room nervously*). No.

No. 8. All right. I want to ask you something. The boy was an experienced knife-fighter. He was even sent to reform school for knifing someone, isn't that so?

No. 12. That's right.

No. 8. Look at this. (NO. 8 *closes the knife, flicks it open, and changes the position of the knife so that he can stab overhanded.*) Doesn't it seem like an awkward way to handle a knife?

No. 3. What are you asking me for?

[NO. 8 *closes the blade and flicks it open, holds it ready to slash underhanded.*]

No. 5. Wait a minute! What's the matter with me? Give me that. (*He reaches out for the knife.*)

No. 8. Have you ever seen a knife fight?

No. 5. Yes, I have.

No. 8. In the movies?

No. 5. In my back yard. On my stoop. In the vacant lot across the street. Too many of them. Switch-knives came with the neighborhood where I lived. Funny I didn't think of it before. I guess you try to forget those things. (*Flicking the knife open*) Anyone who's ever used a switch-knife would never have stabbed downward. You don't handle a switch-knife that way. You use it underhanded.

No. 8. Then he couldn't have made the kind of wound which killed his father.

No. 5. No. He couldn't have. Not if he'd ever had any experience with switch-knives.

No. 3. I don't believe it.

No. 10. Neither do I. You're giving us a lot of mumbo jumbo.

No. 8 (*to* NO. 12). What do you think?

No. 12 (*hesitantly*). Well . . . I don't know.

No. 8 (*to* NO. 7). What about you?

No. 7. Listen, I'll tell you something. I'm a little sick of this whole thing already. We're getting nowhere fast. Let's break it up and go home. I'm changing my vote to not guilty.

No. 3. You're what?

No. 7. You heard me. I've had enough.

No. 3. What do you mean, you've had enough? That's no answer.

No. 11 (*angry*). I think perhaps you're right. This is not an answer. (*to* NO. 7) What kind of a man are you? You have sat here and voted guilty with everyone else because there are some theater tickets burning a hole in your pocket. Now you have changed your vote for the same reason. I do not think you have the right to play like this with a man's life. This is an ugly and terrible thing to do.

No. 7. Now wait a minute. . . . You can't talk like that to me.

No. 11 (*strong*). I can talk like that to you! If you want to vote not guilty, then do it because you are convinced the man is not guilty. If you believe he is guilty, then vote that way. Or don't you have the . . . the . . . guts—the guts to do what you think is right?

No. 7. Now listen . . .

No. 11. Is it guilty or not guilty?

No. 7 (*hesitantly*). I told you. Not . . . guilty.

No. 11 (*hard*). Why?

No. 7. I don't have to——

No. 11. You have to! Say it! Why?

[*They stare at each other for a long while.*]

No. 7 (*low*). I . . . don't think . . . he's guilty.

No. 8 (*fast*). I want another vote.

Foreman. Okay, there's another vote called for. I guess the quickest way is a show of hands. Anybody object?

[*No one does.*]

All right. All those voting not guilty, raise your hands.

[NUMBERS 2, 5, 6, 7, 8, 9, *and* 11 *raise their hands immediately. Then, slowly,* NO. 12 *raises his hand. The* FOREMAN *looks around the table carefully, and then he too raises his hand. He looks around the table, counting silently.*]

Foreman. Nine.

[*The hands go down.*]

All those voting guilty.

[NUMBERS 3, 4, *and* 10 *raise their hands.*]

Foreman. Three.

[*They lower their hands.*]

The vote is nine to three in favor of acquittal.

No. 10. I don't understand you people. How can you believe this kid is innocent? Look, you know how those people lie. I don't have to tell you. They don't know what the truth is. And lemme tell you, they—

[NO. 5 *gets up from table, turns his back to it, and goes to window.*]

—don't need any real big reason to kill someone either. You know, they get drunk, and *bang,* someone's lying in the gutter. Nobody's blaming them. That's how they are. You know what I mean? Violent!

[NO. 9 *gets up and does the same. He is followed by* NO. 11.]

Human life don't mean as much to them as it does to us. Hey, where are you going? Look, these people are drinking and fighting all the time, and if somebody gets killed, so somebody gets killed. They don't care. Oh, sure, there are some good things about them, too. Look, I'm the first to say that.

[NO. 8 *gets up, and then* NO. 2 *and* NO. 6 *follow him to the window.*]

I've known a few who were pretty decent, but that's the exception. Most of them, it's like they have no feelings. They can do anything. What's going on here?

[*The* FOREMAN *gets up and goes to the windows, followed by* NO. 7 *and* NO. 12.]

I'm speaking my piece, and you—Listen to me! They're no good. There's not a one of 'em who's any good. We better watch out. Take it from me. This kid on trial . . .

[NO. 3 *sits at table toying with the knife, and* NO. 4 *gets up and starts for the window. All have their backs to* NO. 10.]

Well, don't you know about them? Listen to me! What are you doing? I'm trying to tell you something. . . .

[NO. 4 *stands over him as he trails off. There is a dead silence. Then* NO. 4 *speaks softly.*]

No. 4. I've had enough. If you open your mouth again, I'm going to split your skull.

[NO. 4 *stands there and looks at him. No one moves or speaks.* NO. 10 *looks at him, then looks down at the table.*]

No. 10 (*softly*). I'm only trying to tell you . . .

[*There is a long pause as* NO. 4 *stares down at* NO. 10.]

No. 4 (*to all*). All right. Sit down everybody.

[*They all move back to their seats. When they are all seated,* NO. 4 *then sits down.*]

No. 4 (*quietly*). I still believe the boy is guilty of murder. I'll tell you why. To me, the most damning evidence was given by the woman across the street who claimed she actually saw the murder committed.
No. 3. That's right. As far as I'm concerned, that's the most important testimony.
No. 8. All right. Let's go over her testimony. What exactly did she say?
No. 4. I believe I can recount it accurately. She said that she went to bed at about eleven o'clock that night. Her bed was next to the open window, and she could look out of the window while lying down and see directly into the window across the street. She tossed and turned for over an hour, unable to fall asleep. Finally she turned toward the window at about twelve-ten and, as she looked out, she saw the boy stab his father. As far as I can see, this is unshakable testimony.
No. 3. That's what I mean. That's the whole case.

[NO. 4 *takes off his eyeglasses and begins to polish them, as they all sit silently watching him.*]

No. 4 (*to the jury*). Frankly, I don't see how you can vote for acquittal. (*To* NO. 12) What do you think about it?
No. 12. Well . . . maybe . . . There's so much evidence to sift.
No. 3. What do you mean, maybe? He's absolutely right. You can throw out all the other evidence.
No. 4. That was my feeling.

[NO. 2, *polishing his glasses, squints at clock, can't see it.* NO. 6 *watches him closely.*]

No. 2. What time is it?
No. 11. Ten minutes of six.
No. 2. It's late. You don't suppose they'd let us go home and finish it in the morning. I've got a kid with mumps.
No. 5. Not a chance.
No. 6 (*to* NO. 2). Pardon me. Can't you see the clock without your glasses?
No. 2. Not clearly. Why?
No. 6. Oh, I don't know. Look, this may be a dumb thought, but what do you do when you wake up at night and want to know what time it is?
No. 2. What do you mean? I put on my glasses and look at the clock.
No. 6. You don't wear them to bed.
No. 2. Of course not. No one wears eyeglasses to bed.
No. 12. What's all this for?
No. 6. Well, I was thinking. You know the woman who testified that she saw the killing wears glasses.
No. 3. So does my grandmother. So what?
No. 8. Your grandmother isn't a murder witness.
No. 6. Look, stop me if I'm wrong. This woman wouldn't wear her eyeglasses to bed, would she?
Foreman. Wait a minute! Did she wear glasses at all? I don't remember.

No. 11 (*excited*). Of course she did! The woman wore bifocals. I remember this very clearly. They looked quite strong.

No. 9. That's right. Bifocals. She never took them off.

No. 4. She did wear glasses. Funny. I never thought of it.

No. 8. Listen, she wasn't wearing them in bed. That's for sure. She testified that in the midst of her tossing and turning she rolled over and looked casually out the window. The murder was taking place as she looked out, and the lights went out a split second later. She couldn't have had time to put on her glasses. Now maybe she honestly thought she saw the boy kill his father. I say that she saw only a blur.

No. 3. How do you know what she saw? Maybe she's farsighted.

[*He looks around. No one answers.*]

No. 3 (*loud*). How does he know all these things?

[*There is silence.*]

No. 8. Does anyone think there still is not a reasonable doubt?

[*He looks around the room, then squarely at* NO. 10. NO. 10 *looks down and shakes his head no.*]

No. 3 (*loud*). I think he's guilty!

No. 8 (*calmly*). Does anyone else?

No. 4 (*quietly*). No. I'm convinced.

No. 8 (*to* NO. 3). You're alone.

No. 3. I don't care whether I'm alone or not! I have a right.

No. 8. You have a right.

[*There is a pause. They all look at* NO. 3.]

No. 3. Well, I told you I think the kid's guilty. What else do you want?

No. 8. Your arguments.

[*They all look at* NO. 3.]

No. 3. I gave you my arguments.
No. 8. We're not convinced. We're waiting to hear them again. We have time.

[NO. 3 *runs to* NO. 4 *and grabs his arm.*]

No. 3 (*pleading*). Listen. What's the matter with you? You're the guy. You made all the arguments. You can't turn now. A guilty man's gonna be walking the streets. A murderer. He's got to die! Stay with me.
No. 4. I'm sorry. There's a reasonable doubt in my mind.
No. 8. We're waiting.

[NO. 3 *turns violently on him.*]

No. 3 (*shouting*). Well, you're not going to intimidate me!

[*They all look at* NO. 3.]

I'm entitled to my opinion!

[*No one answers him.*]

It's gonna be a hung jury! That's it!
No. 8. There's nothing we can do about that, except hope that some night, maybe in a few months, you'll get some sleep.
No. 5. You're all alone.
No. 9. It takes a great deal of courage to stand alone.

[NO. 3 *looks around at all of them for a long time. They sit silently, waiting for him to speak, and all of them despise him for his stubbornness. Then, suddenly, his face contorts as if he is about to cry, and he slams his fist down on the table.*]

No. 3 (*thundering*). All right!

[NO. 3 *turns his back on them. There is silence for a moment, and then the* FOREMAN *goes to the door and knocks on it. It opens. The guard looks in and sees them all standing. The guard holds the door for them as they begin slowly to file out.* NO. 8 *waits at the door as the others file past him. Finally he and* NO. 3 *are the only ones left.* NO. 3 *turns around and sees that they are alone. Slowly he moves toward the door. Then he stops at the table. He pulls the switch-knife out of the table and walks over to* NO. 8 *with it. He holds it in the approved knife-fighter fashion and looks long and hard at* NO. 8, *pointing the knife at his belly.* NO. 8 *stares back. Then* NO. 3 *turns the knife around.* NO. 8 *takes it by the handle.* NO. 3 *exits.* NO. 8 *closes the knife, puts it away and, taking a last look around the room, exits, closing the door. The camera moves in close on the littered table in the empty room, and we clearly see a slip of crumpled paper on which are scribbled the words "Not guilty."*]

FADE OUT

Author's Commentary
Reginald Rose

Of all the plays in this volume[1], *Twelve Angry Men* is certainly the most difficult to read. In reading plays, most of which generally are devoid of any descriptive matter whatsoever (outside of brief outlines of the sets), the first task a reader has is that of separating the characters from each other. In most cases, after several pages have been read, the names of the characters in the play have been memorized by the reader, mental images of these characters have been formed, and it is a relatively simple thing to distinguish between the characters and to know, almost automatically, who is speaking each line. In reading *Twelve Angry Men*, however, I realize that it is almost impossible to form immediate and distinct pictures of each of the twelve men, designated as they are only by number. This play was constructed to fall into shape upon being seen, and since I felt that a dozen names would be quite meaningless to a viewing audience (members of a jury rarely address each other by name), I omitted the sometimes annoying chore of selecting names for my characters. It is for this reason that thumbnail descriptions of characteristics which pertain to the action in this play have been included for purposes of reference.

Twelve Angry Men is the only play I've written which has any relation at all to actual personal experience. A month or so before I began the play I sat on the jury of a manslaughter case in New York's General Sessions Court. This was my first experience on a jury, and it left quite an impression on me. The receipt of my jury notice activated many grumblings and mutterings, most of which began with lines like "My God, eight million people in New York and they have to call me!" All the prospective jurors I met in the waiting room the first day I appeared had

---

1. Commentary is from *Six Television Plays* by Reginald Rose.

the same grim, horribly persecuted attitude. But, strangely, the moment I walked into the courtroom to be empaneled and found myself facing a strange man whose fate was suddenly more or less in my hands, my entire attitude changed. I was hugely impressed with the almost frightening stillness of the courtroom, the impassive, masklike face of the judge, the brisk, purposeful scurrying of the various officials in the room, and the absolute finality of the decision I and my fellow jurors would have to make at the end of the trial. I doubt whether I have ever been so impressed in my life with a role I had to play, and I suddenly became so earnest that, in thinking about it later, I probably was unbearable to the eleven other jurors.

It occurred to me during the trial that no one anywhere ever knows what goes on inside a jury room but the jurors, and I thought then that a play taking place entirely within a jury room might be an exciting and possibly moving experience for an audience.

Actually, the outline of *Twelve Angry Men*, which I began shortly after the trial ended, took longer to write than the script itself. The movements in the play were so intricate that I wanted to have them down on paper to the last detail before I began the construction of the dialogue. I worked on the idea and outline for a week and was stunned by the time I was finished to discover that the outline was twenty-seven typewritten pages long. The average outline is perhaps five pages long, and many are as short as one or two pages. This detailed setting down of the moves of the play paid off, however. The script was written in five days and could have been done in four had I not written it approximately fifteen pages too long.

In writing *Twelve Angry Men* I attempted to blend four elements which I had seen at work in the jury room during my jury service. These elements are (a) the evidence as remembered and interpreted by each individual juror (the disparities here were incredible); (b) the relationship of juror to juror in a life-and-death situation; (c) the emotional pattern of each individual juror; and (d) physical problems such as the weather, the time, the uncomfortable room, etc. All of these elements are of vital importance in any jury room, and all of them presented excellent dramatic possibilities.

Before I began to plot the play, I felt that the basic problem was going to consist of a constant search for drama and movement in order to prevent a normally static situation from becoming too static. Actually, as it turned out, the writing of *Twelve Angry Men* became a struggle to cram all of the detail, action and character I had devised into the less than fifty minutes of air time available.

Before the play went into rehearsal I had to cut large chunks of dialogue, and, since I was dealing with quite an involved plot, all the cuts were made on passages that had been written to give some depth to the characters. This left the bare frame of the plot and the skeletons of the people. To this day I have not been able to decide whether the cuts made *Twelve Angry Men* more effective or not. The men of the play were easily recognizable as types, but I believe that whatever dimension they had as real people was achieved as much by the excellence of the performance as it was by the personal insights revealed in dialogue. What *Twelve Angry Men* has to say about democracy, justice, social responsibilities, and the pressure of the times upon the people who live them has some importance, I believe, and perhaps helps to overshadow the meager development of some of the characters.

As a motion picture, soon to be released, I think that *Twelve Angry Men* has grown in stature. It is nearly twice as long as the television play, and much of the extra time has been spent in exploring the characters and their motivations for behaving as they do toward the defendant and each other.

The time limitations of television tend to restrict the complete development of a play so that it is necessary to show only brief fragments of people if the plot is fairly involved, or the barest sketch of a plot if the characters are to be fully developed. The only way out of this stifling trap is longer, more expensive shows, of which I, for one, am heartily in favor.

The production problems of *Twelve Angry Men* were, for what seemed like a reasonably simple show, incredibly involved.

The set, to be realistic, had to be small and cramped. This, of course, inhibited the movement of cameras and presented director Frank Schaffner with an endless traffic jam which would have had Robert Moses spinning like a ball-bearing top. Somehow, however, Mr. Schaffner managed to capture the speaker of each line on camera at precisely the right moment and composed starkly realistic, tension-filled pictures of the reactions to these lines. This was perhaps the best-directed show I've ever seen on television, and Mr. Schaffner won a mantelpieceful of awards for it, including the Christopher Award, the Sylvania Award and the Academy of Television Arts and Sciences Emmy Award.

Twelve Angry Men, incidentally, was the first of my shows to be seen by my two youngsters—Jonathan, then five and a half, and Richard, three. (Since then, two more small twin boys have joined our family!) I hadn't intended to have them see it at all, but one Sunday afternoon they discovered that I had made arrangements to run off a kinescope of the show for some people who had missed it and they begged to be allowed to see it. Never one to resist the accomplished wheedling of small, determined boys, I agreed, provided that they swore up and down to sit like lumps and not utter a sound. They said they would and they kept their word. From time to time I looked at them, two little figures squatting on hassocks, wide-eyed, unmoving, terribly impressed with the entire situation, and I felt, I must admit, a tinge of pride that they were obviously so fascinated with something I had created. At the end of the show, after much small talk, I went over to the hassock where Jonathan still sat, silent and obviously impressed. With what must have been some smugness I asked, "Well, how'd you like it, Jon?"

He looked at me gravely. The he whispered, "Boy, were they angry!"

He has never mentioned it again and if he thinks I'm going to ask him . . .

Tennessee Williams
(1911–1983)

The Glass Menagerie is an American classic. When it opened on Broadway, in the spring of 1945, the Mississippi-born playwright Tennessee Williams was practically unknown; almost overnight he became an international success.

Though Williams became known principally for his colorful female characters—Blanche in *A Streetcar Named Desire* (1947), Alma in *Summer and Smoke* (1948), Maggie in *Cat on a Hot Tin Roof* (1955)—he also created some great male characters, among them Stanley Kowalski in *A Streetcar Named Desire*. Marlon Brando's portrayal of Stanley in the original production and in the movie established a kind of mumbling, torn-T-shirt technique of acting that was to become popular with many of the younger actors of the next decade.

The Glass Menagerie is a mixture of straightforward, realistic drama and poetic, highly imaginative language. Williams used that combination for most of his works. The structure of his plays is basically conventional, while his vision and his "voice" are imaginative and sensitive.

Because *The Glass Menagerie* is a memory play, its images are hazy. In production, when the curtain goes up, we see the apartment and the alley through a transparent gauze curtain, called a scrim. When the scrim rises, we see the set with pools of light and shadows.

The characters, too, are poetically conceived and seem removed from the daily life of the Great Depression of the 1930s. In a few lines in the opening narration, Williams conveys the social aspects of the period, but he is not really interested in society. What interests him most is the psychological makeup of his characters. In the play, Laura Wingfield passes her life listening to phonograph records and rearranging her collection of glass animals. Tom, her brother, wants to be a writer and to escape to the sea. Amanda, their mother, perpetually revisits her past glories as a southern belle. In contrast to the Wingfield family, the gentleman caller is not poetic. He is from the real world, and it is the touching confrontation between this real man and the unrealistic Laura that provides the climax of the play.

In December 1944, *The Glass Menagerie* was tried out in Chicago. It was poorly attended until the influential drama critic Claudia Cassidy came to its rescue by demanding that people see the play. When it moved to New York in the spring of 1945, it was an instant success.

Williams benefited from two extraordinary collaborators. Amanda was originally played by one of the great actresses of the American stage, Laurette Taylor. She had been in retirement for some years, but she was lured back to the stage by Williams's play. The natural tension of opening night was increased by the question, Would Laurette Taylor make it? She did make it. It was her greatest performance but her last role in the theater.

Williams's other great collaborator was Jo Mielziner, the foremost stage designer of his day.

Though a young playwright, Williams brought his collaborators a play with a passionate and poetic expression of his feelings for his own sister and a brilliantly conceived dramatic structure. Williams's collaborators rose to new heights when they helped him realize this gem of a play.

The Glass Menagerie
Tennessee Williams

Characters

Amanda Wingfield (the mother), a little woman of great but
confused vitality clinging frantically to another time and
place. Her characterization must be carefully created, not
copied from type. She is not paranoiac, but her life is
paranoia.

There is much to admire in Amanda, and as much to love
and pity as there is to laugh at. Certainly she has endurance
and a kind of heroism, and though her foolishness makes
her unwittingly cruel at times, there is tenderness in her
slight person.

Laura Wingfield (her daughter). Amanda, having failed to
establish contact with reality, continues to live vitally in her
illusions, but Laura's situation is even graver. A childhood
illness has left her crippled, one leg slightly shorter than the
other, and held in a brace. This defect need not be more
than suggested on the stage. Stemming from this, Laura's
separation increases till she is like a piece of her own glass
collection, too exquisitely fragile to move from the shelf.

Tom Wingfield (her son), and the narrator of the play. A poet
with a job in a warehouse. His nature is not remorseless, but
to escape from a trap he has to act without pity.

Jim O'Connor (the gentleman caller), a nice, ordinary, young
man.

Scene 1

*The Wingfield apartment is in the rear of the building, one of those vast
hive-like conglomerations of cellular living-units that flower at warty*

growths in overcrowded urban centers of lower middle-class population and are symptomatic of the impulse of this largest and fundamentally enslaved section of American society to avoid fluidity and differentiation and to exist and function as one interfused mass of automatism.

The apartment faces an alley and is entered by a fire escape, a structure whose name is a touch of accidental poetic truth, for all of these huge buildings are always burning with the slow and implacable fires of human desperation. The fire escape is part of what we see—that is, the landing of it and steps descending from it.

The scene is memory and is therefore nonrealistic. Memory takes a lot of poetic license. It omits some details; others are exaggerated, according to the emotional value of the articles it touches, for memory is seated predominantly in the heart. The interior is therefore rather dim and poetic.

At the rise of the curtain, the audience is faced with the dark, grim rear wall of the Wingfield tenement. This building is flanked on both sides by dark, narrow alleys which run into murky canyons of tangled clotheslines, garbage cans, and the sinister latticework of neighboring fire escapes. It is up and down these side alleys that exterior entrances and exits are made during the play. At the end of TOM's *opening commentary, the dark tenement wall slowly becomes transparent and reveals the interior of the ground-floor Wingfield apartment.*

Nearest the audience is the living room, which also serves as a sleeping room for LAURA, *the sofa unfolding to make her bed. Just beyond, separated from the living room by a wide arch or second proscenium with transparent faded portieres (or second curtain), is the dining room. In an old-fashioned whatnot in the living room are seen scores of transparent glass animals. A blown-up photograph of the father hangs on the wall of the living room, to the left of the archway. It is the face of a very handsome young man in a doughboy's First World War cap. He is gallantly smiling, ineluctably smiling, as if to say "I will be smiling forever."*

Also hanging on the wall, near the photograph, are a typewriter keyboard chart and a Gregg shorthand diagram. An upright typewriter on a small table stands beneath the charts.

The audience hears and sees the opening scene in the dining room through both the transparent fourth wall of the building and the transparent gauze portieres of the dining-room arch. It is during this revealing scene that the fourth wall slowly ascends, out of sight. This transparent exterior wall is not brought down again until the very end of the play, during TOM's *final speech.*

The narrator is an undisguised convention of the play. He takes whatever license with dramatic convention is convenient to his purposes.

[TOM *enters, dressed as a merchant sailor, and strolls across to the fire escape. There he stops and lights a cigarette. He addresses the audience.*]

Tom. Yes, I have tricks in my pocket, I have things up my sleeve. But I am the opposite of a stage magician. He gives you illusion that has the appearance of truth. I give you truth in the pleasant disguise of illusion.

To begin with, I turn back time. I reverse it to that quaint period, the thirties, when the huge middle class of America was matriculating in a school for the blind. Their eyes had failed them, or they had failed their eyes, and so they were having their fingers pressed forcibly down on the fiery Braille alphabet of a dissolving economy.

In Spain there was revolution. Here there was only shouting and confusion. In Spain there was Guernica. Here there were disturbances of labor, sometimes pretty violent, in otherwise peaceful cities such as Chicago, Cleveland, Saint Louis. . . . This is the social background of the play.

[*Music begins to play.*]

The play is memory. Being a memory play, it is dimly lighted, it is sentimental, it is not realistic. In memory everything seems to happen to music. That explains the fiddle in the wings.

I am the narrator of the play, and also a character in it. The other characters are my mother, Amanda, my sister, Laura, and a gentleman caller who appears in the final scenes. He is the most realistic character in the play, being an emissary from a world of reality that we were somehow set apart from. But since I have a poet's weakness for symbols, I am using this character also as a symbol; he is the long delayed but always expected something that we live for.

There is a fifth character in the play who doesn't appear except in this larger-than-life-size photograph over the mantel. This is our father who left us a long time ago. He was a telephone man who fell in love with long distances; he gave up his job with the telephone company and skipped the light fantastic out of town. . . .

The last we heard of him was a picture postcard from Mazatlan, on the Pacific coast of Mexico, containing a message of two words: "Hello—— Goodbye!" and no address.

I think the rest of the play will explain itself. . . .

[AMANDA's *voice becomes audible through the portieres.*]

[*Legend on screen:* "Ou sont les neiges?"]

[TOM *divides the portieres and enters the dining room.* AMANDA *and* LAURA *are seated at a dropleaf table. Eating is indicated by gestures without food or utensils.* AMANDA *faces the audience.* TOM *and* LAURA *are seated in profile. The interior has lit up softly and through the scrim we see* AMANDA *and* LAURA *seated at the table.*]

Amanda (*calling*). Tom?
Tom. Yes, mother.
Amanda. We can't say grace until you come to the table!
Tom. Coming, Mother. (*He bows slightly and withdraws, reappearing a few moments later in his place at the table.*)
Amanda (*to her son*). Honey, don't *push* with your *fingers*. If you have to push something, the thing to push with is a crust of bread. And chew—chew! Animals have secretions in their stomachs which enable them to digest food without mastication, but human beings are supposed to chew their food before they swallow it down. Eat food leisurely, son, and really enjoy it. A well-cooked meal has lots of delicate flavors that have to be held in the mouth for appreciation. So chew your food and give your salivary glands a chance to function!

[TOM *deliberately lays his imaginary fork down and pushes his chair back from the table.*]

Tom. I haven't enjoyed one bite of this dinner because of your constant directions on how to eat it. It's you that make me rush through meals with your hawk-like attention to every bite I take. Sickening—spoils my appetite—all this discussion of—animals' secretion—salivary glands—mastication!
Amanda (*lightly*). Temperament like a Metropolitan star!

[TOM *rises and walks toward the living room.*]

You're not excused from the table.
Tom. I'm getting a cigarette.
Amanda. You smoke too much.

[LAURA *rises.*]

Laura. I'll bring in the blanc mange.

[TOM *remains standing with his cigarette by the portieres.*]

Amanda (*rising*). No, sister—you be the lady this time and I'll be the servant.
Laura. I'm already up.
Amanda. Resume your seat, little sister—I want you to stay fresh and pretty—for gentlemen callers!
Laura (*sitting down*). I'm not expecting any gentlemen callers.
Amanda (*crossing out to the kitchenette, airily*). Sometimes they come when they are least expected! Why, I remember one Sunday afternoon in Blue Mountain——

[*She enters the kitchenette.*]

Tom. I know what's coming!
Laura. Yes. But let her tell it.
Tom. Again?

Laura. She loves to tell it.

[AMANDA *returns with a bowl of dessert.*]

Amanda. One Sunday afternoon in Blue Mountain—your mother received—*seventeen*—gentlemen callers! Why, sometimes there weren't chairs enough to accommodate them all. We had to send the servant over to bring in folding chairs from the parish house.

Tom (*remaining at the portieres*). How did you entertain those gentlemen callers?

Amanda. I understood the art of conversation!

Tom. I bet you could talk.

Amanda. Girls in those days *knew* how to talk, I can tell you.

Tom. Yes?

[*Image on screen:* AMANDA *as a girl on a porch, greeting callers.*]

Amanda. They knew how to entertain their gentlemen callers. It wasn't enough for a girl to be possessed of a pretty face and a graceful figure—although I wasn't slighted in either respect. She also needed to have a nimble wit and a tongue to meet all occasions.

Tom. What did you talk about?

Amanda. Things of importance going on in the world! Never anything coarse or common or vulgar.

[*She addresses* TOM *as though he were seated in the vacant chair at the table though he remains by the portieres. He plays this scene as though reading from a script.*]

My callers were gentlemen—all! Among my callers were some of the most prominent young planters of the Mississippi Delta—planters and sons of planters!

[TOM *motions for music and a spot of light on* AMANDA. *Her eyes lift, her face glows, her voice becomes rich and elegiac.*]

[*Screen legend.* "Ou sont les neiges d'antan?"]

There was young Champ Laughlin who later became vice-president of the Delta Planters Bank. Hadley Stevenson who was drowned in Moon Lake and left his widow one hundred and fifty thousand in Government bonds. There were the Cutrere brothers, Wesly and Bates. Bates was one of my bright particular beaux! He got in a quarrel with that wild Wainwright boy. They shot it out on the floor of Moon Lake Casino. Bates was shot through the stomach. Died in the ambulance on his way to Memphis. His widow was also well provided-for, came into eight or ten thousand acres, that's all. She married him on the rebound—never loved her—carried my picture on him the night he died! And there was that boy that every girl in the Delta had set her cap for! That beautiful, brilliant young Fitzhugh boy from Greene County!

Tom. What did he leave his widow?

Amanda. He never married! Gracious, you talk as though all of my old admirers had turned up their toes to the daisies!

Tom. Isn't this the first you've mentioned that still survives?

Amanda. That Fitzhugh boy went North and made a fortune—came to be known as the Wolf of Wall Street! He had the Midas touch, whatever he touched turned to gold! And I could have been Mrs. Duncan J. Fitzhugh, mind you! But—I picked your *father!*

Laura (*rising*). Mother, let me clear the table.

Amanda. No, dear, you go in front and study your typewriter chart. Or practice your shorthand a little. Stay fresh and pretty!—— It's almost time for your gentlemen callers to start arriving. (*She flounces girlishly toward the kitchenette.*) How many do you suppose we're going to entertain this afternoon?

[TOM *throws down the paper and jumps up with a groan.*]

Laura (*alone in the dining room*). I don't believe we're going to receive any, Mother.

Amanda (*reappearing, airily*). What? No one—not one? You must be joking!

[LAURA *nervously echoes her laugh. She slips in a fugitive manner through the half-open portieres and draws them gently behind her. A shaft of very clear light is thrown on her face against the faded tapestry of the curtains. Faintly the music of "The Glass Menagerie" is heard as she continues lightly.*]

Not one gentleman caller? It can't be true! There must be a flood, there must have been a tornado!
Laura. It isn't a flood, it's not a tornado, Mother. I'm just not popular like you were in Blue Mountain. . . .

[TOM *utters another groan.* LAURA *glances at him with a faint, apologetic smile. Her voice catches a little.*]

Mother's afraid I'm going to be an old maid.

[*The scene dims out with "The Glass Menagerie" music.*]

Scene 2

On the dark stage the screen is lighted with the image of blue roses. Gradually LAURA'*s figure becomes apparent and the screen goes out. The music subsides.*

LAURA *is seated in the delicate ivory chair at the small claw-foot table. She wears a dress of soft violet material for a kimono—her hair is tied back from her forehead with a ribbon. She is washing and polishing her collection of glass.* AMANDA *appears on the fire-escape steps. At the sound of her ascent,* LAURA *catches her breath, thrusts the bowl of ornaments away, and seats herself stiffly before the diagram of the typewriter keyboard as though it held her spellbound. Something has happened to* AMANDA. *It is written in her face as she climbs to the landing: a look that is grim and hopeless and a little absurd. She has on one of those cheap or imitation velvety-looking cloth coats with imitation fur collar. Her hat is five or six years old, one of those dreadful cloche hats that were worn in the late Twenties, and she is clutching an enormous black patent-leather pocketbook with nickel clasps and initials. This is her full-dress outfit, the one she usually wears to the D.A.R. Before entering she looks through the door. She purses her lips, opens her eyes very wide, rolls them upward and shakes her head. Then she slowly lets herself in the door. Seeing her mother's expression* LAURA *touches her lips with a nervous gesture.*

Laura. Hello, Mother, I was—— (*She makes a nervous gesture toward the chart on the wall.* AMANDA *leans against the shut door and stares at* LAURA *with a martyred look.*)
Amanda. Deception? Deception? (*She slowly removes her hat and gloves, continuing the sweet suffering stare. She lets the hat and gloves fall on the floor—a bit of acting.*)
Laura (*shakily*). How was the D.A.R. meeting?

[AMANDA *slowly opens her purse and removes a dainty white handkerchief which she shakes out delicately and delicately touches to her lips and nostrils.*]

Didn't you go to the D.A.R. meeting, Mother?
Amanda (*faintly, almost inaudibly*). ——No—— No. (*then more forcibly*) I did not have the strength—to go to the D.A.R. In fact, I did not have the courage! I wanted to find a hole in the ground and hide myself in it forever! (*She crosses slowly to the wall and removes the diagram of the typewriter keyboard. She holds it in front of her for a second, staring at it sweetly and sorrowfully—then bites her lips and tears it in two pieces.*)
Laura (*faintly*). Why did you do that, Mother?

[AMANDA *repeats the same procedure with the chart of the Gregg Alphabet.*]

Why are you——
Amanda. Why? Why? How old are you, Laura?
Laura. Mother, you know my age.
Amanda. I thought that you were an adult; it seems that I was mistaken. (*She crosses slowly to the sofa and sinks down and stares at* LAURA.)

Laura. Please don't stare at me, Mother.

[AMANDA *closes her eyes and lowers her head. There is a ten-second pause.*]

Amanda. What are we going to do, what is going to become of us, what is the future?

[*There is another pause.*]

Laura. Has something happened, Mother?

[AMANDA *draws a long breath, takes out the handkerchief again, goes through the dabbing process.*]

Mother, has—something happened?
Amanda. I'll be all right in a minute. I'm just bewildered— (*She hesitates.*) —by life. . . .
Laura. Mother, I wish that you would tell me what's happened!
Amanda. As you know, I was supposed to be inducted into my office at the D.A.R. this afternoon.

[*Screen image:* A swarm of typewriters.]

But I stopped off at Rubicam's Business College to speak to your teachers about your having a cold and ask them what progress they thought you were making down there.
Laura. Oh . . .
Amanda. I went to the typing instructor and introduced myself as your mother. She didn't know who you were. "Wingfield," she said, "We don't have any such student enrolled at the school!" I assured her she did, that you had been going to classes since early in January. "I wonder," she said, "If you could be talking about that terribly shy little girl who dropped out of school after only a few days' attendance?" "No," I said, "Laura, my daughter, has been going to school every day for the past six weeks!" "Excuse me," she said. She took the attendance book

out and there was your name, unmistakably printed, and all the dates you were absent until they decided that you had dropped out of school. I still said, "No, there must have been some mistake! There must have been some mix-up in the records!" And she said, "No—I remember her perfectly now. Her hands shook so that she couldn't hit the right keys! The first time we gave a speed test, she broke down completely— was sick at the stomach and almost had to be carried into the wash room! After that morning she never showed up any more. We phoned the house but never got any answer"—— While I was working at Famous-Barr, I suppose, demonstrating those—— (*She indicates a brassiere with her hands.*) Oh! I felt so weak I could barely keep on my feet! I had to sit down while they got me a glass of water! Fifty dollars' tuition, all of our plans—my hopes and ambitions for you—just gone up the spout, just gone up the spout like that.

[LAURA *draws a long breath and gets awkwardly to her feet. She crosses to the victrola and winds it up.*]

What are you doing?
Laura. Oh! (*She releases the handle and returns to her seat.*)
Amanda. Laura, where have you been going when you've gone out pretending that you were going to business college?
Laura. I've just been going out walking.
Amanda. That's not true.
Laura. It is. I just went walking.
Amanda. Walking? Walking? In winter? Deliberately courting pneumonia in that light coat? Where did you walk to, Laura?
Laura. All sorts of places—mostly in the park.
Amanda. Even after you'd started catching that cold?
Laura. It was the lesser of two evils, Mother.

[*Screen image:* Winter scene in a park.]

I couldn't go back there. I—threw up—on the floor!
Amanda. From half past seven till after five every day you mean to tell me you walked around in the park, because you

wanted to make me think that you were still going to Rubicam's Business College?

Laura. It wasn't as bad as it sounds. I went inside places to get warmed up.

Amanda. Inside where?

Laura. I went in the art museum and the bird houses at the Zoo. I visited the penguins every day! Sometimes I did without lunch and went to the movies. Lately I've been spending most of my afternoons in the Jewel Box, that big glass house where they raise the tropical flowers.

Amanda. You did all this to deceive me, just for deception?

[LAURA *looks down.*]

Why?

Laura. Mother, when you're disappointed, you get that awful suffering look on your face, like the picture of Jesus' mother in the museum!

Amanda. Hush!

Laura. I couldn't face it.

[*There is a pause. A whisper of strings is heard. Legend on screen:* "The Crust of Humility."]

Amanda (*hopelessly fingering the huge pocketbook*). So what are we going to do the rest of our lives? Stay home and watch the parades go by? Amuse ourselves with the glass menagerie, darling? Eternally play those worn-out phonograph records your father left as a painful reminder of him? We won't have a business career—we've given that up because it gave us nervous indigestion! (*She laughs wearily.*) What is there left but dependency all our lives? I know so well what becomes of unmarried women who aren't prepared to occupy a position. I've seen such pitiful cases in the South—barely tolerated spinsters living upon the grudging patronage of sister's husband or brother's wife—stuck away in some little mousetrap of a room—encouraged by one in-law to visit another—little birdlike women without any nest—eating the crust of humility all their life!

Is that the future that we've mapped out for ourselves? I swear it's the only alternative I can think of! (*She pauses.*) It isn't a very pleasant alternative, is it? (*She pauses again.*) Of course—some girls *do marry.*

[LAURA *twists her hands nervously.*]

Haven't you ever liked some boy?
Laura. Yes. I liked one once. (*She rises.*) I came across his picture a while ago.
Amanda (*with some interest*). He gave you his picture?
Laura. No, it's in the yearbook.
Amanda (*disappointed*). Oh—a high school boy.

[*Screen image:* JIM as the high school hero bearing a silver cup.]

Laura. Yes. His name was Jim. (*She lifts the heavy annual from the claw-foot table.*) Here he is in *The Pirates of Penzance.*
Amanda (*absently*). The what?
Laura. The operetta the senior class put on. He had a wonderful voice and we sat across the aisle from each other Mondays, Wednesdays, and Fridays in the Aud. Here he is with the silver cup for debating! See his grin?
Amanda (*absently*). He must have a jolly disposition.
Laura. He used to call me—Blue Roses.

[*Screen image:* Blue Roses.]

Amanda. Why did he call you such a name as that?
Laura. When I had that attack of pleurosis—he asked me what was the matter when I came back. I said pleurosis—he thought that I said Blue Roses! So that's what he always called me after that. Whenever he saw me, he'd holler, "Hello, Blue Roses!" I didn't care for the girl that he went out with. Emily Meisenbach. Emily was the best-dressed girl at Soldan. She never struck me, though, as being sincere.... It says in the Personal Section—they're engaged. That's—six years ago! They must be married by now.

Amanda. Girls that aren't cut out for business careers usually wind up married to some nice man. (*She gets up with a spark of revival.*) Sister, that's what you'll do!

[LAURA *utters a startled, doubtful laugh. She reaches quickly for a piece of glass.*]

Laura. But, Mother——
Amanda. Yes? (*She goes over to the photograph.*)
Laura (*in a tone of frightened apology*). I'm—crippled!
Amanda. Nonsense! Laura, I've told you never, never to use that word. Why, you're not crippled, you just have a little defect—hardly noticeable, even! When people have some slight disadvantage like that, they cultivate other things to make up for it—develop charm—and vivacity—and—*charm!* That's all you have to do! (*She turns again to the photograph.*) One thing your father had *plenty* of—was *charm!*

[*The scene fades out with music.*]

Scene 3

Legend on screen: "After the fiasco——"

TOM *speaks from the fire-escape landing.*

Tom. After the fiasco at Rubicam's Business College, the idea of getting a gentleman caller for Laura began to play a more and more important part in Mother's calculations. It became an obsession. Like some archetype of the universal unconscious, the image of the gentleman caller haunted our small apartment. . . .

[*Screen image:* A young man at the door of a house with flowers.]

An evening at home rarely passed without some allusion to this image, this specter, this hope. . . . Even when he wasn't mentioned, his presence hung in Mother's preoccupied look and in my sister's frightened, apologetic manner—hung like a sentence passed upon the Wingfields!

Mother was a woman of action as well as words. She began to take logical steps in the planned direction. Late that winter and in the early spring—realizing that extra money would be needed to properly feather the nest and plume the bird—she conducted a vigorous campaign on the telephone, roping in sub-scribers to one of those magazines for matrons called *The Homemaker's Companion*, the type of journal that features the seri-alized sublimations of ladies of letters who think in terms of deli-cate cuplike breasts, slim, tapering waists, rich, creamy thighs, eyes like wood smoke in autumn, fingers that soothe and caress like strains of music, bodies as powerful as Etruscan sculpture.

[*Screen image:* The cover of a glamor magazine.]

[AMANDA *enters with the telephone on a long extension cord. She is spotlighted in the dim stage.*]

Amanda. Ida Scott? This is Amanda Wingfield! We *missed* you at the D.A.R. last Monday! I said to myself: She's probably suf-fering with that sinus condition! How is that sinus condition? Horrors! Heaven have a mercy!—— You're a Christian martyr, yes, that's what you are, a Christian martyr. Well, I just now happened to notice that your subscription to the *Companion*'s about to expire. Yes, it expires with the next issue, honey!— just when that wonderful new serial by Bessie Mae Hopper is getting off to such an exciting start. Oh, honey, it's something that you can't miss! You remember how *Gone with the Wind* took everybody by storm? You simply couldn't go out if you hadn't read it. All everybody *talked* was Scarlett O'Hara. Well, this is a book that critics already compare to *Gone with the Wind*. It's the *Gone with the Wind* of the post-World-War generation!—— What?—— Burning?—— Oh, honey, don't let them burn, go take a look in the oven and I'll hold the wire! Heavens—I think she's hung up!

[*The scene dims out.*]

[*Legend on screen:* "You think I'm in love with Continental Shoemakers?"]

[*Before the lights come up again, the violent voices of* TOM *and* AMANDA *are heard. They are quarreling behind the portieres. In front of them stands* LAURA *with clenched hands and panicky expression. A clear pool of light is on her figure throughout this scene.*]

Tom. What in hell am I——
Amanda (*shrilly*). Don't you use that——
Tom. ——supposed to do!
Amanda. ——expression! Not in my——
Tom. Ohhh!
Amanda. ——presence! Have you gone out of your senses?
Tom. I have, that's true, *driven* out!
Amanda. What is the matter with you, you—big—big—IDIOT!
Tom. Look!—— I've got *no thing*, no single thing——
Amanda. Lower your voice!
Tom. ——in my life here that I can call my OWN! Everything is——
Amanda. Stop that shouting!
Tom. Yesterday you confiscated my books! You had the nerve to——
Amanda. I took that horrible novel back to the library—yes! That hideous book by that insane Mr. Lawrence.

[TOM *laughs wildly.*]

I cannot control the output of diseased minds or people who cater to them——

[TOM *laughs still more wildly.*]

BUT I WON'T ALLOW SUCH FILTH BROUGHT INTO MY HOUSE! No, no, no, no, no!

Tom. House, house! Who pays rent on it, who makes a slave of himself to——

Amanda (*fairly screeching*). Don't you DARE to——

Tom. No, no, I mustn't say things! *I've* got to just——

Amanda. Let me tell you——

Tom. I don't want to hear any more!

[*He tears the portieres open. The dining-room area is lit with a turgid smoky red glow. Now we see* AMANDA; *her hair is in metal curlers and she is wearing a very old bathrobe, much too large for her slight figure, a relic of the faithless* MR. WINGFIELD. *The upright typewriter now stands on the drop-leaf table, along with a wild disarray of manuscripts. The quarrel was probably precipitated by* AMANDA's *interruption of* TOM's *creative labor. A chair lies overthrown on the floor. Their gesticulating shadows are cast on the ceiling by the fiery glow.*]

Amanda. You *will* hear more, you——

Tom. No, I won't hear more, I'm going out!

Amanda. You come right back in——

Tom. Out, out, out! Because I'm——

Amanda. Come back here, Tom Wingfield! I'm not through talking to you!

Tom. Oh, go——

Laura (*desperately*). Tom!

Amanda. You're going to listen, and no more insolence from you! I'm at the end of my patience!

[*He comes back toward her.*]

Tom. What do you think I'm at? Aren't I supposed to have any patience to reach the end of, Mother? I know, I know. It seems unimportant to you, what I'm *doing*—what I *want* to do—having a little *difference* between them! You don't think that——

Amanda. I think you've been doing things that you're ashamed of. That's why you act like this. I don't believe that you go every night to the movies. Nobody goes to the movies night after night. Nobody in their right minds goes to the

movies as often as you pretend to. People don't go to the movies
at nearly midnight, and movies don't let out at two A.M. Come
in stumbling. Muttering to yourself like a maniac! You get three
hours' sleep and then go to work. Oh, I can picture the way
you're doing down there. Moping, doping, because you're in
no condition.

Tom (*wildly*). No, I'm in no condition!

Amanda. What right have you got to jeopardize your job?
Jeopardize the security of us all? How do you think we'd manage if you were——

Tom. Listen! You think I'm crazy about the *warehouse?* (*He
bends fiercely toward her slight figure.*) You think I'm in love with
the Continental Shoemakers? You think I want to spend fifty-
five *years* down there in that—*celotex interior!* with—*fluorescent—
tubes!* Look! I'd rather somebody picked up a crowbar and
battered out my brains—than go back mornings! I *go!* Every
time you come in yelling that damn *"Rise and Shine!" "Rise and
Shine!"* I say to myself, "How *lucky dead* people are!" But I get
up. I *go!* For sixty-five dollars a month I give up all that I dream
of doing and being *ever!* and you say self—*self's* all I ever think
of. Why, listen, if self is what I thought of, Mother, I'd be where
he is—GONE! (*He points to his father's picture.*) As far as the system of transportation reaches! (*He starts past her. She grabs his
arm.*) Don't grab at me, Mother!

Amanda. Where are you going?

Tom. I'm going to the *movies!*

Amanda. I don't believe that lie!

[TOM *crouches toward her, overtowering her tiny figure. She backs
away, gasping.*]

Tom. I'm going to opium dens! Yes, opium dens, dens of vice
and criminals' hangouts, Mother. I've joined the Hogan Gang,
I'm a hired assassin, I carry a tommy gun in a violin case! I run
a string of cat houses in the Valley! They call me Killer, Killer
Wingfield, I'm leading a double-life, a simple, honest warehouse worker by day, by night a dynamic *czar* of the *underworld*,

Mother. I go to gambling casinos, I spin away fortunes on the roulette table! I wear a patch over one eye and a false mustache, sometimes I put on green whiskers. On those occasions they call me—*El Diablo!* Oh, I could tell you many things to make you sleepless! My enemies plan to dynamite this place. They're going to blow us all sky-high some night! I'll be glad, very happy, and so will you! You'll go up, up on a broomstick, over Blue Mountain with seventeen gentlemen callers! You ugly— babbling old—*witch* . . . (*He goes through a series of violent, clumsy movements, seizing his overcoat, lunging to the door, pulling it fiercely open. The women watch him, aghast. His arm catches in the sleeve of the coat as he struggles to pull it on. For a moment he is pinioned by the bulky garment. With an outraged groan he tears the coat off again, splitting the shoulder of it, and hurls it across the room. It strikes against the shelf of Laura's glass collection, and there is a tinkle of shattering glass. Laura cries out as if wounded.*)

[*Music.*]

[*Screen legend:* "The Glass Menagerie."]

Laura (*shrilly*). *My glass!*—menagerie . . . (*She covers her face and turns away.*)

[*But* AMANDA *is still stunned and stupefied by the "ugly witch" so that she barely notices this occurrence. Now she recovers her speech.*]

Amanda (*in an awful voice*). I won't speak to you—until you apologize!

[*She crosses through the portieres and draws them together behind her.* TOM *is left with* LAURA. LAURA *clings weakly to the mantel with her face averted.* TOM *stares at her stupidly for a moment. Then he crosses to the shelf. He drops awkwardly on his knees to collect the fallen glass, glancing at* LAURA *as if he would speak but couldn't.*]

[*"The Glass Menagerie" music steals in as the scene dims out.*]

Scene 4

The interior of the apartment is dark. There is a faint light in the alley. A deep-voiced bell in a church is tolling the hour of five.

TOM *appears at the top of the alley. After each solemn boom of the bell in the tower, he shakes a little noisemaker or rattle as if to express the tiny spasm of man in contrast to the sustained power and dignity of the Almighty. This and the unsteadiness of his advance make it evident that he has been drinking. As he climbs the few steps to the fire-escape landing light steals up inside.* LAURA *appears in the front room in a nightdress. She notices that* TOM's *bed is empty.* TOM *fishes in his pockets for his door key, removes a motley assortment of articles in the search, including a shower of movie ticket stubs and an empty bottle. At last he finds the key, but just as he is about to insert it, it slips from his fingers. He strikes a match and crouches below the door.*

Tom (*bitterly*). One crack—and it falls through!

[LAURA *opens the door.*]

Laura. Tom! Tom, what are you doing?
Tom. Looking for a door key.
Laura. Where have you been all this time?
Tom. I have been to the movies.
Laura. All this time at the movies?
Tom. There was a very long program. There was a Garbo picture and a Mickey Mouse and a travelogue and a newsreel and a preview of coming attractions. And there was an organ solo and a collection for the Milk Fund—simultaneously—which ended up in a terrible fight between a fat lady and an usher!
Laura (*innocently*). Did you have to stay through everything?
Tom. Of course! And, oh, I forgot! There was a big stage show! The headliner of this stage show was Malvolio the Magician. He performed wonderful tricks, many of them, such as pouring water back and forth between pitchers. First it turned to wine and then it turned to beer and then it turned to whisky.

I know it was whisky it finally turned into because he needed somebody to come up out of the audience to help him, and I came up—both shows! It was Kentucky Straight Bourbon. A very generous fellow, he gave souvenirs. (*He pulls from his back pocket a shimmering rainbow-colored scarf.*) He gave me this. This is his magic scarf. You can have it, Laura. You wave it over a canary cage and you get a bowl of goldfish. You wave it over the goldfish bowl and they fly away canaries. . . . But the wonderfullest trick of all was the coffin trick. We nailed him into a coffin and he got out of the coffin without removing one nail. (*He has come inside.*) There is a trick that would come in handy for me—get me out of this two-by-four situation! (*He flops onto the bed and starts removing his shoes.*)

Laura. Tom—shhh!

Tom. What're you shushing me for?

Laura. You'll wake up Mother.

Tom. Goody, goody! Pay 'er back for all those "Rise an' Shines." (*He lies down, groaning.*) You know it don't take much intelligence to get yourself into a nailed-up coffin, Laura. But who ever got himself out of one without removing one nail?

[*As if in answer, the father's grinning photograph lights up. The scene dims out.*]

[*Immediately following, the church bell is heard striking six. At the sixth stroke the alarm clock goes off in* AMANDA's *room, and after a few moments we hear her calling: "Rise and Shine! Rise and Shine! Laura, go tell your brother to rise and shine!"*]

Tom (*sitting up slowly*). I'll rise—but I won't shine.

[*The light increases.*]

Amanda. Laura, tell your brother his coffee is ready.

[LAURA *slips into the front room.*]

Laura. Tom!—It's nearly seven. Don't make Mother nervous.

[*He stares at her stupidly.*]

(*Beseechingly*) Tom, speak to Mother this morning. Make up with her, apologize, speak to her!

Tom. She won't to me. It's her that started not speaking.

Laura. If you just say you're sorry she'll start speaking.

Tom. Her not speaking—is that such a tragedy?

Laura. Please—please!

Amanda (*calling from the kitchenette*). Laura, are you going to do what I asked you to do, or do I have to get dressed and go out myself?

Laura. Going, going—soon as I get on my coat!

[*She pulls on a shapeless felt hat with a nervous, jerky movement, pleadingly glancing at* TOM. *She rushes awkwardly for her coat. The coat is one of* AMANDA's, *inaccurately made-over, the sleeves too short for* LAURA.]

Butter and what else?

Amanda (*entering from the kitchenette*). Just butter. Tell them to charge it.

Laura. Mother, they make such faces when I do that.

Amanda. Sticks and stones can break our bones, but the expression on Mr. Garfinkel's face won't harm us! Tell your brother his coffee is getting cold.

Laura (*at the door*). Do what I asked you, will you, will you, Tom?

[*He looks sullenly away.*]

Amanda. Laura, go now or just don't go at all!

Laura (*rushing out*). Going—going!

[*A second later she cries out.* TOM *springs up and crosses to the door.* TOM *opens the door.*]

Tom. Laura?

Laura. I'm all right. I slipped, but I'm all right.

Amanda (*peering anxiously after her*). If anyone breaks a leg on those fire-escape steps, the landlord ought to be sued for every cent he possesses! (*She shuts the door. Now she remembers she isn't speaking to* TOM *and returns to the other room.*)

[*As* TOM *comes listlessly for his coffee, she turns her back to him and stands rigidly facing the window on the gloomy gray vault of the areaway. Its light on her face with its aged but childish features is cruelly sharp, satirical as a Daumier print.*]

[*The music of "Ave Maria" is heard softly.*]

[TOM *glances sheepishly but sullenly at her averted figure and slumps at the table. The coffee is scalding hot; he sips it and gasps and spits it back in the cup. At his gasp,* AMANDA *catches her breath and half turns. Then she catches herself and turns back to the window.* TOM *blows on his coffee, glancing sidewise at his mother. She clears her throat.* TOM *clears his. He starts to rise, sinks back down again, scratches his head, clears his throat again.* AMANDA *coughs.* TOM *raises his cup in both hands to blow on it, his eyes staring over the rim of it at his mother for several moments. Then he slowly sets the cup down and awkwardly and hesitantly rises from the chair.*]

Tom (*hoarsely*). Mother. I—I apologize, Mother.

[AMANDA *draws a quick, shuddering breath. Her face works grotesquely. She breaks into childlike tears.*]

I'm sorry for what I said, for everything that I said, I didn't mean it.
Amanda (*sobbingly*). My devotion has made me a witch and so I make myself hateful to my children!
Tom. No, you *don't.*
Amanda. I worry so much, don't sleep, it makes me nervous!
Tom (*gently*). I understand that.
Amanda. I've had to put up a solitary battle all these years. But you're my right-hand bower! Don't fall down, don't fail!

Tom (*gently*). I try, Mother.

Amanda (*with great enthusiasm*). Try and you will *succeed!* (*The notion makes her breathless.*) Why, you—you're just *full* of natural endowments! Both of my children—they're *unusual* children! Don't you think I know it? I'm so—*proud!* Happy and—feel I've— so much to be thankful for but—promise me one thing, son!

Tom. What, Mother?

Amanda. Promise, son, you'll—never be a drunkard!

Tom (*turns to her grinning*). I will never be a drunkard, Mother.

Amanda. That's what frightened me so, that you'd be drinking! Eat a bowl of Purina!

Tom. Just coffee, Mother.

Amanda. Shredded wheat biscuit?

Tom. No. No, Mother, just coffee.

Amanda. You can't put in a day's work on an empty stomach. You've got ten minutes—don't gulp! Drinking too-hot liquids makes cancer of the stomach. . . . Put cream in.

Tom. No, thank you.

Amanda. To cool it.

Tom. No! No, thank you. I want it black.

Amanda. I know, but it's not good for you. We have to do all we can to build ourselves up. In these trying times we live in, all that we have to cling to is—each other. . . . That's why it's so important to—Tom, I—I sent out your sister so I could discuss something with you. If you hadn't spoken I would have spoken to you. (*She sits down.*)

Tom (*gently*). What is it, Mother, that you want to discuss?

Amanda. *Laura!*

[TOM *puts his cup down slowly.*]

[*Legend on screen:* "Laura." *Music:* "The Glass Menagerie."]

Tom. ——Oh—Laura . . .

Amanda (*touching his sleeve*). You know how Laura is. So quiet but—still water runs deep! She notices things and I think she— broods about them.

[TOM *looks up.*]

A few days ago I came in and she was crying.

Tom. What about?

Amanda. You.

Tom. Me?

Amanda. She has an idea that you're not happy here.

Tom. What gave her that idea?

Amanda. What gives her any idea? However, you do act strangely. I—I'm not criticizing, understand *that!* I know your ambitions do not lie in the warehouse, that like everybody in the whole wide world—you've had to—make sacrifices, but— Tom—Tom—life's not easy, it calls for—Spartan endurance! There's so many things in my heart that I cannot describe to you! I've never told you but I—*loved* your father. . . .

Tom (*gently*). I know that, Mother.

Amanda. And you—when I see you taking after his ways! Staying out late—and—well, you *had* been drinking the night you were in that—terrifying condition! Laura says that you hate the apartment and that you go out nights to get away from it! Is that true, Tom?

Tom. No. You say there's so much in your heart that you can't describe to me. That's true of me, too. There's so much in my heart that I can't describe to *you!* So let's respect each other's——

Amanda. But, why—*why*, Tom—are you always so *restless?* Where do you *go* to, nights?

Tom. I—go to the movies.

Amanda. Why do you go to the movies so much, Tom?

Tom. I go to the movies because—I like adventure. Adventure is something I don't have much of at work, so I go to the movies.

Amanda. But, Tom, you go to the movies *entirely* too *much!*

Tom. I like a lot of adventure.

[AMANDA *looks baffled, then hurt. As the familiar inquisition resumes,* TOM *becomes hard and impatient again.* AMANDA *slips back into her querulous attitude toward him.*]

[*Image on screen:* A sailing vessel with Jolly Roger.]

Amanda. Most young men find adventure in their careers.

Tom. Then most young men are not employed in a warehouse.

Amanda. The world is full of young men employed in warehouses and offices and factories.

Tom. Do all of them find adventure in their careers?

Amanda. They do or they do without it! Not everybody has a craze for adventure.

Tom. Man is by instinct a lover, a hunter, a fighter, and none of those instincts are given much play at the warehouse!

Amanda. Man is by instinct! Don't quote instinct to me! Instinct is something that people have got away from! It belongs to animals! Christian adults don't want it!

Tom. What do Christian adults want, then, Mother?

Amanda. Superior things! Things of the mind and the spirit! Only animals have to satisfy instincts! Surely your aims are somewhat higher than theirs! Than monkeys—pigs——

Tom. I reckon they're not.

Amanda. You're joking. However, that isn't what I want to discuss.

Tom (*rising*). I haven't much time.

Amanda (*pushing his shoulders*). Sit down.

Tom. You want me to punch in red at the warehouse, Mother?

Amanda. You have five minutes. I want to talk about Laura.

[*Screen legend:* "Plans and Provisions."]

Tom. All right! What about Laura?

Amanda. We have to be making some plans and provisions for her. She's older than you, two years, and nothing has happened. She just drifts along doing nothing. It frightens me terribly how she just drifts along.

Tom. I guess she's the type that people call home girls.

Amanda. There's no such type, and if there is, it's a pity! That is unless the home is hers, with a husband!

Tom. What?

Amanda. Oh, I can see the handwriting on the wall as plain as I see the nose in front of my face! It's terrifying! More and more you remind me of your father! He was out all hours without explanation—— Then *left! Goodbye!* And me with the bag to hold. I saw that letter you got from the Merchant Marine. I know what you're dreaming of. I'm not standing here blind-folded. (*She pauses.*) Very well, then. Then *do* it! But not till there's somebody to take your place.

Tom. What do you mean?

Amanda. I mean that as soon as Laura has got somebody to take care of her, married, a home of her own, independent—why, then you'll be free to go wherever you please, on land, on sea, whichever way the wind blows you! But until that time you've got to look out for your sister. I don't say me because I'm old and don't matter! I say for your sister because she's young and dependent.

I put her in business college—a dismal failure! Frightened her so it made her sick at the stomach. I took her over to the Young People's League at the church. Another fiasco. She spoke to nobody, nobody spoke to her. Now all she does is fool with those pieces of glass and play those worn-out records. What kind of a life is that for a girl to lead?

Tom. What can I do about it?

Amanda. Overcome selfishness! Self, self, self is all that you ever think of!

[TOM *springs up and crosses to get his coat. It is ugly and bulky. He pulls on a cap with earmuffs.*]

Where is your muffler? Put your wool muffler on!

[*He snatches it angrily from the closet, tosses it around his neck and pulls both ends tight.*]

Tom! I haven't said what I had in mind to ask you.

Tom. I'm too late to——

Amanda (*catching his arm—very importunately; then shyly*). Down at the warehouse, aren't there some—nice young men?

Tom. No!

Amanda. There *must* be—*some* . . .

Tom. Mother—— (*He gestures.*)
Amanda. Find out one that's clean-living—doesn't drink and ask him out for sister!
Tom. What?
Amanda. For *sister*! To *meet*! Get *acquainted*!
Tom (*stamping to the door*). Oh, my *go-osh*!
Amanda. Will you?

[*He opens the door. She says, imploringly:*]

Will you?

[*He starts down the fire escape.*]

Will you? *Will* you dear?
Tom (*calling back*). Yes!

[AMANDA *closes the door hesitantly with a troubled but faintly hopeful expression.*]

[*Screen image:* The cover of a glamor magazine.]

[*The spotlight picks up* AMANDA *at the phone.*]

Amanda. Ella Cartwright? This is Amanda Wingfield! How are you, honey? How is that kidney condition?

[*There is a five-second pause.*]

Horrors!

[*There is another pause.*]

You're a Christian martyr, yes, honey, that's what you are, a Christian martyr! Well, I just now happened to notice in my little red book that your subscription to the *Companion* has just run out! I know that you wouldn't want to miss out on the wonderful serial starting in this new issue. It's by Bessie Mae Hopper, the first thing she's written since *Honeymoon for Three*. Wasn't that a strange and interesting story? Well, this one is even lovelier, I believe. It has a sophisticated, society background. It's all about the horsey set on Long Island!

[*The light fades out.*]

Scene 5

Legend on the screen: "Annunciation."

Music is heard as the light slowly comes on.

It is early dusk of a spring evening. Supper has just been finished in the Wingfield apartment. AMANDA *and* LAURA, *in light-colored dresses, are removing dishes from the table in the dining room, which is shadowy, their movements formalized almost as a dance or ritual, their moving forms as pale and silent as moths.* TOM, *in white shirt and trousers, rises from the table and crosses toward the fire escape.*

Amanda (*as he passes her*). Son, will you do me a favor?
Tom. What?
Amanda. Comb your hair! You look so pretty when your hair is combed!

[TOM *slouches on the sofa with the evening paper. Its enormous headline reads:* "*Franco Triumphs.*"]

There is only one respect in which I would like you to emulate your father.
Tom. What respect is that?
Amanda. The care he always took of his appearance. He never allowed himself to look untidy.

[*He throws down the paper and crosses to the fire escape.*]

Where are you going?
Tom. I'm going out to smoke.
Amanda. You smoke too much. A pack a day at fifteen cents a pack. How much would that amount to in a month? Thirty times fifteen is how much, Tom? Figure it out and you will be astounded at what you could save. Enough to give you a night-school course in accounting at Washington U.! Just think what a wonderful thing that would be for you, son!

[TOM *is unmoved by the thought.*]

Tom. I'd rather smoke. (*He steps out on the landing, letting the screen door slam.*)
Amanda (*sharply*). I know! That's the tragedy of it. . . . (*Alone, she turns to look at her husband's picture.*)

[*Dance music:* "The World Is Waiting for the Sunrise!"]

Tom (*to the audience*). Across the alley from us was the Paradise Dance Hall. On evenings in Spring the windows and doors were open and the music came outdoors. Sometimes the lights were turned out except for a large glass sphere that hung from the ceiling. It would turn slowly about and filter the dusk with delicate rainbow colors. Then the orchestra played a waltz or a tango, something that had a slow and sensuous rhythm. Couples would come outside, to the relative privacy of the alley. You could see them kissing behind ash pits and telephone poles. This was the compensation for lives that passed like mine, without any change or adventure. Adventure and change were imminent in this year. They were waiting around the corner for all these kids. Suspended in the mist over Berchtesgaden, caught in the folds of Chamberlain's umbrella. In Spain there was Guernica! But here there was only hot swing music and liquor, dance halls, bars, and movies, and sex that hung in the gloom like a chandelier and flooded the world with brief, deceptive rainbows. . . . All the world was waiting for bombardments!

[AMANDA *turns from the picture and comes outside.*]

Amanda (*sighing*). A fire escape landing's a poor excuse for a porch. (*She spreads a newspaper on a step and sits down, gracefully and demurely as if she were settling into a swing on a Mississippi veranda.*) What are you looking at?

Tom. The moon.

Amanda. Is there a moon this evening?

Tom. It's rising over Garfinkel's Delicatessen.

Amanda. So it is! A little silver slipper of a moon. Have you made a wish on it yet?

Tom. Um-hum.

Amanda. What did you wish for?

Tom. That's a secret.

Amanda. A secret, huh? Well, I won't tell mine either. I will be just as mysterious as you.

Tom. I bet I can guess what yours is.

Amanda. Is my head so transparent?

Tom. You're not a sphinx.

Amanda. No. I don't have secrets. I'll tell you what I wished for on the moon. Success and happiness for my precious children! I wish for that whenever there's a moon, and when there isn't a moon, I wish for it, too.

Tom. I thought perhaps you wished for a gentleman caller.

Amanda. Why do you say that?

Tom. Don't you remember asking me to fetch one?

Amanda. I remember suggesting that it would be nice for your sister if you brought home some nice young man from the warehouse. I think that I've made that suggestion more than once.

Tom. Yes, you have made it repeatedly.

Amanda. Well?

Tom. We are going to have one.

Amanda. *What?*

Tom. A gentleman caller!

[*The annunciation is celebrated with music.*]

[AMANDA *rises.*]

[*Image on screen:* A caller with a bouquet.]

Amanda. You mean you have asked some nice young man to come over?
Tom. Yep. I've asked him to dinner.
Amanda. You really did?
Tom. I did!
Amanda. You did, and did he—*accept?*
Tom. He did!
Amanda. Well, well—well, well! That's—lovely!
Tom. I thought that you would be pleased.
Amanda. It's definite then?
Tom. Very definite.
Amanda. Soon?
Tom. Very soon.
Amanda. For heaven's sake, stop putting on and tell me some things, will you?
Tom. What things do you want me to tell you?
Amanda. *Naturally* I would like to know when he's *coming!*
Tom. He's coming tomorrow.
Amanda. *Tomorrow?*
Tom. Yep. Tomorrow.
Amanda. But, Tom!
Tom. Yes, Mother?
Amanda. Tomorrow gives me no time!
Tom. Time for what?
Amanda. Preparations! Why didn't you phone me at once, as soon as you asked him, the minute that he accepted? Then, don't you see, I could have been getting ready!
Tom. You don't have to make any fuss.
Amanda. Oh, Tom, Tom, Tom, of course I have to make a fuss! I want things nice, not sloppy! Not thrown together. I'll certainly have to do some fast thinking, won't I?
Tom. I don't see why you have to think at all.

Amanda. You just don't know. We can't have a gentleman caller in a pigsty! All my wedding silver has to be polished, the monogrammed table linen ought to be laundered! The windows have to be washed and fresh curtains put up. And how about clothes? We have to *wear* something, don't we?

Tom. Mother, this boy is no one to make a fuss over!

Amanda. Do you realize he's the first young man we've introduced to your sister? It's terrible, dreadful, disgraceful that poor little sister has never received a single gentleman caller! Tom, come inside! (*She opens the screen door.*)

Tom. What for?

Amanda. I want to ask you some things.

Tom. If you're going to make such a fuss, I'll call it off, I'll tell him not to come!

Amanda. You certainly won't do anything of the kind. Nothing offends people worse than broken engagements. It simply means I'll have to work like a Turk! We won't be brilliant, but we will pass inspection. Come on inside.

[TOM *follows her inside, groaning.*]

Sit down.

Tom. Any particular place you would like me to sit?

Amanda. Thank heavens I've got that new sofa! I'm also making payments on a floor lamp I'll have sent out! And put the chintz covers on, they'll brighten things up! Of course I'd hoped to have these walls re-papered. . . . What is the young man's name?

Tom. His name is O'Connor.

Amanda. That, of course, means fish—tomorrow is Friday! I'll have that salmon loaf—with Durkee's dressing! What does he do? He works at the warehouse?

Tom. Of course! How else would I——

Amanda. Tom, he—doesn't drink?

Tom. Why do you ask me that?

Amanda. Your father *did!*

Tom. Don't get started on that!

Amanda. He *does* drink, then?

Tom. Not that I know of!

Amanda. Make sure, be certain! The last thing I want for my daughter's a boy who drinks!

Tom. Aren't you being a little bit premature? Mr. O'Connor has not yet appeared on the scene!

Amanda. But will tomorrow. To meet your sister, and what do I know about his character? Nothing! Old maids are better off than wives of drunkards!

Tom. Oh, my God!

Amanda. Be still!

Tom (*leaning forward to whisper*). Lots of fellows meet girls whom they don't marry!

Amanda. Oh, talk sensibly, Tom—and don't be sarcastic! (*She has gotten a hairbrush.*)

Tom. What are you doing?

Amanda. I'm brushing that cowlick down! (*She attacks his hair with the brush.*) What is this young man's position at the warehouse?

Tom (*submitting grimly to the brush and the interrogation*). This young man's position is that of a shipping clerk, Mother.

Amanda. Sounds to me like a fairly responsible job, the sort of a job *you* would be in if you just had more *get-up*. What is his salary? Have you any idea?

Tom. I would judge it to be approximately eighty-five dollars a month.

Amanda. Well—not princely, but——

Tom. Twenty more than I make.

Amanda. Yes, how well I know! But for a family man, eighty-five dollars a month is not much more than you can just get by on. . . .

Tom. Yes, but Mr. O'Connor is not a family man.

Amanda. He might be, mightn't he? Some time in the future?

Tom. I see. Plans and provisions.

Amanda. You are the only young man that I know of who ignores the fact that the future becomes the present, the present the past, and the past turns into everlasting regret if you don't plan for it!

Tom. I will think that over and see what I can make of it.

Amanda. Don't be supercilious with your mother! Tell me some more about this—what do you call him?

Tom. James D. O'Conner. The D. is for Delaney.

Amanda. Irish on *both* sides! *Gracious!* And doesn't drink?

Tom. Shall I call him up and ask him right this minute?

Amanda. The only way to find out about those things is to make discreet inquiries at the proper moment. When I was a girl in Blue Mountain and it was suspected that a young man drank, the girl whose attentions he had been receiving, if any girl *was*, would sometimes speak to the minister of his church, or rather her father would if her father was living, and sort of feel him out on the young man's character. That is the way such things are discreetly handled to keep a young woman from making a tragic mistake!

Tom. Then how did you happen to make a tragic mistake?

Amanda. That innocent look of your father's had everyone fooled! He *smiled*—the world was *enchanted!* No girl can do worse than put herself at the mercy of a handsome appearance! I hope that Mr. O'Connor is not too good-looking.

Tom. No, he's not too good-looking. He's covered with freckles and hasn't too much of a nose.

Amanda. He's not right-down homely, though?

Tom. Not right-down homely. Just medium homely, I'd say.

Amanda. Character's what to look for in a man.

Tom. That's what I've always said, Mother.

Amanda. You've never said anything of the kind and I suspect you would never give it a thought.

Tom. Don't be so suspicious of me.

Amanda. At least I hope he's the type that's up and coming.

Tom. I think he really goes in for self-improvement.

Amanda. What reason have you to think so?

Tom. He goes to night school.

Amanda (*beaming*). Splendid! What does he do, I mean study?

Tom. Radio engineering and public speaking!

Amanda. Then he has visions of being advanced in the world! Any young man who studies public speaking is aiming to have an executive job some day! And radio engineering? A thing for the future! Both of these facts are very illuminating. Those are the sort of things that a mother should know concerning any young man who comes to call on her daughter. Seriously or—not.

Tom. One little warning. He doesn't know about Laura. I didn't let on that we had dark ulterior motives. I just said, why don't you come and have dinner with us? He said okay and that was the whole conversation.

Amanda. I bet it was! You're eloquent as an oyster. However, he'll know about Laura when he gets here. When he sees how lovely and sweet and pretty she is, he'll thank his lucky stars he was asked to dinner.

Tom. Mother, you mustn't expect too much of Laura.

Amanda. What do you mean?

Tom. Laura seems all those things to you and me because she's ours and we love her. We don't even notice she's crippled any more.

Amanda. Don't say crippled! You know that I never allow that word to be used!

Tom. But face facts, Mother. She is and—that's not all——

Amanda. What do you mean "not all?"

Tom. Laura is very different from other girls.

Amanda. I think the difference is all to her advantage.

Tom. Not quite all—in the eyes of others—strangers—she's terribly shy and lives in a world of her own and those things make her seem a little peculiar to people outside the house.

Amanda. Don't say peculiar.

Tom. Face the facts. She is.

[*The dance hall music changes to a tango that has a minor and somewhat ominous tone.*]

Amanda. In what way is she peculiar—may I ask?

Tom (*gently*). She lives in a world of her own—a world of little glass ornaments, Mother. . . .

[*He gets up.* AMANDA *remains holding the brush, looking at him, troubled.*]

She plays old phonograph records and—that's about all——

[*He glances at himself in the mirror and crosses to the door.*]

Amanda (*sharply*). Where are you going?
Tom. I'm going to the movies. (*He goes out the screen door.*)
Amanda. Not to the movies, every night to the movies! (*She follows quickly to the screen door.*) I don't believe you always go to the movies!

[*He is gone.* AMANDA *looks worriedly after him for a moment. Then vitality and optimism return and she turns from the door, crossing to the portieres.*]

Laura! Laura!

[LAURA *answers from the kitchenette.*]

Laura. Yes, Mother.
Amanda. Let those dishes go and come in front!

[LAURA *appears with a dish towel.* AMANDA *speaks to her gaily.*]

Laura, come here and make a wish on the moon!

[*Screen image:* The Moon.]

Laura (*entering*). Moon—moon?
Amanda. A little silver slipper of a moon. Look over your left shoulder, Laura, and make a wish!

[LAURA *looks faintly puzzled as if called out of sleep.* AMANDA *seizes her shoulders and turns her at an angle by the door.*]

Now! Now, darling, *wish!*

Laura. What shall I wish for, Mother?
Amanda (*her voice trembling and her eyes suddenly filling with tears*). Happiness! Good fortune!

[*The sound of the violin rises and the stage dims out.*]

Scene 6

The light comes up on the fire-escape landing. TOM *is leaning against the grill, smoking.*

[*Screen image:* The high school hero.]

Tom. And so the following evening I brought Jim home to dinner. I had known Jim slightly in high school. In high school Jim was a hero. He had tremendous Irish good nature and vitality with the scrubbed and polished look of white chinaware. He seemed to move in a continual spotlight. He was a star in basketball, captain of the debating club, president of the senior class and the glee club and he sang the male lead in the annual light operas. He was always running or bounding, never just walking. He seemed always at the point of defeating the law of gravity. He was shooting with such velocity through his adolescence that you would logically expect him to arrive at nothing short of the White House by the time he was thirty. But Jim apparently ran into more interference after his graduation from Soldan. His speed had definitely slowed. Six years after he left high school he was holding a job that wasn't much better than mine.

[*Screen image:* The Clerk.]

He was the only one at the warehouse with whom I was on friendly terms. I was valuable to him as someone who could remember his former glory, who had seen him win basketball games and the silver cup in debating. He knew of my secret practice of retiring to a cabinet of the washroom to work on poems when business was slack in the warehouse. He called me Shakespeare. And while the other boys in the warehouse regarded me with suspicious hostility, Jim took a humorous attitude toward me. Gradually his attitude affected the others, their hostility wore off and they also began to smile at me as people smile at an oddly fashioned dog who trots across their path at some distance.

I knew that Jim and Laura had known each other at Soldan, and I had heard Laura speak of his voice. I didn't know if Jim remembered her or not. In high school Laura had been as unobtrusive as Jim had been astonishing. If he did remember Laura, it was not as my sister; for when I asked him to dinner, he grinned and said, "You know, Shakespeare, I never thought of you as having folks!"

He was about to discover that I did. . . .

[*Legend on screen:* "The accent of a coming foot."]

[*The light dims out on* TOM *and comes up in the Wingfield living room—a delicate lemony light. It is about five on a Friday evening of late spring which comes "scattering poems in the sky."*]

[AMANDA *has worked in preparation for the gentleman caller. The results are astonishing. The new floor lamp with its rose silk shade is in place, a colored paper lantern conceals the broken light fixture in the ceiling, new billowing white curtains are at the windows, chintz covers are on the chairs and sofa, a pair of new sofa pillows make their initial appearance. Open boxes and tissue paper are scattered on the floor.*]

[LAURA *stands in the middle of the room with lifted arms while* AMANDA *crouches before her, adjusting the hem of a new dress, devout and ritualistic. The dress is colored and designed by memory. The arrangement of* LAURA*'s hair is changed; it is softer and more becoming. A fragile unearthly prettiness has come out in* LAURA; *she is like a piece of translucent glass touched by light, given a momentary radiance, not actual, not lasting.*]

Amanda (*impatiently*). Why are you trembling?
Laura. Mother, you've made me so nervous!
Amanda. How have I made you nervous?
Laura. By all this fuss! You make it seem so important!
Amanda. I don't understand you, Laura. You couldn't be satisfied with just sitting home, and yet whenever I try to arrange something for you, you seem to resist it. (*She gets up.*) Now take a look at yourself. No, wait! Wait just a moment—— I have an idea!
Laura. What is it now?

[AMANDA *produces two powder puffs which she wraps in handkerchiefs and stuffs in* LAURA's *bosom.*]

Laura. Mother, what are you doing?
Amanda. They call them "Gay Deceivers"!
Laura. I won't wear them!
Amanda. You will!
Laura. Why should I?
Amanda. Because, to be painfully honest, your chest is flat.
Laura. You make it seem like we were setting a trap.
Amanda. All pretty girls are a trap, a pretty trap, and men expect them to be.

[*Legend on screen:* "A pretty trap."]

Now look at yourself, young lady. This is the prettiest you will ever be! (*She stands back to admire* LAURA.) I've got to fix myself now! You're going to be surprised by your mother's appearance!

[AMANDA *crosses through the portieres, humming gaily.* LAURA *moves slowly to the long mirror and stares solemnly at herself. A wind blows the white curtains inward in a slow, graceful motion and with a faint, sorrowful sighing.*]

Amanda (*from somewhere behind the portieres*). It isn't dark enough yet.

[LAURA *turns slowly before the mirror with a troubled look.*]

[*Legend on screen:* "This is my sister: Celebrate her with strings!" *Music plays.*]

Amanda (*laughing, still not visible*). I'm going to show you something. I'm going to make a spectacular appearance!
Laura. What is it, Mother?
Amanda. Possess your soul in patience—you will see! Something I've resurrected from that old trunk! Styles haven't changed so terribly much after all. . . . (*She parts the portieres.*) Now just look at your mother! (*She wears a girlish frock of yellowed voile with a blue silk sash. She carries a bunch of jonquils—the legend of her youth is nearly revived. Now she speaks feverishly:*) This is the dress in which I led the cotillion. Won the cakewalk twice at Sunset Hill, wore one spring to the Governor's Ball in Jackson! See how I sashayed around the ballroom, Laura? (*She raises her skirt and does a mincing step around the room.*) I wore it on Sundays for my gentlemen callers! I had it on the day I met your father. . . . I had malaria fever all that spring. The change of climate from East Tennessee to the Delta—weakened resistance. I had a little temperature all the time—not enough to be serious—just enough to make me restless and giddy! Invitations poured in— parties all over the Delta! "Stay in bed," said Mother, "you have fever!"—but I just wouldn't. I took quinine but kept on going, going! Evenings, dances! Afternoons, long, long rides! Picnics— lovely! So lovely, that country in May—all lacy with dogwood, literally flooded with jonquils! That was the Spring I had the craze for jonquils. Jonquils became an absolute obsession. Mother said, "Honey, there's no more room for jonquils." And still I kept on bringing in more jonquils. Whenever, wherever I saw them, I'd say, "Stop! Stop! I see jonquils!" I made the young men help me gather the jonquils! It was a joke, Amanda and her jonquils. Finally there were no more vases to hold them, every available space was filled with jonquils. No vases to hold them? All right, I'll hold them myself! And then I—— (*She stops in front of the picture. Music plays.*) met your father! Malaria fever

and jonquils and then—this—boy. . . . (*She switches on the rose-colored lamp.*) I hope they get here before it starts to rain. (*She crosses the room and places the jonquils in a bowl on the table.*) I gave your brother a little extra change so he and Mr. O'Connor could take the service car home.

Laura (*with an altered look*). What did you say his name was?

Amanda. O'Connor.

Laura. What is his first name?

Amanda. I don't remember. Oh, yes, I do. It was—Jim!

[LAURA *sways slightly and catches hold of a chair.*]

[*Legend on screen:* "Not Jim!"]

Laura (*faintly*). Not—Jim!

Amanda. Yes, that was it, it was Jim! I've never known a Jim that wasn't nice!

[*The music becomes ominous.*]

Laura. Are you sure his name is Jim O'Connor?

Amanda. Yes. Why?

Laura. Is he the one that Tom used to know in high school?

Amanda. He didn't say so. I think he just got to know him at the warehouse.

Laura. There was a Jim O'Connor we both knew in high school—— (*Then, with effort*) If that is the one that Tom is bringing to dinner—you'll have to excuse me, I won't come to the table.

Amanda. What sort of nonsense is this?

Laura. You asked me once if I'd ever liked a boy. Don't you remember I showed you this boy's picture?

Amanda. You mean the boy you showed me in the yearbook?

Laura. Yes, that boy.

Amanda. Laura, Laura, were you in love with that boy?

Laura. I don't know, Mother. All I know is I couldn't sit at the table if it was him!

Amanda. It won't be him! It isn't the least bit likely. But whether it is or not, you will come to the table. You will not be excused.
Laura. I'll have to be, Mother.
Amanda. I don't intend to humor your silliness, Laura. I've had too much from you and your brother, both! So just sit down and compose yourself till they come. Tom has forgotten his key so you'll have to let them in, when they arrive.
Laura (*panicky*). Oh, Mother—*you* answer the door!
Amanda (*lightly*). I'll be in the kitchen—busy!
Laura. Oh, Mother, please answer the door, don't make me do it!
Amanda (*crossing into the kitchenette*). I've got to fix the dressing for the salmon. Fuss, fuss—silliness!—over a gentleman caller!

[*The door swings shut.* LAURA *is left alone.*]

[*Legend on screen:* "Terror!"]

[*She utters a low moan and turns off the lamp—sits stiffly on the edge of the sofa, knotting her fingers together.*]

[*Legend on screen:* "The Opening of a Door!"]

[TOM *and* JIM *appear on the fire-escape steps and climb to the landing. Hearing their approach,* LAURA *rises with a panicky gesture. She retreats to the portieres. The doorbell rings.* LAURA *catches her breath and touches her throat. Low drums sound.*]

(*Calling*) Laura, sweetheart! The door!

[LAURA *stares at it without moving.*]

Jim. I think we just beat the rain.
Tom. Uh-huh. (*He rings again, nervously.* JIM *whistles and fishes for a cigarette.*)
Amanda (*very, very gaily*). Laura, that is your brother and Mr. O'Connor! Will you let them in, darling?

[LAURA *crosses toward the kitchenette door.*]

Laura (*breathlessly*). Mother—you go to the door!

[AMANDA *steps out of the kitchenette and stares furiously at* LAURA. *She points imperiously at the door.*]

Laura. Please, please!
Amanda (*in a fierce whisper*). What is the matter with you, you silly thing?
Laura (*desperately*). Please, you answer it, *please!*
Amanda. I told you I wasn't going to humor you, Laura. Why have you chosen this moment to lose your mind?
Laura. Please, please, please, you go!
Amanda. You'll have to go to the door because I can't!
Laura (*despairingly*). I can't either!
Amanda. *Why?*
Laura. I'm *sick!*
Amanda. I'm sick too—of your nonsense! Why can't you and your brother be normal people? Fantastic whims and behavior!

[TOM *gives a long ring.*]

Preposterous goings on! Can you give me one reason—— (*She calls out lyrically.*) *Coming! Just one second!*—why you should be afraid to open a door? Now you answer it, Laura!
Laura. Oh, oh, oh . . . (*She returns through the portieres, darts to the victrola, winds it frantically and turns it on.*)
Amanda. Laura Wingfield, you march right to that door!
Laura. *Yes—yes, Mother!*

[*A faraway, scratchy rendition of* "Dardanella" *softens the air and gives her strength to move through it. She slips to the door and draws it cautiously open.* TOM *enters with the caller,* JIM O'CONNOR.]

Tom. Laura, this is Jim. Jim, this is my sister, Laura.
Jim (*stepping inside*). I didn't know that Shakespeare had a sister!
Laura (*retreating, stiff and trembling, from the door*). How—how do you do?

Jim (*heartily, extending his hand*). Okay!

[LAURA *touches it hesitantly with hers.*]

Jim. Your hand's *cold*, Laura!

Laura. Yes, well—I've been playing the victrola.

Jim. Must have been playing classical music on it! You ought to play a little hot swing music to warm you up!

Laura. Excuse me—I haven't finished playing the victrola. . . . (*She turns awkwardly and hurries into the front room. She pauses a second by the victrola. Then she catches her breath and darts through the portieres like a frightened deer.*)

Jim (*grinning*). What was the matter?

Tom. Oh—with Laura? Laura is—terribly shy.

Jim. Shy, huh? It's unusual to meet a shy girl nowadays. I don't believe you ever mentioned you had a sister.

Tom. Well, now you know. I have one. Here is the *Post Dispatch*. You want a piece of it?

Jim. Uh-huh.

Tom. What piece? The comics?

Jim. Sports! (*He glances at it.*) Ole Dizzy Dean is on his bad behavior.

Tom (*uninterested*). Yeah? (*He lights a cigarette and goes over to the fire-escape door.*)

Jim. Where are *you* going?

Tom. I'm going out on the terrace.

Jim (*going after him*). You know, Shakespeare—I'm going to sell you a bill of goods!

Tom. What goods?

Jim. A course I'm taking.

Tom. Huh?

Jim. In public speaking! You and me, we're not the warehouse type.

Tom. Thanks—that's good news. But what has public speaking got to do with it?

Jim. It fits you for—executive positions!

Tom. Awww.

Jim. I tell you it's done a helluva lot for me.

[*Image on screen:* Executive at his desk.]

Tom. In what respect?

Jim. In every! Ask yourself what is the difference between you an' me and men in the office down front? Brains?—— No!—— Ability?—— No! Then what? Just one little thing——

Tom. What is that one little thing?

Jim. Primarily it amounts to—social poise! Being able to square up to people and hold your own on any social level!

Amanda (*from the kitchenette*). Tom?

Tom. Yes, Mother?

Amanda. Is that you and Mr. O'Connor?

Tom. Yes, Mother.

Amanda. Well, you just make yourselves comfortable in there.

Tom. Yes, Mother.

Amanda. Ask Mr. O'Connor if he would like to wash his hands.

Jim. Aw, no—no—thank you—I took care of that at the warehouse. Tom——

Tom. Yes?

Jim. Mr. Mendoza was speaking to me about you.

Tom. Favorably?

Jim. What do you think?

Tom. Well——

Jim. You're going to be out of a job if you don't wake up.

Tom. I am waking up——

Jim. You show no signs.

Tom. The signs are interior.

[*Image on screen:* The sailing vessel with the Jolly Roger again.]

Tom. I'm planning to change. (*He leans over the fire-escape rail, speaking with quiet exhilaration. The incandescent marquees and signs of the first-run movie houses light his face from across the alley. He looks like a voyager.*) I'm right at the point of committing myself to a future that doesn't include the warehouse and Mr. Mendoza or even a night-school course in public speaking.

Jim. What are you gassing about?

Tom. I'm tired of the movies.

Jim. Movies!

Tom. Yes, movies! Look at them—— (*A wave toward the marvels of Grand Avenue*) All of these glamorous people—having adventures—hogging it all, gobbling the whole thing up! You know what happens? People go to the *movies* instead of *moving!* Hollywood characters are supposed to have all the adventures for everybody in America, while everybody in America sits in a dark room and watches them have them! Yes, until there's a war. That's when adventure becomes available to the masses! *Everyone's* dish, not only Gable's! Then the people in the dark room come out of the dark room to have some adventures themselves—goody, goody! It's our turn now, to go to the South Sea Island—to make a safari—to be exotic, far off! But I'm not patient. I don't want to wait till then. I'm tired of the *movies* and I am *about* to *move!*

Jim (*incredulously*). Move?

Tom. Yes.

Jim. When?

Tom. Soon!

Jim. Where? Where?

[*The music seems to answer the question, while* TOM *thinks it over. He searches in his pockets.*]

Tom. I'm starting to boil inside. I know I seem dreamy, but inside—well, I'm boiling! Whenever I pick up a shoe, I shudder a little thinking how short life is and what I am doing! Whatever that means, I know it doesn't mean shoes—except as something to wear on a traveler's feet! (*He finds what he has been searching for in his pockets and holds out a paper to* JIM.) Look——

Jim. What?

Tom. I'm a member.

Jim (*reading*). The Union of Merchant Seamen.

Tom. I paid my dues this month, instead of the light bill.

Jim. You will regret it when they turn the lights off.

Tom. I won't be here.

Jim. How about your mother?

Tom. I'm like my father. . . . Did you notice how he's grinning in his picture in there? And he's been absent going on sixteen years!

Jim. You're just talking, you drip. How does your mother feel about it?

Tom. Shhh! Here comes Mother! Mother is not acquainted with my plans!

Amanda (*coming through the portieres*). Where are you all?

Tom. On the terrace, Mother.

[*They start inside. She advances to them.* TOM *is distinctly shocked at her appearance. Even* JIM *blinks a little. He is making his first contact with girlish Southern vivacity and in spite of the night-school course in public speaking is somewhat thrown off the beam by the unexpected outlay of social charm. Certain responses are attempted by* JIM *but are swept aside by* AMANDA's *gay laughter and chatter.* TOM *is embarrassed but after the first shock* JIM *reacts very warmly. He grins and chuckles, is altogether won over.*]

[*Image on screen:* AMANDA *as a girl.*]

Amanda (*coyly smiling, shaking her girlish ringlets*). Well, well, well, so this is Mr. O'Connor. Introductions entirely unnecessary. I've heard so much about you from my boy. I finally said to him, Tom—good gracious!—why don't you bring this paragon to supper? I'd like to meet this nice young man at the warehouse!—instead of just hearing him sing your praises so much! I don't know why my son is so stand-offish—that's not Southern behavior!

Let's sit down and—I think we could stand a little more air in here! Tom, leave the door open. I felt a nice fresh breeze a moment ago. Where has it gone to? Mmm, so warm already! And not quite summer, even. We're going to burn up when summer really gets started. However, we're having—we're having a very light supper. I think light things are better fo' this time of year. The same as light clothes are. Light clothes an' light food are what warm weather calls fo'. You know our blood gets so thick during th' winter—it takes a while fo' us to *adjust* ou'selves!—when the season changes. . . . It's come so quick this year. I wasn't prepared. All of a sudden—heavens! Already summer! I ran to the trunk an' pulled out this light dress—terribly old! Historical almost! But feels so good—so good an' co-ol, y' know . . .

Tom. Mother——

Amanda. Yes, honey?

Tom. How about—supper?

Amanda. Honey, you go ask Sister if supper is ready! You know that Sister is in full charge of supper! Tell her you hungry boys are waiting for it. (*To* JIM) Have you met Laura?

Jim. She——

Amanda. Let you in? Oh, good, you've met already! It's rare for a girl as sweet an' pretty as Laura to be domestic! But Laura is, thank heavens, not only pretty but also very domestic. I'm not at all. I never was a bit. I never could make a thing but angel-food cake. Well, in the South we had so many servants. Gone, gone, gone. All vestige of gracious living! Gone completely! I wasn't prepared for what the future brought me. All of my gentlemen callers were sons of planters and so of course I assumed that I would be married to one and raise my family on a large piece of land with plenty of servants. But man proposes— and woman accepts the proposal! To vary that old, old saying a little bit—I married no planter! I married a man who worked for the telephone company! That gallantly smiling gentleman over there! (*She points to the picture.*) A telephone man who—fell in love with long-distance! Now he travels and I don't even know where! But what am I going on for about my—tribulations? Tell me yours—— I hope you don't have any! Tom?

Tom (*returning*). Yes, Mother?

Amanda. Is supper nearly ready?

Tom. It looks to me like supper is on the table.

Amanda. Let me look—— (*She rises prettily and looks through the portieres.*) Oh, lovely! But where is Sister?

Tom. Laura is not feeling well and she says that she thinks she'd better not come to the table.

Amanda. What? Nonsense! Laura? Oh, Laura!

Laura (*from the kitchenette, faintly*). Yes, Mother.

Amanda. You really must come to the table. We won't be seated until you come to the table! Come in, Mr. O'Connor. You sit over there, and I'll ... Laura? Laura Wingfield! You're keeping us waiting, honey! We can't say grace until you come to the table!

[*The kitchenette door is pushed weakly open and* LAURA *comes in: She is obviously quite faint, her lips trembling, her eyes wide and staring. She moves unsteadily toward the table.*]

[*Screen legend:* "Terror!"]

[*Outside a summer storm is coming on abruptly. The white curtains billow inward at the windows and there is a sorrowful murmur from the deep blue dusk.*]

[LAURA *suddenly stumbles; she catches at a chair with a faint moan.*]

Tom. Laura!

Amanda. Laura!

[*There is a clap of thunder.*]

[*Screen legend:* "Ah!"]

(*Despairingly*) Why, Laura, you *are* ill, darling! Tom, help your sister into the living room, dear! Sit in the living room, Laura—rest on the sofa. Well! (*To* JIM *as* TOM *helps his sister to the sofa in the living room*) Standing over the hot stove made her ill! I told her that it was just too warm this evening, but——

[TOM *comes back to the table.*]

Is Laura all right now?

Tom. Yes.

Amanda. What *is* that? Rain? A nice cool rain has come up! (*She gives* JIM *a frightened look.*) I think we may—have grace— now. . . . (TOM *looks at her stupidly.*) Tom, honey—you say grace!
Tom. Oh . . . "For these and all thy mercies—"

[*They bow their heads,* AMANDA *stealing a nervous glance at* JIM. *In the living room* LAURA, *stretched on the sofa, clenches her hand to her lips, to hold back a shuddering sob.*]

"God's Holy Name be praised——"

[*The scene dims out.*]

Scene 7

It is half an hour later. Dinner is just being finished in the dining room, LAURA *is still huddled upon the sofa, her feet drawn under, her head resting on a pale blue pillow, her eyes wide and mysteriously watchful. The new floor lamp with its shade of rose-colored silk gives a soft, becoming light to her face, bringing out the fragile, unearthly prettiness which usually escapes attention. From outside there is a steady murmur of rain, but it is slackening and soon stops; the air outside becomes pale and luminous as the moon breaks through the clouds. A moment after the curtain rises, the lights in both rooms flicker and go out.*

Jim. Hey, there, Mr. Light Bulb!

[AMANDA *laughs nervously.*]

[*Legend on screen:* "Suspension of a public service."]

Amanda. Where was Moses when the lights went out? Ha-ha. Do you know the answer to that one, Mr. O'Connor?
Jim. No, Ma'am, what's the answer?
Amanda. In the dark!

[JIM *laughs appreciatively.*]

Everybody sit still. I'll light the candles. Isn't it lucky we have them on the table? Where's a match? Which of you gentlemen can provide a match?

Jim. Here.

Amanda. Thank you, Sir.

Jim. Not at all, Ma'am!

Amanda (*as she lights the candles*). I guess the fuse has burnt out. Mr. O'Connor, can you tell a burnt-out fuse? I know I can't and Tom is a total loss when it comes to mechanics.

[*They rise from the table and go into the kitchenette, from where their voices are heard.*]

Oh, be careful you don't bump into something. We don't want our gentleman caller to break his neck. Now wouldn't that be a fine howdy-do?

Jim. Ha-ha! Where is the fuse-box?

Amanda. Right here next to the stove. Can you see anything?

Jim. Just a minute.

Amanda. Isn't electricity a mysterious thing? Wasn't it Benjamin Franklin who tied a key to a kite? We live in such a mysterious universe, don't we? Some people say that science clears up all the mysteries for us. In my opinion it only creates more! Have you found it yet?

Jim. No, Ma'am. All these fuses look okay to me.

Amanda. Tom!

Tom. Yes, Mother?

Amanda. That light bill I gave you several days ago. The one I told you we got the notices about?

[*Legend on screen: "Ha!"*]

Tom. Oh—yeah.

Amanda. You didn't neglect to pay it by any chance?

Tom. Why, I——

Amanda. Didn't! I might have known it!

Jim. Shakespeare probably wrote a poem on that light bill, Mrs. Wingfield.

Amanda. I might have known better than to trust him with it! There's such a high price for negligence in this world!

Jim. Maybe the poem will win a ten-dollar prize.

Amanda. We'll just have to spend the remainder of the evening in the nineteenth century, before Mr. Edison made the Mazda lamp!

Jim. Candlelight is my favorite kind of light.

Amanda. That shows you're romantic! But that's no excuse for Tom. Well, we got through dinner. Very considerate of them to let us get through dinner before they plunged us into everlasting darkness, wasn't it, Mr. O'Connor?

Jim. Ha-ha!

Amanda. Tom, as a penalty for your carelessness you can help me with the dishes.

Jim. Let me give you a hand.

Amanda. Indeed you will not!

Jim. I ought to be good for something.

Amanda. Good for something? (*Her tone is rhapsodic.*) *You?* Why, Mr. O'Connor, nobody, *nobody's* given me this much entertainment in years—as you have!

Jim. Aw, now, Mrs. Wingfield!

Amanda. I'm not exaggerating, not one bit! But Sister is all by her lonesome. You go keep her company in the parlor! I'll give you this lovely old candelabrum that used to be on the altar at the Church of the Heavenly Rest. It was melted a little out of shape when the church burnt down. Lightning struck it one Spring. Gypsy Jones was holding a revival at the time and he intimated that church was destroyed because the Episcopalians gave card parties.

Jim. Ha-ha.

Amanda. And how about you coaxing Sister to drink a little wine? I think it would be good for her! Can you carry both at once?

Jim. Sure. I'm Superman!

Amanda. Now, Thomas, get into this apron!

[JIM *comes into the dining room, carrying the candelabrum, its candles lighted, in one hand and a glass of wine in the other. The door of the kitchenette swings closed on* AMANDA's *gay laughter; the flickering light approaches the portieres.* LAURA *sits up nervously as* JIM *enters. She can hardly speak from the almost intolerable strain of being alone with a stranger.*]

[*Screen legend:* "I don't suppose you remember me at all!"]

[*At first, before* JIM's *warmth overcomes her paralyzing shyness,* LAURA's *voice is thin and breathless, as though she had just run up a steep flight of stairs.* JIM's *attitude is gently humorous. While the incident is apparently unimportant, it is to* LAURA *the climax of her secret life.*]

Jim. Hello there, Laura.
Laura (*faintly*). Hello.

[*She clears her throat.*]

Jim. How are you feeling now? Better?
Laura. Yes. Yes, thank you.
Jim. This is for you. A little dandelion wine. (*He extends the glass toward her with extravagant gallantry.*)
Laura. Thank you.
Jim. Drink it—but don't get drunk!

[*He laughs heartily.* LAURA *takes the glass uncertainly; she laughs shyly.*]

Where shall I set the candles?
Laura. Oh—oh, anywhere . . .
Jim. How about here on the floor? Any objections?
Laura. No.
Jim. I'll spread a newspaper under to catch the drippings. I like to sit on the floor. Mind if I do?

Laura. Oh, no.

Jim. Give me a pillow?

Laura. What?

Jim. A pillow!

Laura. Oh . . . (*She hands him one quickly.*)

Jim. How about you? Don't you like to sit on the floor?

Laura. Oh—yes.

Jim. Why don't you, then?

Laura. I—will.

Jim. Take a pillow!

[LAURA *does. She sits on the floor on the other side of the candelabrum.* JIM *crosses his legs and smiles engagingly at her.*]

I can't hardly see you sitting way over there.

Laura. I can—see you.

Jim. I know, but that's not fair, I'm in the limelight.

[LAURA *moves her pillow closer.*]

Good! Now I can see you! Comfortable?

Laura. Yes.

Jim. So am I. Comfortable as a cow! Will you have some gum?

Laura. No, thank you.

Jim. I think that I will indulge, with your permission. (*He musingly unwraps a stick of gum and holds it up.*) Think of the fortune made by the guy that invented the first piece of chewing gum. Amazing, huh? The Wrigley Building is one of the sights of Chicago—I saw it when I went up to the Century of Progress. Did you take in the Century of Progress?

Laura. No, I didn't.

Jim. Well, it was quite a wonderful exposition. What impressed me most was the Hall of Science. Gives you an idea of what the future will be in America, even more wonderful than the present time is! (*There is a pause.* JIM *smiles at her.*) Your brother tells me you're shy. Is that right, Laura?

Laura. I—don't know.

Jim. I judge you to be an old-fashioned type of girl. Well, I think that's a pretty good type to be. Hope you don't think I'm being too personal—do you?

Laura (*hastily, out of embarrassment*). I believe I *will* take a piece of gum, if you—don't mind. (*Clearing her throat*) Mr. O'Connor, have you—kept up with your singing?

Jim. Singing? Me?

Laura. Yes. I remember what a beautiful voice you had.

Jim. When did you hear me sing?

[LAURA *does not answer, and in the long pause which follows a man's voice is heard singing off-stage.*]

VOICE:
"Oh blow, ye winds, heigh-ho,
A-roving I will go!
I'm off to my love
With a boxing glove——
Ten thousand miles away!"

Jim. You say you've heard me sing?

Laura. Oh, yes! Yes, very often ... I don't suppose—you remember me—at all?

Jim (*smiling doubtfully*). You know I have an idea I've seen you before. I had that idea soon as you opened the door. It seemed almost like I was about to remember your name. But the name that I started to call you—wasn't a name! And so I stopped myself before I said it.

Laura. Wasn't it—Blue Roses?

Jim (*springing up, grinning*). Blue Roses! My gosh, yes—Blue Roses! That's what I had on my tongue when you opened the door! Isn't it funny what tricks your memory plays? I didn't connect you with high school somehow or other. But that's where it was; it was high school. I didn't even know you were Shakespeare's sister! Gosh, I'm sorry.

Laura. I didn't expect you to. You—barely knew me!

Jim. But we did have a speaking acquaintance, huh?

Laura. Yes, we—spoke to each other.

Jim. When did you recognize me?

Laura. Oh, right away!

Jim. Soon as I came in the door?

Laura. When I heard your name I thought it was probably you. I knew that Tom used to know you a little in high school. So when you came in the door—well, then I was—sure.

Jim. Why didn't you *say* something, then?

Laura (*breathlessly*). I didn't know what to say, I was—too surprised!

Jim. For goodness' sakes! You know, this sure is funny!

Laura. Yes! Yes, isn't it, though . . .

Jim. Didn't we have a class in something together?

Laura. Yes, we did.

Jim. What class was that?

Laura. It was—singing—chorus!

Jim. Aw!

Laura. I sat across the aisle from you in the Aud.

Jim. Aw.

Laura. Mondays, Wednesdays, and Fridays.

Jim. Now I remember—you always came in late.

Laura. Yes, it was so hard for me, getting upstairs. I had that brace on my leg—it clumped so loud!

Jim. I never heard any clumping.

Laura (*wincing at the recollection*). To me it sounded like—thunder!

Jim. Well, well, well, I never even noticed.

Laura. And everybody was seated before I came in. I had to walk in front of all those people. My seat was in the back row. I had to go clumping all the way up the aisle with everyone watching!

Jim. You shouldn't have been self-conscious.

Laura. I know, but I was. It was always such a relief when the singing started.

Jim. Aw, yes, I've placed you now! I used to call you Blue Roses. How was it that I got started calling you that?

Laura. I was out of school a little while with pleurosis. When I came back you asked me what was the matter. I said I had pleurosis—you thought I said *Blue Roses*. That's what you always called me after that!

Jim. I hope you didn't mind.

Laura. Oh, no—I liked it. You see, I wasn't acquainted with many—people. . . .

Jim. As I remember you sort of stuck by yourself.

Laura. I—I—never have had much luck at—making friends.

Jim. I don't see why you wouldn't.

Laura. Well, I—started out badly.

Jim. You mean being——

Laura. Yes, it sort of—stood between me——

Jim. You shouldn't have let it!

Laura. I know, but it did, and——

Jim. You were shy with people!

Laura. I tried not to be but never could——

Jim. Overcome it?

Laura. No, I—I never could!

Jim. I guess being shy is something you have to work out of kind of gradually.

Laura (*sorrowfully*). Yes—I guess it——

Jim. Takes time!

Laura. Yes——

Jim. People are not so dreadful when you know them. That's what you have to remember! And everybody has problems, not just you, but practically everybody has got some problems. You think of yourself as having the only problems, as being the only one who is disappointed. But just look around you and you will see lots of people as disappointed as you are. For instance, I hoped when I was going to high school that I would be further along at this time, six years later, than I am now. You remember that wonderful write-up I had in *The Torch*?

Laura. Yes! (*She rises and crosses to the table.*)

Jim. It said I was bound to succeed in anything I went into!

[LAURA *returns with the high school year book.*]

Holy Jeez! *The Torch!*

[*He accepts it reverently. They smile across the book with mutual wonder.* LAURA *crouches beside him and they begin to turn the pages.* LAURA's *shyness is dissolving in his warmth.*]

Laura. Here you are in *The Pirates of Penzance!*
Jim (*wistfully*). I sang the baritone lead in that operetta.
Laura (*raptly*). So—*beautifully!*
Jim (*protesting*). Aw——
Laura. Yes, yes—beautifully—beautifully!
Jim. You heard me?
Laura. All three times!
Jim. No!
Laura. Yes!
Jim. All three performances?
Laura (*looking down*). Yes.
Jim. Why?
Laura. I—wanted to ask you to—autograph my program. (*She takes the program from the back of the year book and shows it to him.*)
Jim. Why didn't you ask me to?
Laura. You were always surrounded by your own friends so much that I never had a chance to.
Jim. You should have just——
Laura. Well, I—thought you might think I was——
Jim. Thought I might think you was—what?
Laura. Oh——
Jim (*with reflective relish*). I was beleaguered by females in those days.
Laura. You were terribly popular!
Jim. Yeah——
Laura. You had such a—friendly way——
Jim. I was spoiled in high school.
Laura. Everybody—liked you!
Jim. Including you?
Laura. I—yes, I—did, too—— (*She gently closes the book in her lap.*)
Jim. Well, well, well! Give me that program, Laura.

[*She hands it to him. He signs it with a flourish.*]

There you are—better late than never!

Laura. Oh, I—what a—surprise!

Jim. My signature isn't worth very much right now. But some-day—maybe—it will increase in value! Being disappointed is one thing and being discouraged is something else. I am disappointed but I am not discouraged. I'm twenty-three years old. How old are you?

Laura. I'll be twenty-four in June.

Jim. That's not old age!

Laura. No, but——

Jim. You finished high school?

Laura (*with difficulty*). I didn't go back.

Jim. You mean you dropped out?

Laura. I made bad grades in my final examinations. (*She rises and replaces the book and the program on the table. Her voice is strained.*) How is—Emily Meisenbach getting along?

Jim. Oh, that kraut-head!

Laura. Why do you call her that?

Jim. That's what she was.

Laura. You're not still—going with her?

Jim. I never see her.

Laura. It said in the "Personal" section that you were—engaged!

Jim. I know, but I wasn't impressed by that—propaganda!

Laura. It wasn't—the truth?

Jim. Only in Emily's optimistic opinion!

Laura. Oh——

[*Legend:* "What have you done since high school?"]

[JIM *lights a cigarette and leans indolently back on his elbows smiling at* LAURA *with a warmth and charm which lights her inwardly with altar candles. She remains by the table, picks up a piece from the glass menagerie collection, and turns it in her hands to cover her tumult.*]

Jim (*after several reflective puffs on his cigarette*). What have you done since high school?

[*She seems not to hear him.*]

Huh?

[LAURA *looks up.*]

I said what have you done since high school, Laura?
Laura. Nothing much.
Jim. You must have been doing something these six long years.
Laura. Yes.
Jim. Well, then, such as what?
Laura. I took a business course at business college——
Jim. How did that work out?
Laura. Well, not very—well—I had to drop out, it gave me—indigestion——

[JIM *laughs gently.*]

Jim. What are you doing now?
Laura. I don't do anything—much. Oh, please don't think I sit around doing nothing! My glass collection takes up a good deal of time. Glass is something you have to take good care of.
Jim. What did you say—about glass?
Laura. Collection I said—I have one—— (*She clears her throat and turns away again, acutely shy.*)
Jim (*abruptly*). You know what I judge to be the trouble with you? Inferiority complex! Know what that is? That's what they call it when someone low-rates himself! I understand it because I had it, too. Although my case was not so aggravated as yours seems to be. I had it until I took up public speaking, developed my voice, and learned that I had an aptitude for science. Before that time I never thought of myself as being outstanding in any way whatsoever! Now I've never made a regular study of it, but I have a friend who says I can analyze people better than doctors that make a profession of it. I don't claim that to be necessarily true, but I can sure guess a person's psychology, Laura! (*He takes out his gum.*) Excuse me, Laura. I always take it out when the flavor is gone. I'll use this scrap of paper to wrap it in. I know how it is to get it stuck on a shoe. (*He wraps the gum in paper and puts it in his pocket.*) Yep—that's what I judge to be

your principal trouble. A lack of confidence in yourself as a person. You don't have the proper amount of faith in yourself. I'm basing that fact on a number of your remarks and also on certain observations I've made. For instance that clumping you thought was so awful in high school. You say that you even dreaded to walk into class. You see what you did? You dropped out of school, you gave up an education because of a clump, which as far as I know was practically non-existent! A little physical defect is what you have. Hardly noticeable even! Magnified thousands of times by imagination! You know what my strong advice to you is? Think of yourself as *superior* in some way!

Laura. In what way would I think?

Jim. Why, man alive, Laura! Just look about you a little, what do you see? A world full of common people! All of 'em born and all of 'em going to die! Which of them has one-tenth of your good points! Or mine! Or anyone else's, as far as that goes—gosh! Everybody excels in some one thing. Some in many! (*He unconsciously glances at himself in the mirror.*) All you've got to do is discover in *what!* Take me, for instance. (*He adjusts his tie at the mirror.*) My interest happens to lie in electrodynamics. I'm taking a course in radio engineering at night school, Laura, on top of a fairly responsible job at the warehouse. I'm taking that course and studying public speaking.

Laura. Ohhhh.

Jim. Because I believe in the future of television! (*Turning his back to her.*) I wish to be ready to go up right along with it. Therefore I'm planning to get in on the ground floor. In fact I've already made the right connections and all that remains is for the industry itself to get under way! Full steam—— (*His eyes are starry.*) *Knowledge*—— Zzzzzp! *Money*— Zzzzzzp!—— *Power!* That's the cycle democracy is built on!

[*His attitude is convincingly dynamic.* LAURA *stares at him, even her shyness eclipsed in her absolute wonder. He suddenly grins.*]

I guess you think I think a lot of myself!

Laura. No—o-o-o, I——

Jim. Now how about you? Isn't there something you take more interest in than anything else?

Laura. Well, I do—as I said—have my—glass collection——

[*A peal of girlish laughter rings from the kitchenette.*]

Jim. I'm not sure I know what you're talking about. What kind of glass is it?

Laura. Little articles of it, they're ornaments mostly! Most of them are little animals made out of glass, the tiniest little animals in the world. Mother calls them a glass menagerie! Here's an example of one, if you'd like to see it! This one is one of the oldest. It's nearly thirteen.

[*Music:* "The Glass Menagerie."]

[*He stretches out his hand.*]

Oh, be careful—if you breathe, it breaks!

Jim. I'd better not take it. I'm pretty clumsy with things.

Laura. Go on, I trust you with him! (*She places the piece in his palm.*) There now—you're holding him gently! Hold him over the light, he loves the light! You see how the light shines through him?

Jim. It sure does shine!

Laura. I shouldn't be partial, but he is my favorite one.

Jim. What kind of a thing is this one supposed to be?

Laura. Haven't you noticed the single horn on his forehead?

Jim. A unicorn, huh?

Laura. Mmmm-hmmm!

Jim. Unicorns—aren't they extinct in the modern world?

Laura. I know!

Jim. Poor little fellow, he must feel sort of lonesome.

Laura (*smiling*). Well, if he does, he doesn't complain about it. He stays on a shelf with some horses that don't have horns and all of them seem to get along nicely together.

Jim. How do you know?

Laura (*lightly*). I haven't heard any arguments among them!

Jim (*grinning*). No arguments, huh? Well, that's a pretty good sign! Where shall I set him?

Laura. Put him on the table. They all like a change of scenery once in a while!

Jim. Well, well, well, well—— (*He places the glass piece on the table, then raises his arms and stretches.*) Look how big my shadow is when I stretch!

Laura. Oh, oh, yes—it stretches across the ceiling!

Jim (*crossing to the door*). I think it's stopped raining. (*He opens the fire-escape door and the background music changes to a dance tune.*) Where does the music come from?

Laura. From the Paradise Dance Hall across the alley.

Jim. How about cutting the rug a little, Miss Wingfield?

Laura. Oh, I——

Jim. Or is your program filled up? Let me have a look at it. (*He grasps an imaginary card.*) Why, every dance is taken! I'll just have to scratch some out.

[*Waltz music:* "La Golondrina."]

Ahhh, a waltz! (*He executes some sweeping turns by himself, then holds his arms toward* LAURA.)

Laura (*breathlessly*). I—can't dance!

Jim. There you go, that inferiority stuff!

Laura. I've never danced in my life!

Jim. Come on, try!

Laura. Oh, but I'd step on you!

Jim. I'm not made out of glass.

Laura. How—how—how do we start?

Jim. Just leave it to me. You hold your arms out a little.

Laura. Like this?

Jim (*taking her in his arms*). A little bit higher. Right. Now don't tighten up, that's the main thing about it—relax.

Laura (*laughing breathlessly*). It's hard not to.

Jim. Okay.

Laura. I'm afraid you can't budge me.

Jim. What do you bet I can't? (*He swings her into motion.*)

Laura. Goodness, yes, you can!

Jim. Let yourself go, now, Laura, just let yourself go.

Laura. I'm——

Jim. Come on!

Laura. ——trying!

Jim. Not so stiff—easy does it!

Laura. I know but I'm——

Jim. Loosen th' backbone! There now, that's a lot better.

Laura. Am I?

Jim. Lots, lots better! (*He moves her about the room in a clumsy waltz*).

Laura. Oh, my!

Jim. Ha-ha!

Laura. Oh, my goodness!

Jim. Ha-ha-ha!

[*They suddenly bump into the table, and the glass piece on it falls to the floor.* JIM *stops the dance.*]

What did we hit on?

Laura. Table.

Jim. Did something fall off it? I think——

Laura. Yes.

Jim. I hope that it wasn't the little glass horse with the horn!

Laura. Yes. (*She stoops to pick it up.*)

Jim. Aw, aw, aw. Is it broken?

Laura. Now it is just like all the other horses.

Jim. It's lost its—

Laura. Horn! It doesn't matter. Maybe it's a blessing in disguise.

Jim. You'll never forgive me. I bet that that was your favorite piece of glass.

Laura. I don't have favorites much. It's no tragedy, Freckles. Glass breaks so easily. No matter how careful you are. The traffic jars the shelves and things fall off them.

Jim. Still I'm awfully sorry that I was the cause.
Laura (*smiling*). I'll just imagine he had an operation. The horn was removed to make him feel less—freakish!

[*They both laugh.*]

Now he will feel more at home with the other horses, the ones that don't have horns. . . .
Jim. Ha-ha, that's very funny! (*Suddenly he is serious.*) I'm glad to see that you have a sense of humor. You know—you're—well—very different! Surprisingly different from anyone else I know! (*His voice becomes soft and hesitant with a genuine feeling.*) Do you mind me telling you that?

[LAURA *is abashed beyond speech.*]

I mean it in a nice way——

[LAURA *nods shyly, looking away.*]

You make me feel sort of—I don't know how to put it! I'm usually pretty good at expressing things, but—this is something that I don't know how to say!

[LAURA *touches her throat and clears it—turns the broken unicorn in her hands. His voice becomes softer.*]

Has anyone ever told you that you were pretty?

[*There is a pause, and the music rises slightly.* LAURA *looks up slowly, with wonder, and shakes her head.*]

Well, you are! In a very different way from anyone else. And all the nicer because of the difference, too.

[*His voice becomes low and husky.* LAURA *turns away, nearly faint with the novelty of her emotions.*]

I wish that you were my sister. I'd teach you to have some confidence in yourself. The different people are not like other people, but being different is nothing to be ashamed of. Because other people are not such wonderful people. They're one hundred times one thousand. You're one times one! They walk all over the earth. You just stay here. They're common as—weeds, but—you—well, you're—*Blue Roses!*

[*Image on screen:* Blue Roses.]

[*The music changes.*]

Laura. But blue is wrong for—roses. . . .
Jim. It's right for you! You're—pretty!
Laura. In what respect am I pretty?
Jim. In all respects—believe me! Your eyes—your hair—are pretty! Your hands are pretty! (*He catches hold of her hand.*) You think I'm making this up because I'm invited to dinner and have to be nice. Oh, I could do that! I could put on an act for you, Laura, and say lots of things without being very sincere. But this time I am. I'm talking to you sincerely. I happened to notice you had this inferiority complex that keeps you from feeling comfortable with people. Somebody needs to build your confidence up and make you proud, instead of shy and turning away and—blushing. Somebody—ought to—*kiss* you, Laura!

[*His hand slips slowly up her arm to her shoulder as the music swells tumultuously. He suddenly turns her about and kisses her on the lips. When he releases her,* LAURA *sinks on the sofa with a bright, dazed look.* JIM *backs away and fishes in his pocket for a cigarette.*]

[*Legend on screen:* "A souvenir."]

Stumblejohn!

[*He lights the cigarette, avoiding her look. There is a peal of girlish laughter from* AMANDA *in the kitchenette.* LAURA *slowly raises and opens her hand. It still contains the little broken glass animal. She looks at it with a tender, bewildered expression.*]

Stumblejohn! I shouldn't have done that—that was way off the beam. You don't smoke, do you?

[*She looks up, smiling, not hearing the question. He sits beside her rather gingerly. She looks at him speechlessly—waiting. He coughs decorously and moves a little farther aside as he considers the situation and senses her feelings, dimly, with perturbation. He speaks gently.*]

Would you—care for a—mint?

[*She doesn't seem to hear him but her look grows brighter even.*]

Peppermint? Life Saver? My pocket's a regular drug store— wherever I go. . . . (*He pops a mint in his mouth. Then he gulps and decides to make a clean breast of it. He speaks slowly and gingerly.*) Laura, you know, if I had a sister like you, I'd do the same thing as Tom. I'd bring out fellows and—introduce her to them. The right type of boys—of a type to—appreciate her. Only—well—he made a mistake about me. Maybe I've got no call to be saying this. That may not have been the idea in having me over. But what if it was? There's nothing wrong about that. The only trouble is that in my case—I'm not in a situation to—do the right thing. I can't take down your number and say I'll phone. I can't call up next week and—ask for a date. I thought I had better explain the situation in case you—misunderstood it and—I hurt your feelings. . . .

[*There is a pause. Slowly, very slowly,* LAURA's *look changes, her eyes returning slowly from his to the glass figure in her palm.* AMANDA *utters another gay laugh in the kitchenette.*]

Laura (*faintly*). You—won't—call again?
Jim. No, Laura, I can't. (*He rises from the sofa.*) As I was just explaining, I've—got strings on me. Laura, I've—been going steady! I go out all the time with a girl named Betty. She's a

home-girl like you, and Catholic, and Irish, and in a great many ways we—get along fine. I met her last summer on a moonlight boat trip up the river to Alton, on the *Majestic*. Well—right away from the start it was—love!

[*Legend:* Love!]

[LAURA *sways slightly forward and grips the arm of the sofa. He fails to notice, now enrapt in his own comfortable being.*]

Being in love has made a new man of me!

[*Leaning stiffly forward, clutching the arm of the sofa,* LAURA *struggles visibly with her storm. But* JIM *is oblivious; she is a long way off.*]

The power of love is really pretty tremendous! Love is something that—changes the whole world, Laura!

[*The storm abates a little and* LAURA *leans back. He notices her again.*]

It happened that Betty's aunt took sick, she got a wire and had to go to Centralia. So Tom—when he asked me to dinner—I naturally just accepted the invitation, not knowing that you—that he—that I—— (*He stops awkwardly.*) Huh—I'm a stumblejohn!

[*He flops back on the sofa. The holy candles on the altar of* LAURA's *face have been snuffed out. There is a look of almost infinite desolation.* JIM *glances at her uneasily.*]

I wish that you would—say something.

[*She bites her lip which was trembling and then bravely smiles. She opens her hand again on the broken glass figure. Then she gently takes his hand and raises it level with her own. She carefully places the unicorn in the palm of his hand, then pushes his fingers closed upon it.*]

What are you—doing that for? You want me to have him? Laura?

[*She nods.*]

What for?
Laura. A—souvenir . . .

[*She rises unsteadily and crouches beside the victrola to wind it up.*]

[*Legend on screen:* "Things have a way of turning out so badly!"
Or image: "Gentleman caller waving goodbye—gaily."]

[*At this moment* AMANDA *rushes brightly back into the living room.
She bears a pitcher of fruit punch in an old-fashioned cut-glass pitcher,
and a plate of macaroons. The plate has a gold border and poppies
painted on it.*]

Amanda. Well, well, well! Isn't the air delightful after the
shower? I've made you children a little liquid refreshment. (*She
turns gaily to* JIM.) Jim, do you know that song about lemonade?

> "Lemonade, lemonade
> Made in the shade and stirred with a spade—
> Good enough for any old maid!"

Jim (*uneasily*). Ha-ha! No—I never heard it.
Amanda. Why, Laura! You look so serious!
Jim. We were having a serious conversation.
Amanda. Good! Now you're better acquainted!
Jim (*uncertainly*). Ha-ha! Yes.
Amanda. You modern young people are much more serious-
minded than my generation. I was so gay as a girl!
Jim. You haven't changed, Mrs. Wingfield.
Amanda. Tonight I'm rejuvenated! The gaiety of the occasion,
Mr. O'Connor! (*She tosses her head with a peal of laughter, spilling
some lemonade.*) Oooo! I'm baptizing myself!
Jim. Here—let me——
Amanda (*setting the pitcher down*). There now. I discovered we
had some maraschino cherries. I dumped them in, juice and all!

Jim. You shouldn't have gone to that trouble, Mrs. Wingfield.

Amanda. Trouble, trouble? Why, it was loads of fun! Didn't you hear me cutting up in the kitchen? I bet your ears were burning! I told Tom how outdone with him I was for keeping you to himself so long a time! He should have brought you over much, much sooner! Well, now that you've found your way, I want you to be a very frequent caller! Not just occasional but all the time. Oh, we're going to have a lot of gay times together! I see them coming! Mmm, just breathe that air! So fresh, and the moon's so pretty! I'll skip back out—I know where my place is when young folks are having a—serious conversation!

Jim. Oh, don't go out, Mrs. Wingfield. The fact of the matter is I've got to be going.

Amanda. Going, now! You're joking! Why, it's only the shank of the evening, Mr. O'Connor!

Jim. Well, you know how it is.

Amanda. You mean you're a young workingman and have to keep workingmen's hours. We'll let you off early tonight. But only on the condition that next time you stay later. What's the best night for you? Isn't Saturday night the best night for you workingmen?

Jim. I have a couple of time-clocks to punch, Mrs. Wingfield. One at morning, another one at night!

Amanda. My, but you *are* ambitious! You work at night, too?

Jim. No, Ma'am, not work but—Betty!

[*He crosses deliberately to pick up his hat. The band at the Paradise Dance Hall goes into a tender waltz.*]

Amanda. Betty? Betty? Who's—Betty?

[*There is an ominous cracking sound in the sky.*]

Jim. Oh, just a girl. The girl I go steady with!

[*He smiles charmingly. The sky falls.*]

[*Legend:* "The Sky Falls."]

Amanda (*a long-drawn exhalation*). Ohhhh … Is it a serious romance, Mr. O'Connor?

Jim. We're going to be married the second Sunday in June.

Amanda. Ohhhh—how nice! Tom didn't mention that you were engaged to be married.

Jim. The cat's not out of the bag at the warehouse yet. You know how they are. They call you Romeo and stuff like that. (*He stops at the oval mirror to put on his hat. He carefully shapes the brim and the crown to give a discreetly dashing effect.*) It's been a wonderful evening, Mrs. Wingfield. I guess this is what they mean by Southern hospitality.

Amanda. It really wasn't anything at all.

Jim. I hope it don't seem like I'm rushing off. But I promised Betty I'd pick her up at the Wabash depot, an' by the time I get my jalopy down there her train'll be in. Some women are pretty upset if you keep 'em waiting.

Amanda. Yes, I know—the tyranny of women! (*She extends her hand.*) Goodbye, Mr. O'Connor. I wish you luck—and happiness—and success! All three of them, and so does Laura! Don't you, Laura?

Laura. Yes!

Jim (*taking Laura's hand*). Goodbye, Laura. I'm certainly going to treasure that souvenir. And don't you forget the good advice I gave you. (*He raises his voice to a cheery shout.*) So long, Shakespeare! Thanks again, ladies. Good night!

[*He grins and ducks jauntily out. Still bravely grimacing,* AMANDA *closes the door on the gentleman caller. Then she turns back to the room with a puzzled expression. She and* LAURA *don't dare to face each other.* LAURA *crouches beside the victrola to wind it.*]

Amanda (*faintly*). Things have a way of turning out so badly. I don't believe that I would play the victrola. Well, well—well! Our gentleman caller was engaged to be married! (*She raises her voice.*) Tom!

Tom (*from the kitchenette*). Yes, Mother?

Amanda. Come in here a minute. I want to tell you something awfully funny.

Tom (*entering with a macaroon and a glass of the lemonade*). Has the gentleman caller gotten away already?

Amanda. The gentleman caller has made an early departure. What a wonderful joke you played on us!

Tom. How do you mean?

Amanda. You didn't mention that he was engaged to be married.

Tom. Jim? Engaged?

Amanda. That's what he just informed us.

Tom. I'll be jiggered! I didn't know about that.

Amanda. That seems very peculiar.

Tom. What's peculiar about it?

Amanda. Didn't you call him your best friend down at the warehouse?

Tom. He is, but how did I know?

Amanda. It seems extremely peculiar that you wouldn't know your best friend was going to be married!

Tom. The warehouse is where I work, not where I know things about people!

Amanda. You don't know things anywhere! You live in a dream; you manufacture illusions!

[*He crosses to the door.*]

Where are you going?

Tom. I'm going to the movies.

Amanda. That's right, now that you've had us make such fools of ourselves. The effort, the preparations, all the expense! The new floor lamp, the rug, the clothes for Laura! All for what? To entertain some other girl's fiancé! Go to the movies, go! Don't think about us, a mother deserted, an unmarried sister who's crippled and has no job! Don't let anything interfere with your selfish pleasure! Just go, go, go—to the movies!

Tom. All right, I will! The more you shout about my selfishness to me the quicker I'll go, and I won't go to the movies!

Amanda. Go, then! Go to the moon—you selfish dreamer!

[TOM *smashes his glass on the floor. He plunges out on the fire escape, slamming the door.* LAURA *screams in fright. The dance-hall music becomes louder.* TOM *stands on the fire escape, gripping the rail. The moon breaks through the storm clouds, illuminating his face.*]

[*Legend on screen:* "And so goodbye . . ."]

[TOM's *closing speech is timed with what is happening inside the house. We see, as though through soundproof glass, that* AMANDA *appears to be making a comforting speech to* LAURA, *who is huddled upon the sofa. Now that we cannot hear the mother's speech, her silliness is gone and she has dignity and tragic beauty.* LAURA's *hair hides her face until, at the end of the speech, she lifts her head to smile at her mother.* AMANDA's *gestures are slow and graceful, almost dance-like, as she comforts her daughter. At the end of her speech she glances a moment at the father's picture—then withdraws through the portieres. At the close of* TOM's *speech,* LAURA *blows out the candles, ending the play.*]

Tom. I didn't go to the moon, I went much further—for time is the longest distance between two places. Not long after that I was fired for writing a poem on the lid of a shoe box. I left Saint Louis. I descended the steps of this fire escape for a last time and followed, from then on, in my father's footsteps, attempting to find in motion what was lost in space. I traveled around a great deal. The cities swept about me like dead leaves, leaves that were brightly colored but torn away from branches. I would have stopped, but I was pursued by something. It always came upon me unawares, taking me altogether by surprise. Perhaps it was a familiar bit of music. Perhaps it was only a piece of transparent glass. Perhaps I am walking along a street at night, in some strange city, before I have found companions. I pass the lighted window of a shop where perfume is sold. The window is filled with pieces of colored glass, tiny transparent bottles in delicate colors, like bits of a shattered rainbow. Then all at once my sister touches my shoulder. I turn around and look into her eyes. Oh, Laura, Laura, I tried to leave you behind me, but I am more faithful than I intended to be! I reach for a cigarette, I cross the street, I run into the movies or a bar, I buy a drink, I speak to the nearest stranger—anything that can blow your candles out!

[LAURA *bends over the candles.*]

For nowadays the world is lit by lightning! Blow out your candles, Laura—and so goodbye. . . .

[*She blows the candles out.*]

The Model for Laura
from **Memoirs**
Tennessee Williams

The story of my sister Rose's tragedy begins a few years before I commenced my three-year break from college to work for the Continental Shoemakers branch of the International Shoe Company.

I have mentioned that Rose suffered for several years from mysterious stomach trouble. She was several times hospitalized for this digestive trouble but no ulcer, no physical cause for the illness, could be determined. At last, it was recommended that she have "an exploratory operation."

Luckily, our family doctor, a brilliant physician, intervened at this point and told my mother, much to her dismay, that it was his (quite accurate) opinion that Rose needed psychiatric attention, the mysterious digestive upset being due, he thought, to psychic or psychosomatic reasons that could be determined only through the course of analysis.

You can imagine how this struck Miss Edwina. I am afraid that dear Mother has at times seemed to me to have been a moderately controlled hysteric all her life—and in her family tree (on both sides of it, Dakins and Ottes) have been alarming incidences of mental and nervous breakdowns. . . .

In her early twenties Rose was sent to Knoxville with a few inexpensive party dresses to "make her debut." A formal debutante party had been planned by Aunt Belle, but the death of her husband's mother intervened and the debut was "informal." A party was given at the Knoxville Country Club, for Rose's informal presentation to society. Aunt Belle had to buy Rose quite a few more dresses during this debut season: Even so, the debut was not exactly a howling success. I think Miss Rose fell in love with a young man who did not altogether respond in kind; and Rose was never quite the same. A shadow had fallen over her that was to deepen steadily through the next four or five years.

When Rose returned from her Knoxville debut, I said, "How was your visit, Rose?"

She said, "Aunt Ella and Aunt Belle only like charming people and I'm not charming.". . .

There were years when I was in the shoe company and summers when I was a student at the State University of Missouri when my sister and I spent nearly all our evenings together aside from those which I spent with Hazel.

What did we do those evenings, Rose and I? Well, we strolled about the business streets of University City. It was a sort of ritual with a pathos that I assure you was never caught in *Menagerie* nor in my story "Portrait of Girl in Glass," on which *Menagerie* was based.

I think it was Delmar—that long, long street which probably began near the Mississippi River in downtown St. Louis and continued through University City and on out into the country— that Rose and I strolled along in the evenings. There was a root-beer stand at which we always stopped. Rose was inordinately fond of root beer, especially on warm summer evenings. And before and after our root-beer stop, we would window-shop. Rose's passion . . . was clothes. And all along that part of Delmar that cut through University City were little shops with lighted windows at night in which were displayed dresses and accessories for women. Rose did not have much of a wardrobe, and so her window-shopping on Delmar was like a hungry child's gazing through the window-fronts of restaurants. Her taste in clothes was excellent.

"How about *that* dress, Rose?"

"Oh, no, that's tacky. But this one here's very nice."

The evening excursions lasted about an hour and a half, and I'd usually follow her into her bedroom when we came home, to continue our warmly desultory chats. I felt most at home in that room, which was furnished with the white ivory bedroom set that had been acquired with the family's furnished apartment on Westminster Place when we first moved to St. Louis in 1918.

It was the only attractive room in the apartment—or did it seem so because it was my sister's?

Dad had subleased our first real residence in St. Louis, a very charming two-story Georgian house in the suburb of Clayton, only a block or two from Washington University. . . . Miss Rose's mind again began to slip. Not violently but gradually.

I remember a drive in the country with young friends. We started, the young friends and I, to laugh at the outrageous behavior of an acquaintance who was losing his mind. Miss Rose turned very grave and stiff in the back seat of the car.

"You must never make fun of insanity," she reproved us. "It's worse than death."